Politics Ideology & Education

Federal Policy During the Clinton and Bush Administrations

Politics Ideology & Education

Federal Policy During the Clinton and Bush Administrations

Elizabeth H. DeBray

Foreword by Carl Kaestle

Teachers College Press

Teachers College, Columbia University
New York and London

Published by Teachers College Press, 1234 Amsterdam Avenue, New York, NY 10027

The financial assistance of the Spencer and William and Flora Hewlett Foundations, through the Advanced Studies Fellowship Program at Brown University, is gratefully acknowledged.

Library of Congress Cataloging-in-Publication Data

Debray, Elizabeth H.
Politics, ideology, & education : federal policy during the Clinton and Bush administrations / Elizabeth H. Debray ; foreword by Carl Kaestle.
p. cm.
Includes bibliographical references and index.
ISBN-13: 978-0-8077-4667-7 (pbk.)
ISBN-10: 0-8077-4667-3 (pbk.)
1. Education and state—United States. 2. Education—Political aspects—United States. I. Title: Politics, ideology, and education. II. Title

LC89.D43 2006
379.73'09049—dc22

2005055456

ISBN-13: 978-0-8077-4667-7 (paper)
ISBN-10: 0-8077-4667-3 (paper)

Printed on acid-free paper

Manufactured in the United States of America

12 11 10 09 08 07 06 8 7 6 5 4 3 2 1

For Richard Elmore and Gary Orfield

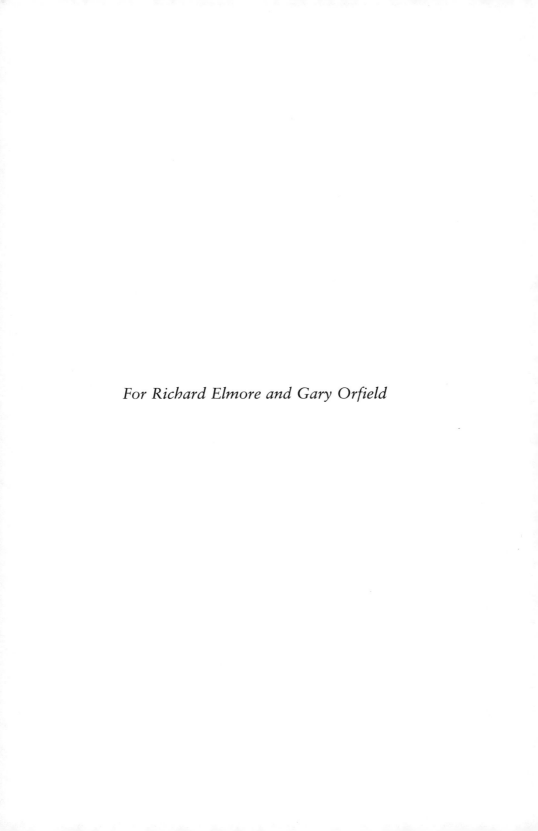

Contents

Part II: The 106th Congress, 1999–2000

Foreword

President George W. Bush's education policy, famously embodied in the No Child Left Behind Act of 2001 (NCLB), is a central topic of discussion in education today. NCLB has pervasively influenced schools' daily activities and preoccupied state departments of education, both of which are responsible for carrying out its mandates. NCLB divides policy advocates and befuddles policy commentators, who continually debate its merits and failings. Across America, scholars and policymakers also debate whether NCLB simply builds upon and augments a well-established movement or is an unprecedented escalation of the federal role in education.

As an evolutionary document, NCLB is the federal embodiment of an education movement called Standards-Based Reform (SBR), which emerged in response to the 1983 *A Nation at Risk* report. *A Nation at Risk* was a thunderclap, widely held to have awakened the American public to the dangerous mediocrity of the public schools and, as a result, sparked two decades of reform efforts. If *A Nation at Risk* provided the political will to reform schools, the SBR movement provided the means to do it. SBR provided new theories about "systemic" reform, which emphasized renewing academic focus in schools, holding teachers accountable for educational outcomes, measured by students' academic achievement, and aligning teacher preparation and pedagogical practice with content standards, curriculum, classroom practice, and performance standards.[1]

The first phases of the standards movement were initiated at the state level, the principal locus of standards reform. Recognizing this fact, President George H. W. Bush tried to partner with the states to foster the movement, but his education bill, America 2000, encountered election year politics in 1992, and it failed. Upon entering office, Bush's successor, President Bill Clinton, eagerly accepted the challenge of forging a federal role in the standards-based reform movement. Clinton enjoyed a reputation as a successful "education" governor in Arkansas, and he recruited Richard Riley of South Carolina, another education governor, to become Secretary of Education and help him in this task. Their central legislative achievements—the Goals 2000 Act of 1993 and the Improving America's Schools Act of 1994—

defined a federal role in the movement. Soon thereafter, Clinton's forward momentum in education policy hit a roadblock with the arrival of a Republican-dominated Congress hostile to federal intervention in education.

When George W. Bush became President in 2001, some observers expected him to embrace the emerging, robust Republican education agenda that advocated market-based reform, parental choice, and a minimal federal role in education. But his experience as an "education governor" in Texas led him instead to adopt more centrist policies. Rather than turning education policy in an entirely new direction, Bush sought to continue the standards-based reform work and strengthen the federal role in schooling. The fascinating piece of legislative history by Elizabeth DeBray that you are about to read chronicles why and how this happened.

Although much of the NCLB story is a continuation of the Standards-Based Reform movement, the legislation has some novel features. For example, it requires that student test scores be reported by ethnic subgroups, and it provides private choices for tutoring. It also places the federal government in a more aggressive stance, defining when students will be tested, on what subjects, which methods of instruction should be used, how an underperforming school is defined, and what the consequences for underperformance are. However, even when this new mix of components and a newly aggressive federal government are taken into account, NCLB represents more evolution than revolution. The disaggregated scores and private tutoring had been in the policy stream for some time, awaiting an opportunity. The aggressive enforcement from the Education Department, Professor DeBray explains, stemmed from the fact that Republicans controlled Congress as well as the White House, along with a general impression across party lines that compliance with the 1994 assessment requirements had been tardy and ineffective. Nonetheless, even against this phalanx of a "unified" federal government, state and district resistance to NCLB has led to more flexibility and softer talk in the second Bush administration. Nor is the intrusiveness of NCLB unprecedented, if one recalls regional and Congressional resistance to the enforcement of desegregation requirements of ESEA in the late 1960s. NCLB's level of muscle-flexing does not seem to be unprecedented or unrelenting.

But what if the political system *itself* has changed over the past eight years? Was NCLB the product of a new set of institutional relationships? If Congress did not operate the way it had before the 106th and 107th Congresses, are the changes temporary or durable? If the latter, what are the implications for the future? Professor DeBray handily explores all of these questions. When one is in the midst of a complex change, it is difficult to discern just how transitory it will be; however, there is no better starting place than this book to start ruminating over these interesting questions. It is a fine blend of legislative history and political theory, enlivened by a huge treasure trove of interviews with Congressional and agency staff.

The political theories most relevant to this analysis revolve around interest groups. In the 1960s, a widely accepted theory featured the metaphor of the "iron triangle," representing a stable and effective political alliance comprised of a government agency, relevant Congressional committees, and a long-term coalition of interest groups. The heyday of the "iron triangle" in the area of federal education policy was from the mid-1960s through the late 1970s. In the 1980s and 1990s this model became less persuasive as a description of reality, and political scientists gravitated toward the idea of "interest networks," a new metaphor coined by Hugh Heclo. "Interest networks" are more fluid than "iron triangles." They are made up of looser, more temporary coalitions of interest groups that work together on particular focused issues.[2] Of course, some elements of the old iron triangle survived after the advent of "interest networks." For example, the Office (later Department) of Education continued to play a strong role in shaping federal education policy well into the 1990s. But as Elizabeth DeBray shows, the power dynamics changed strikingly in the 106th and 107th Congresses.

Each point of the old triangle experienced disruption and displacement. The 106th Congress barely consulted the Department of Education in matters of education policy; in the 107th, even with a "unified" Republican government, the Department's role was entirely passive. Internal relationships within the Congress changed as well. In the 107th, for example, the Republican leadership of the Senate bypassed the relevant committee and created its own informal coalition. New power relationships abounded. The opportunity for interest groups to influence the legislative process also shifted. One might have expected that in a Republican-dominated Congress, liberal interest groups would suffer restricted access, while conservative think tanks and foundations would enjoy increased influence; this was certainly true during Republican administrations during the 1980s and 1990s. But during the passage of NCLB in the 107th Congress, the access of almost all interest groups was dramatically curtailed. DeBray explores this and other puzzles in her analysis.

Understanding the complex and changing workings of the federal government is like looking at a kaleidoscope. When a few pieces fall into a new position, other pieces get configured differently, creating an entirely new picture. For example, in the 106th Congress, conservative Republicans, armed with their newly robust market-based education agenda, were eager to attack the centrist consensus on standards-based reform, especially because this education policy was a signature accomplishment of President Bill Clinton. But when those same conservatives were faced with NCLB in the 107th, they were reluctant to criticize their new President, George W. Bush, because, as

Professor DeBray points out, they also believed in party loyalty. They correctly believed that they could rely upon the President to be conservative in most other policy areas and, along with most Americans, they believed Congress should promptly move ahead with a domestic agenda in the wake of 9/11. While this piece was settling into place, a second piece—a set of compromises that drew key Democrats into the alliance—fell into place as well. A new picture emerged: A strong bipartisan victory for NCLB was assured, with liberal and conservative dissenters relegated to the margins. Elizabeth DeBray illuminates these interesting and notable changes in the way Congress did its work on education policy—a veritable transformation of Congressional procedures and politics—and she probes their implications for the future.

—Carl Kaestle

NOTES

1. Marshall S. Smith and Jennifer O'Day, "Systemic School Reform," *Politics of Education Association Yearbook* (1990), 233–267.
2. Hugh Heclo, "Issue Networks and the Executive Establishments," in *The New American Political System* ed. Anthony King (Washington, D.C.: American Enterprise Institute, 1978), 87–123.

Acknowledgments

There are many people and institutions to thank for the support that made this book possible.

My deepest gratitude is to Richard Elmore and Gary Orfield, who spent countless hours during my five years as a student developing my intellectual perspective on the federal role in education and encouraging me to pursue my interest. I dedicate this work to them. Only an advisor as patient and broad-minded as Richard would have enthusiastically supported a study that began with my surprising announcement to him in 1999 that I wanted to start *immediately*, continued at an erratic pace over the course of a year, and culminated with the death of a bill. He was a steadying influence throughout the unpredictability of studying legislation, keeping my mind focused on what I was discovering. This project benefited in so many ways from Gary's generous spirit and considerable expertise about Congress. He convinced me to undertake the study, helped me devise questions before my research trips to Washington, and gave me pointers on interviewing public officials. My discussions with both of them about politics and Congress opened up a whole world of fascination. Their enthusiasm about my work buoyed me through many of the difficult periods of writing and research. Richard, at my doctoral robing ceremony, charged my exhausted self to finish the story of the legislation, which at that point was only half told—and so I did.

Three others at Harvard who deserve special thanks are Jerome Murphy, who readily agreed to serve on my dissertation committee in his final year as dean of the School of Education; and Robert Schwartz and Paul Reville, who offered me many opportunities for participation in discussions of federal and national-level issues. My friends Eileen Coppola, Katie Woodworth, and most especially my writing buddies, Antonia Rudenstine and Mary-Priscilla Stevens, read drafts and offered invaluable feedback at various stages of conceptualization, research, and writing. For moral support, there are many other friends from my years at Harvard Graduate School of Education to acknowledge; among those who saw me through are Cecilia Wu, Joanne Marshall, Lee and Stela Balderas Holcombe, Alixe Callen, Joel Vargas, Erica Walker, Michal Kurlaender, Dave Ferrero, and Hui Paik.

There were also significant outside resources invested in this project. A research apprenticeship grant from the Spencer Foundation at a critical juncture in 1999–2000 permitted me to turn an idea into a study. The Advanced Studies Fellowship Program on Federal and National Strategies of School Reform at Brown University, jointly funded by the Spencer and William and Flora Hewlett Foundations, provided me with a paid research leave in 2002–03. This enabled me to finish the analysis and complete the manuscript. Equally important, the program exposed me to the energy and ideas of the nine other fellows and the affiliated faculty members, who read my work and offered valuable feedback over the fellowship's three-year period. I particularly thank my two faculty mentors there, Professors Carl Kaestle of the Education Department and Wendy Schiller of the Political Science Department, for the time they spent reading drafts and offering candid input. My thanks to our core group of fellows for their suggestions and encouragement: Beth Rose, Nora Gordon, Doug Reed, Adam Nelson, Marguerite Clarke, Katie McDermott, Kim Freeman, David Gamson, and Chris Lubienski. It was a great privilege to work so closely and become friends with all of them. In addition, I thank Emily Ackman at the University of Georgia for her research assistance and Brian Ellerbeck at Teachers College Press for shepherding me through the publication process. Finally, I am grateful to the congressional aides and many others in Washington who spoke with me.

Then there is the DeBray family—my parents, Don and Dee, brother, Ted, and sister-in-law, Jeannine—who offered me love and encouragement as they always have. My dear grandparents, Susan and the late Edward Dawson, were a steadfast rooting section. On the home front, I am fortunate to have Louis Pelot's love, good humor, and drumming.

—E.D.
Athens, Georgia

Chapter 1

Introduction

In January 1995 a coalition of House freshmen from the newly elected Republican majority called for the abolition of the United States Department of Education. They declared their intent to dissolve the agency and turn programs over to the states. In May 1995 the leader of the group, Representative Joe Scarborough (R-FL), said "The great federal experiment in education is over. It is failed. It is time to move on."[1] On May 18 the House of Representatives passed a budget blueprint for the next 7 years that would cut education programs, including the Head Start and Safe and Drug Free Schools programs, by $40 billion. The House also put the school lunch program into block grants to the states and set funding $10 billion below the projected growth in demand. Majority Leader Newt Gingrich (R-GA) invoked the building of the "opportunity society" as justification for cutting social programs for children and families. In the summer of 1995 the House voted to eliminate funding for President Bill Clinton's Goals 2000 legislation and to cut funding for Title I, the major federal compensatory education program, by 17 percent.

During the ensuing six years many observers believed that the federal role in education was in decline. The Clinton administration's enforcement of compliance with the Improving America's Schools Act (IASA) was weak, and almost all of Clinton's new education proposals, from national testing to class-size reduction, were fought by the Republican House and Senate. In 1996 Republican presidential nominee Robert Dole's major proposals were elimination of the U.S. Department of Education, teaching moral values in schools, and a multibillion dollar proposal for school vouchers.[2]

Six years later, in January of 2002, Republican president George W. Bush signed into law the No Child Left Behind Act (NCLB). The most conservative congressional Republicans, who opposed the bill's extensive new testing mandates and absence of school voucher provisions, were largely left out in the cold as the president picked up a major domestic political victory. In fact, the House Committee on Education and the Workforce chairman, John Boehner (R-OH), an ardent Gingrich loyalist, threw his support behind Bush's bill.

This book attempts to answer questions about the politics of the adoption of this law in Congress over the three-year period 1999–2002, and more broadly, about the dramatic shift in the Republican Party's positions on federal education policy. Because No Child Left Behind is the reauthorized Elementary and Secondary Education Act (ESEA) and thus the centerpiece of federal education policy, Congress's legislative treatment of the bill provides an opportunity for a fresh analysis of political and institutional relationships and how they may shape federal policy in the future. Not only is the content of legislation different, but the very way that Congress makes education policy has changed since the 1960s. What political factors enabled this dramatic and relatively rapid shift to occur? How did the No Child Left Behind legislation develop with both houses of Congress controlled by Republicans?

The study spans two Congresses, first the 106th, when Bill Clinton was president, and then the 107th, during the administration of the newly arrived George W. Bush. The events over the course of the two Congresses—gridlock in one and the passage of legislation in the other—highlight different aspects of the political environment during this period. The battle over the ESEA illustrates how ideological, political, and institutional factors affecting the development of federal education policy have changed from earlier periods—how prior political coalitions came apart, new ones formed, and partisan gridlock was overcome.

A NEW LEGISLATIVE HISTORY

The book is intended to update the earlier legislative histories of the ESEA. In these studies, scholars offered explanations for why Congress acted after years of failing to pass general aid provision to school districts.[3] These histories focused on such factors as the shift in the House Education and Labor Committee membership to a majority of federal aid supporters, the realization by the Catholic Church's leaders that special purpose aid would help their schools, and the leadership of President Lyndon Johnson. Aside from Jack Jennings's book about the national standards movement and federal education legislation of 1994,[4] there has not been a legislative history examining these conditions of the formation of the ESEA since these early accounts. Thirty-five years later the composition of the congressional committees, the institutional environment surrounding education policy, and the makeup and ideological character of both parties have changed. The number and influence of northern liberal Republicans has dwindled, while the former Democratic base in the South has largely defected to the Republican Party. My premise is that changes to federal education policy should be analyzed in light of these changes in Congress.

The focus of my study was the politics of the reauthorization of the ESEA, with a particular emphasis on Title I, its single largest program. Centered on services for economically disadvantaged students, its present appropriation of approximately $12.7 billion a year represents more than 40 percent of all federal aid to elementary and secondary education. Because of the program's political significance to members of Congress, the Education Department, and interest groups, as well as its substantive importance in terms of policy for schools, Title I is a useful illustration of how political coalitions have shifted in Congress over the past two decades. In both Congresses there was ample criticism of the Title I program's record of effectiveness; both Democrats and Republicans advanced proposals for how it should be reformed to better serve students' needs. Thus my primary focus is on the dynamics of educational policymaking in Congress that led to No Child Left Behind, while the substance of the legislative proposals for changing Title I is my secondary focus, a means of showing how policy development and agenda formation worked on Capitol Hill.

I drew on John Kingdon's work on agenda setting and the specification of alternatives in the policy process to guide my inquiry about what coalitions were forming, what kinds of bargaining and negotiation were taking place, and which political actors were setting the agenda.[5] The research consisted of multiple sources of data, the primary one being interviews with congressional aides and representatives of interest groups involved in education policy. Over a three-year period I conducted approximately forty-five interviews (see Appendix B). There were five major waves of interviews inside Congress and one with members of interest groups. The interviews with aides were designed to elicit information about both the members' ideologies and why they were advancing their particular policy proposals for Title I. Interviewees were asked the following central questions: What were their perceptions of who or what was driving the legislative agenda? What were the political positions of their bosses and the party? How did they believe that Title I or the ESEA or both needed to be amended? On which sources of information in the external environment did they draw when forming their positions or proposals? I focused mainly on the policy issues of choice (both vouchers and public school choice), accountability, testing, and flexibility and traced their trajectories through the legislative process in detail.

My other sources of data were media accounts, press releases from members of Congress, the *Congressional Record*, committee reports and hearings, presidential campaign literature, and public opinion data. Appendix A discusses the study's methods in greater detail.

Following a brief overview of the structure of the book, I provide a brief history of the Title I program. Finally, I introduce a common theme to be traced across both Congresses: institutional relationships among Congress, the executive agencies and the White House, and interest groups in the formation of education legislation.

OVERVIEW OF THE BOOK'S FOUR SECTIONS

During the 1990s the bipartisan consensus in federal education policy was premised on support for high academic standards for all students. Part I describes the decade-long development of a federal and national education strategy promoting state-level standards-based reform over the course of the presidencies of George H. W. Bush and Bill Clinton, a set of policies that Bush chose to fortify rather than dismantle. Between 1992 and 1998 the Clinton administration advanced this coherent standards-based reform, codified in legislation in 1994 with the passage of the Improving America's Schools Act and the Goals 2000: Educate America Act. The Bush education agenda would later build on the momentum of the standards and accountability movement.

The two Congresses acted quite differently on education policy, and comparing them reveals major factors about how the federal role in education is changing. Part II covers the events of the 106th Congress, during Clinton's second term in office. This segment of the reauthorization reveals heightened partisanship and ideological division between the parties during the period leading up to the 2000 presidential election. The Republican Party advanced proposals to change dramatically the administration of the Title I program. These divisions set the stage for the 107th Congress, described in Part III, when the leadership and tenor of the debate shifted as President Bush urged the education committee chairs to reach an agreement on his top domestic priority from the campaign. Despite continuing disputes between the GOP and the Democrats about how to hold schools accountable, as well as the switch of the Senate to Democratic control midyear in 2001, leaders found a way to bridge the previous ideological gulf between the two parties in order to pass NCLB.

While the focus of this book is not on implementation, I do consider some of the law's immediate policy implications. Part IV gives an overview of the major controversies during the initial phase of implementation, the response of the education and policy communities between 2002 and 2004, and the enforcement stance of Bush's appointed officials in the Education Department. I consider the implications of the 2004 presidential and congressional elections for education policy for the 109th Congress and beyond, in particular, the realignment of both parties' positions. As one Democratic aide put it months after the bill had passed, "The Democrats have tied this issue up with a bow and handed it to Bush."[6] Yet in spite of the president's victory and Congress's having located a new equilibrium with NCLB, I argue that there is little evidence that the parties' long-held ideologies about education policy permanently shifted. The centrist compromise has held so far during the Bush second term, insofar as Congress has made no major amendments to the law. Yet Republican-controlled statehouses, such as Virginia and Utah, have passed resolutions declaring the law as an unfunded mandate, while congressional Democrats' 2005 "Strengthen Our Schools" agenda calls for subsidization of school construction and more funding for both No Child Left Behind and the Individuals with Disabilities Education Act.[7] Thus, it is clear that the two parties' core ideologies on education are intact and may drive policymaking in unpredictable directions in the near term.

Since it is a important prologue to the legislative history of No Child Left Behind, I next present a brief history of Title I and its major policy developments over a thirty-year period.

TITLE I FROM 1965 TO 1994

Title I is the centerpiece of the ESEA. The legislative history of the ESEA reveals a set of programs whose development is characterized by "incrementalism,"[8] or gradual changes to its policy content. After the bill's passage in the 89th Congress, which was a nonincremental adoption of major policies, Congress has tended to proceed from the original base of the program and make minor adjustments with each reauthorization, recurring roughly every six years.

There are two critical points about the initial passage of the bill in Congress. First, the bill passed as part of a much larger legislative and political strategy of the Johnson administration called the Great Society programs, or as Johnson proclaimed it, the War on Poverty. Thus the 89th Congress passed ESEA along with many other pieces of legislation, such as the Economic Opportunities Act, which was designed to ameliorate conditions of poverty, particularly in economically depressed parts of the country that were not sharing in prosperity.[9]

Poverty as an issue on Capitol Hill had been discovered in the 1950s when a series of Labor Department reports documented that many depressed areas in America were not keeping pace with the prosperity in the rest. Thus there was a bloc of "depressed area" Congressmen in the early 1960s. A multitude of scholarly articles and books, including Harrington's *The Other America*, gradually brought the issue to the attention of the Kennedy and then Johnson administrations.[10] Further, civil rights issues also brought new attention to the lower economic status of African American citizens. As John Bibby and Roger Davidson write, "Not all blacks were below the poverty threshold, and not all below the poverty threshold were black. But burgeoning statistics on the race question made it transparently clear that a disproportionate number of blacks were to be found in the ranks of the unskilled, the unemployed, and the poverty-stricken."[11] Thus the ESEA was passed as part of a package of broader social programs that were framed by Johnson as addressing problems of national importance. In introducing the Economic Opportunity Act, Johnson called for a "total victory" in the war against poverty.[12]

Second, the passage of the ESEA signified the end of a lengthy congressional stalemate in approving federal aid to schools. Several legislative histories explain the stalemate and offer explanations for why it was broken.[13] The early legislative histories explored such factors as the changing composition of the House Education and Labor Committee to a majority of supporters,[14] and the realization by opposition groups—such as the Catholic Church's leaders—that special purpose aid would help their schools.[15] Eidenberg and Morey also emphasize the change of Congress's composition in the 1964 elections. Specifically, they point to the rise of "northern urban-oriented Democrats" in the 89th Congress: "The Democratic leadership could make all strategic and tactical decisions without consulting the Republicans. Republican support for the Democratic majorities was welcome but unnecessary."[16] The 89th Congress moved nonincrementally to adopt the ESEA, but subsequent Congresses maintained Title I via incremental changes.

Prior legislative histories concur that a central reason for the bill's passage was that its proponents advanced it as a "special purpose" bill for the neediest students. It was not to be general aid, opposed for decades out of a fear of federal control and the inability to settle religious and racial conflicts.[17] Congress was successful because "the new special purpose was 'the education of children of needy families and children living in areas of substantial unemployment.'"[18] The aligned relationship between Congress and the presidential agenda was also considered a critical factor for the passage of the bill. As he did with all of the Great Society legislation, Johnson assumed the role of "Chief Legislator"[19] during the ESEA's passage, first appointing the education task force chaired by Carnegie Corporation President John Gardner that made recommendations for aid to poor schools and then, once clear that the favorable constellation of political interests had aligned in the 89th Congress, urging Commissioner Keppel to expedite the committee hearings.[20] President Johnson stated in 1965 that what was important was not whether the passed law was "good" or "bad" in policy terms; the point was whether there was ever going to be elementary and secondary federal aid at all. The details would have to be worked out later.[21]

The ESEA was identified as a priority by the administration and members of Congress because they saw that state and local governments were not acting adequately to ameliorate poverty. As former Democratic congressman John Brademas writes, members of both parties perceived that there were problems related to poverty that state and city leaders were not adequately addressing.

> Many of us in Congress and some presidents of both parties perceived that there were indeed genuine needs—in housing, health, and education—to which state and city governments were simply not responding. It was this inattention by state and local political leaders, therefore, that prompted us at the federal level to say, "We're going to do something about these problems." And we did.[22]

In other words, Congress's initiation of a partnership across federal, state, and local levels of government was necessary to solve national problems. While not all members of Congress supported this new partnership, an underlying theory of the new federal role was that it was becoming a "complex and uneasy partnership whose collective aims are transforming educational priorities and methods."[23] Bailey and Mosher characterized the new federal role in education as a "marble cake," rather than a "layer cake"[24]—federalism was part of a complex, intergovernmental web addressing social problems.

ESEA was enacted for a limited time period. Since 1965, Congress has extended and amended the act eight times. In general, the evolution of the Title I program can be thought of in three broad periods.[25] In the first period, roughly 1965 to 1980, federal, state, and local administrators were trying to reach an agreement about what the funds' exact purposes ought to be. Many school officials did not understand the intent of the legislation: targeted aid for poor students, rather than general aid. The law did not specify a use for the monies, but focused on the formulas by which students would qualify and funds would be targeted.[26] According to Jerome Murphy, many congressmen themselves differed about whether "Title I was an antipoverty measure or a thinly disguised general aid-to-education bill"[27]; in fact, a House committee publication listed a wide array of allowable uses for Title I funds, from extra equipment to health services. By 1969 a civil rights report documented the misuse of funds, from swimming pools to band uniforms.[28] And there were incentives, both from those in Congress and from school administrators benefiting from funding, that built middle-class support for the program.[29] While targeting the funds was the deal that Congress struck out of political necessity, there have historically been pressures for the program to become general aid in practice. In a May 1966 national survey of school administrators, "approximately 70 percent stated that Title I funds should not be allocated on the basis of poverty. Moreover, [administrators] were confused and dismayed when they learned of the specific language of Title I showing that the program was not general aid to the schools."[30] Thus there has always been a tension in the implementation of Title I between targeting the money on the poorest students and using the funds for general purposes. The 1970s was a period of administrative retrenchment, as the U.S. Office of Education worked to ensure that the monies reached the intended recipients. In the 1969 amendments, Congress concentrated the program on the poorest districts.[31]

In the second phase, from roughly 1980 to 1990, during the Reagan and Bush administrations, there were major debates about the governance of the program, but no overall increases in the number of children served. The Reagan administration block-granted several education programs to states through the Educational Consolidation and Improvement Act. Title I, which was not block-granted, was renamed Chapter I during this period. While the compliance and accountability requirements in the program continued, the overall funding and number of children served did not increase during the decade.[32] This meant that by 1990 supporters of the program had to work just to restore funding levels in real dollars (i.e., adjust it for inflation). The Reagan administration's overall lack of support for the program had another implication: there were no major policy discussions at the federal level about quality of program services.[33]

Bipartisan support in Congress for federal education programs had held together during the 1970s and 1980s despite the opposition of Republican presidents Nixon, Reagan, and Ford. As Harvey Kantor writes of this period,

> Democrats were not the only ones who supported the continuation of federal aid for low-income and other special-needs students. Although most Republicans in Congress favored efforts to limit the expansion of the federal role in educational policymaking, many of them also supported the continuation of federal aid for low-income students and other special-needs legislation as well.[34]

By the early 1980s, researchers had begun to play an important role in identifying negative organizational effects of the program. Kaestle and Smith[35] and Elmore and McLaughlin[36] both noted that federal programs had a "fragmenting" effect on school organizations, by creating such different instructional programs. By 1988 there was a growing recognition that federal categorical programs were often not well integrated into the entire school, and moreover, that remedial instruction and "pull-out" programs were not supporting higher levels of learning.

Recognizing the principle that Title I schools needed to have comprehensive instructional programs that served all students' learning needs, starting with the 1988 reauthorization, Congress turned policy in the direction of support for schoolwide projects, use of funds for instructional enrichment of the entire school's academic program. Through the 1988 Hawkins-Stafford amendments, Congress established a school-level threshold of 75 percent of students in poverty as the level at which funds could be used to serve all students in the school rather than running a pull-out program.

Also in 1988, as Jack Jennings observed, Congress began to move the program toward accountability for outcomes:

> A major shift in Chapter I is occurring; it emphasizes that educational improvements are intended results, not just fiscal and programmatic compliance. Such a shift toward educational accountability has not only begun to change the program at the local level, but it has also attracted substantial additional dollars in appropriations to the program.[37]

By the 1990s—when the third phase begins—evaluations offered evidence that the program was not effective in producing achievement gains for high-poverty schools. To address this, reformers attempted to change the program so that it would support the same academic expectations for all students. This third phase is described in greater detail in Chapter 3.

Overall, Title I has shown weak effectiveness in improving the academic performance of schools attended by economically disadvantaged students. While Title I funding has increased the variation of programs offered to children in poverty and may have provided a compensatory effect by preventing further declines of recipient students' achievement,[38] the program has not been associated with an overall narrowing of the achievement gap between children participating in the program and nonparticipants. The Department of Education's 1997 evaluation of student outcomes from *Prospects*, the congressionally mandated study of Title I, confirmed this finding.[39] While more recent studies from the department claim that the 1994 reforms have begun to reap achievement gains on the National Assessment of Educational Progress, no independent evaluations had yet documented such a trend.[40] Proponents of preserving the program could only assert that better results would follow.

CHANGED INSTITUTIONAL RELATIONSHIPS: INTEREST GROUPS, CAPITOL HILL, AGENCIES, AND THE WHITE HOUSE

A common theme I trace across the story of the two Congresses is the relationship among committee staff, the executive branch, and the education interest group and lobbying sector in the legislative process. When the original legislation passed in 1965, a "subgovernment"[41]—or alliance—among congressional committees, interest group lobbyists, and a federal agency, was a reasonably accurate model of how education legislation was put together. Political scientists called these alliances "iron triangles."[42] The traditional education subgovernment was sustained by ties between committees and fragmented political parties during the 1960s and 1970s, as committees had to negotiate the demands of diverse and pluralistic interests.

But by the mid-1970s, political reality seemed to have changed; "iron triangle" gave way to what Hugh Heclo termed "issue networks," open and shifting networks of interests and expertise looking to affect governmental policy.[43] The education policy environment grew more pluralistic in the 1980s and 1990s, as well as more conservative. Following the U.S. Department of Education's alarming and stern report, *A Nation at Risk*,[44] education issues became linked to economic productivity and anxieties about America's declining world position. The business community and governors played a correspondingly prominent role in both the standards movement and federal Goals 2000 legislation during the presidential administrations of George H. W. Bush and Bill Clinton.[45] Until the Republican Party took control of both houses of Congress in 1995, a network of aides to House and Senate committee members, administration officials, and advocacy groups for teachers, practitioners, and urban schools had shared information and coordinated the drafting of education legislation. Both standards-based reform and whole-school reform in Title I were approved by a bipartisan majority in 1994.

What is different about the period I document here is not the conservative education agenda itself, but the new sources of input utilized by GOP congressional staff to shape an ESEA bill. The influence of new kinds of interests not associated with the traditional "left" was growing. The heightened polarization between parties and the growing coherence of the Republicans' policy positions now made the political process more closed than in the past to outside interests, except those most closely aligned with the party. It is my argument that these questions of which groups and interests gain access to the legislative process have enormous implications for the substance of federal education policy in the coming decades. With this context in mind, I turn in the next chapter to an overview of my theory of partisanship driving the politics of education in Congress between 1998 and 2001.

PART I

EDUCATION POLICY AND POLITICS, 1990–2004

How party polarization in Congress and the standards movement led to an unusual convergence of political forces.

Chapter 2

The Increasing Role of Partisanship in Congress

The broad support in Congress for Title I and other federal education programs was, until 1995, largely dependent on the liberal-moderate Democratic alliance behind them. The chief reason why congressional Republicans lent their support for the Great Society programs in spite of their ideological tenets was that Title I benefited their constituents through resource distribution. The conservative presidential administrations of Nixon, Ford, and Reagan would all call for cuts to federal education spending, but the coalition of support for Title I remained strong in Congress. As Harvey Kantor writes, Title I "dispersed funds to nearly every congressional district in the country, [making] it attractive not only to liberal Democrats but also to more conservative Republicans who in principle objected to it."[1]

The period covering the turnabout in the Republican Party's stance on education—the partisan division in the 106th Congress and the passage of No Child Left Behind in the 107th—is best understood in the context of changes in Congress over the past several decades. These include shifts in party composition, growing ideological differences between parties, and changes in the institutional environment in Washington since the 1970s. The fact of Republican control of both houses of Congress was in itself a new political factor for the reauthorization of the ESEA. Only twice between 1930 and 1994—in 1946 and 1954—had Republicans held the majority in both House and Senate, and it had not happened since the time that the Great Society programs were enacted. Now, during the first 6 months of the 107th Congress (i.e., prior to Jeffords's switch), there was "unified party government"[2]—a Republican president was working with a Republican House (with a 221–212 majority) and Senate (with a 50–50 split, with Vice President Richard Cheney the tie-breaking vote in the Republicans' favor). The 2000 election did not significantly shift the balance between parties in the House of Representatives; the Republicans lost a net of two seats from the 106th Congress.

I posit that theories of "unified party government" are a large part of the explanation for why George W. Bush was able to secure passage of the reauthorization bill when Clinton during his second term could not. Sarah Binder summarizes the theory:

> Under unified government, shared electoral and policy motivations of the president and congressional majorities give majority party legislative leaders the incentive and capacity to use their tools and resources to pass legislation. In contrast, under divided government, competing policy views and electoral incentives are said to reinforce institutional rivalries between Congress and the president, which makes it difficult to assemble the coherent policy majorities necessary to forge major legislation.[3]

Thus Clinton battled the GOP-controlled 106th Congress, while Bush could readily find the support he needed in the 107th. Nevertheless, the theory of unified party government alone does not entirely account for the passage of No Child Left Behind.

The Republican Party's attack on the effectiveness of Title I and other federal programs in the 106th Congress was also a function of the party leadership's crafting an active message about education and competing with Democrats on their long-held domination of leadership on that issue. As Larry Evans writes, when political parties compete over the same issue, one strategy that party leaders employ is *interpretation*, which "refers to the parties' attempts to influence media coverage and public opinion by emphasizing different dimensions or policy images for evaluating an issue."[4] While the Democrats in the 106th pushed Clinton's second-term education initiatives such as school construction, class-size reduction, and new money for teachers, Republicans, to set their proposals apart, emphasized state and local flexibility, reduced regulation, and choice. The Republicans' Straight A's block-grant proposal in the 106th, drafted under the direction of the party leadership and released at a leadership press conference, exemplified this strategy of interpretation of what Evans calls a "shared message priority"[5]—an issue that both parties attempted to promote as "theirs" in the public's eyes.

Although this message competition between congressional Republicans and Democrats continued into the 107th, President Bush's education proposal contained several substantive policies that were inconsistent with his own party's emphasis on the primacy of local control in education. This created intraparty divisions among the Republican caucus. Substantively, most of what Bush proposed had been developed during the 106th Congress by both parties, and the majority of the content of the proposal had been voted upon in some form in 1999. Despite Bush's ability to set the legislative agenda, his advocacy of annual testing for all students in every state as a prerequisite for federal aid was new, and it landed rather uncomfortably in the 107th Congress. While one common interpretation has been that No Child Left Behind was a bipartisan compromise, NCLB must also be understood as an ideological defection, made possible by the concessions of members of the Republican House out of loyalty to President Bush during the post–9/11 period of national crisis.

An accurate understanding of the future of federal education policy is dependent on understanding changes in Congress since the Great Society reforms were enacted. The remainder of this chapter describes the enormous demographic changes in Congress, growing ideological coherence within each party and growing polarization between them, changes made to committees beginning with the Gingrich Congress in 1995, and the strengthened role of the party leadership in agenda setting. I also provide a brief overview of one aspect of the institutional environment that would affect the development of education legislation during this period: the growth of the conservative think-tank sector during the 1990s, which provided a fresh source of policy proposals for Title I and other ESEA programs.

INCREASING PARTY POLARIZATION AND IDEOLOGICAL COHERENCE

The Southern Realignment and Increasing Party Cohesion

There is a variety of explanations for increased partisanship in Congress. The first is related to party demographics: The South had begun to send Republicans to Congress as the party ideologies had changed. As the Voting Rights Act of 1965 enfranchised southern blacks as Democrats, conservative southern whites dropped their long-standing allegiance to the Democratic Party in favor of the GOP.[6] Davidson and Oleszek write: "The Democratic party has become more liberal and the Republican party more conservative than in the past . . . the South is now in the GOP camp, so the once-prominent conservative coalition of Republicans and southern Democrats no longer is an important voting bloc in today's Congress."[7] The moderate "Rockefeller Republicans" had mostly disappeared. Democrats in 1996 made gains in the House in the East, Midwest, and West and held their gains in the Senate in those regions. The Republican gains in the South led to greater party conservatism and homogeneity because elected Republicans from the South are almost always conservative.[8] Many Southern Democrats, who had been in the moderate wing of their party, retired only to be replaced by conservative Republicans. While in 1961 there was not a single southern Republican senator, there were fourteen in 2000, which represents 64 percent of the senators from the Old Democratic South.[9] The rise of Senate Majority Leader Trent Lott (R-MS) and Representatives Newt Gingrich (R-GA) and Majority Whip Tom DeLay (R-TX) as dominant powers in the GOP leadership during the 1990s illustrates the heightened party conservatism. Twenty years ago these officials would have been viewed as part of the extreme right faction of the Republican Party. Notwithstanding Lott's replacement as Republican majority leader by the more moderate Bill Frist in January of 2003, it has unquestionably been conservative Republicans who have set the legislative agenda in recent years. Democrats in both the House and Senate after 1996 were also more homogeneous, but tended more toward the liberal side.[10] This rounded out the demographic reasons for the increased ideological polarization.

A second set of explanations for increased partisanship has to do with changes in the electorate over the past several decades. At the time of this reauthorization, there was a far stronger correlation between party identification and issue positions in the electorate than was true in the 1970s. Gary Jacobson, for instance, found that in the 1972 House elections voters' position on various issues—ideology, jobs, aid to blacks, and women's role—predicted party identification with only 62 percent accuracy, compared with 74 percent accuracy in 1998. He writes, "Clearly, citizens now sort themselves into the appropriate party (given their ideological leanings and positions on issues) a good deal more consistently than they did in the 1970s, with the largest increases in consistency occurring in the 1990s."[11] This efficiency in electoral self-sorting has been reinforced by the drawing of congressional districts. After the 2000 census the parties agreed to keep 90 percent of districts drawn in such a way that they were safely either Democrats or Republicans, so the partisan division in the House was almost certain to continue. This in turn fed ideological divisions, as candidates had fewer incentives to reach across party lines during the primary phase of campaigning than to toe their party's line.[12] Candidates and lawmakers were more responsive to the active coalitions that elect them than in the past. As Davidson and Oleszek write, "as voting turnout has gone down, lawmakers are more beholden to activists who vote in the primary and general elections. As a result, lawmakers may be reluctant to vote for bipartisan compromises that antagonize the vocal concerns of well-organized groups, such as the Christian Coalition, the National Rifle Association, or labor unions."[13]

The House

The move toward polarization of parties in Congress, particularly in the House, began almost twenty years ago. Koopman[14] argues that after 1980 "GOP activism became far more conservative and distant from that of the

Democrats, and the Democratic strategy was to shut off both GOP conservatives and moderates from policy cooperation. Conservative activism and Democratic exclusion drove Republican activists of all stripes together." Throughout the 1970s and during the first two years of the Reagan administration, Democrats tended to divide on many issues; while the Democrats held a House majority, they did not vote as a partisan bloc. House Democrats tended to divide along North-South lines.[15] But the policy preferences of House Democrats would become more unified from the early 1980s through 1994. As Rohde explains,

> Changes occurred that made the constituencies of northern and southern Democrats, and the members selected from them, more similar to each other and more different from those of Republicans. On the one hand, enfranchisement of black voters in the South by the Voting Rights Act and the increasing propensity of conservative white voters to shift their allegiance to the Republican party, made average policy preferences among Democrats in Southern districts more liberal and made average Republican preferences more conservative.[16]

The liberal and moderate wings of the Republican Party lost ground in Congress between 1964 and 1984 because there was a dynamic process by which the economic and population bases of the northeast declined while the GOP gained strength in the South. As the Northeast lost influence within the GOP as a whole, the party lost more electoral support in New England and the mid-Atlantic regions: "New Liberal" northern Democrats got elected, replacing Republicans from formerly Republican districts. These trends led to an upswing in the conservatism of the national Republican Party, and the importance of candidates' adherence to the party's positions.[17]

During the twelve years of the Reagan and George H. W. Bush administrations, bashing of the Democratic-controlled House was particularly marked.[18] Those two administrations comprised the "longest continuous period of divided government in the nation's history."[19] As Burdett Loomis and Wendy Schiller observe, during this period "the Democratic caucus empowered its leaders to act aggressively as its agents," which was accomplished "through an initial set of decisions at the beginning of each Congress and through continuing conversations between party leaders and Democratic members, both in groups and one on one."[20] With the White House in GOP hands, Republicans were limited to blaming Democrats in Congress for policy failures.

With the Republican victory in 1994, the Gingrich era ushered in a culture of "attack politics." The partisan rancor was so marked in the 105th and 106th that "civility retreats" with members' families were arranged, with the hope that they might be able to work better on a bipartisan basis. Clinton's impeachment caused more hard feelings on both sides.[21] *Congressional Quarterly*'s analysis suggests, however, that the Republican freshmen in the House had become less ideologically conservative by 1998.[22] While most of these House freshmen were conservative four years after their election in 1994, many had learned that they needed to work incrementally and to forge compromise. Their service on committees, attempts to get funding for their home districts, and support for incremental policy changes are all indications of the assimilation of many of them into the institution.[23]

The Senate

While the Senate came later to the divisions, it too eventually followed the House's partisan pattern in the 1990s. From 1990 to 1994, Democratic Majority Leader George Mitchell began to run the body in a more partisan manner, setting up floor debates and votes in such a way as to highlight policy differences with President George H. W. Bush.[24] As Loomis and Schiller write, 1994 brought about two major shifts that led to greater partisanship in the Senate. First, Republicans took control of both houses, which had not occurred in forty years. Second, for the first time, Republicans reached parity with Democrats in most southern states. Because in the North many moderate Democrats were taking the seats of liberal Republicans, "the differences between the two parties in the Senate became greater than the differences within each party."[25] Majority Leader Robert Dole found that he was leading a very different group of Republicans than he had in the past. Many of the southern conservative Republican senators had come from the House, and they pressed for more aggressive partisan leadership, electing Trent Lott (R-MS) assistant majority leader over Alan Simpson of Wyoming. When Dole began his 1996 presidential bid, Lott was elected majority leader. Lott, who held this position during all of the 106th and 107th Congresses (with the exception of the last six months of 2001, following Senator James Jeffords's party switch), is considered a strong partisan.[26]

The Senate's institutional rules, which are generally looser than the House's—and more reliant on civility—also ended up contributing to partisan gridlock in the reauthorization of the education bill. Much of the way that the Senate accomplishes work on important bills is by developing a procedural agreement, or a unanimous consent agreement, specifying how it will consider a particular measure.[27] Senators must rely more on working across party lines to reach consensus to keep functioning, because the Senate lacks the rigid rules that the House has. Senators, for instance, enjoy the freedom to debate and offer any and as many amendments as they choose, whether germane or not. A supermajority of sixty votes is required to bring debate to cloture for a vote.[28] In a climate of partisanship, though, those same less restrictive rules can be used for obstructionist ends. Observing the Senate in 2000, a *Washington Post* writer predicted: "When that consensus breaks down, the Senate is likely to break down too, because members can use their looser—but often intricate—rules to tie the place in knots."[29] Indeed, this situation had implications for the reauthorization.

In the 106th Congress, Minority Leader Tom Daschle (D-SD) often tried to block Majority Leader Lott from bringing up bills under conditions that set limits on Democratic amendments. Democratic senators were infuriated at what they saw as Lott's precluding their traditional prerogative as senators to debate, offer amendments, and vote on measures. Lott's strategy of trying to stifle debate before it started on a bill favored by the Democrats was particularly unfair, the Democrats claimed; past majority leaders had generally forced votes, defeated measures, and moved on. Republicans, however, charged that Democrats, in an effort to portray the Republicans as "do-nothings" in an election year, were attaching irrelevant amendments to bills and threatening filibusters.[30] These tactics contributed even more to the breakdown of comity. Gordon Smith (R-OR) observed: "The contest for control is poisoning every debate," and Charles Schumer (D-NY) warned that unless the leaders' tactics changed, the "whole order and comity of this body will break down."[31]

PROMINENCE OF PARTIES AND WEAKENING OF COMMITTEES

A major change was that in the post-Gingrich Congresses, committees had less power. Committee chairs still held sway in agenda setting, but it was contingent on the priorities of the party caucuses. In the postreform Congress, committee power was "real, but contingent": contingent on the power and authority of the Democratic and Republican caucuses.[32] Committees are "powerful, but not all-powerful." Committees in the Senate often "bolster the individualism" of the Senate; Senate party leaders have far less power to shape committee actions than do leaders in the House.[33]

The weakening of the power of authorizing committees, such as the House Committee on Education and the Workforce, began during the Reagan administration, with the Omnibus Budget Reconciliation Act of 1981. The appropriations committees gained power, as they set specified deficit-reducing targets; this in turn curtailed the ability of the authorizing committees to initiate legislation.[34] However, the most recent radical weakening of committee prerogatives is associated with the GOP takeover of Congress in 1995.

In that year, House committee staff was reduced by 38 percent, and Senate positions by nearly 25 percent. When budget and appropriations are figured in, the size of the Senate staff in 1995 approximated that of 1971, while the size of the House staff was equivalent to its 1973 level.[35] All staff was to be controlled by the chair.[36] Committee strength, in other words, prior to these changes, had been based not only in the power of members to set a legislative agenda, but also in the expertise of staff. The 1995 reforms diminished the power of committees in two ways. First, they diminished the capacity of staff by cutting their numbers and thus their expertise. Second, with the GOP leadership asserting its power to set the legislative agenda, individual committee members became less able to do so. The story of the ESEA reauthorization has several examples of both Democratic and Republican party leaders attempting to control the agendas beyond the committees. With the capacity and policymaking influence of committees reduced, the environment was far more receptive to that of outside interests.

The committee now called the House Committee on Education and the Workforce has historically been party led in its policy dealings and coalitions. Richard Fenno observed in 1973 that what was then called the House Education and Labor Committee was marked by a "partisan-ideological character" when the Democrats were in the majority: "The Committee confronts policy demands in geological layers: some are long-settled, cold, and solidified; some are unresolved, hot, and volatile. It is the latter type which, at any point in time, give the Committee environment its distinctive characteristics."[37] During the 1980s and 1990s, the two education committees continued to be characterized by more "party infighting" than many others because of the contentious social issues.[38] This was particularly true after 1994.

CHANGES TO THE HOUSE AND SENATE EDUCATION COMMITTEES

The 1995 institutional reforms in the House and subsequent ones in the Senate had some intended consequences such as diminishing the size of the Democratic committee staff and consolidating power in the hands of party leaders. Yet they also had one unintended consequence: diminished expertise and capacity of committee staff to generate new proposals and to draft legislation. This is a partial explanation as to why outside conservative interests so successfully advanced their education policy proposals in the 106th and 107th Congresses. At the same time, changes to the membership of the education committees had led to higher levels of political and ideological bifurcation than at any time over the past two decades.

In the House

After 1994 there was an influx of very conservative members onto the House Committee on Education and the Workforce, which paved the way for the success of conservative education proposals in the 106th Congress. Majority Leader Richard Armey played a role in loading the committee with more conservative members, and the result was a lack of ideological uniformity among the Republicans. A few moderate Republicans still served, but the trend was toward a mobilized right. Marge Roukema (R-NJ), for instance, was a moderate Republican who had been involved in higher education legislation, as was Thomas Petri (R-WI); Chairman Bill Goodling (R-PA), a former high school teacher, had been the original sponsor of the Even Start Family Literacy Program. Petri, Roukema, and Michael Castle (R-DE) were three of the remaining moderate Republicans, out of a total of 27 Republicans, on the House committee. The net effect was that the Republican caucus had become divided, and thus it became harder for chairman Goodling to be effective.

Tables 2.1 and 2.2 show the American Conservative Union's 2000 ratings for the members of the House Committee on Education and the Workforce in the 106th Congress. These ratings are based on a monitoring of members' votes on various issues, and are on a 100-point scale, with 100 as the highest ranking for conservatism.[39]

The result was that by the opening of the 106th Congress, the House Committee on Education and the Workforce was politically bifurcated, even though that had not been its reputation of long standing. On one side were fairly liberal Democrats, and on the other, very conservative Republicans like Peter Hoekstra (R-MI), Tom Tancredo (R-CO), and Bob Schaffer (R-CO), who opposed the federal role in education and favored returning dollars to the local level. Many Republican committee staff, being new, lacked ideological commitment to existing ESEA programs. All these conditions created a political climate that was receptive to outside ideological interests and conservative members' proposals for radical change.

In the Senate

The Senate Health, Education, Labor, and Pensions Committee also grew in party polarization after 1994. The Republican membership was composed of a range of ideologies. It was chaired by a moderate Republican, James Jeffords (R-VT); another moderate Republican member, Michael DeWine (R-OH) had been a champion of the Safe and Drug Free Schools program. More conservative Republicans, such as Jeff Sessions (R-AL), Tim Hutchinson (R-AR), and Judd Gregg (R-NH), joined the committee after 1994. Perhaps

Table 2.1. Rankings of Republican Members of the House Committee on Education and the Workforce by Declining Levels of Conservatism

Lindsay Graham, SC	100	Mark Souder, IN	88
Bob Schaffer, CO	100	Bill Goodling, PA	88
Charlie Norwood, GA	100	Bill Barrett, NE	87
Sam Johnson, TX	100	John Boehner, OH	87
Jim DeMint, SC	100	Thomas Petri, WI	84
Tom Tancredo, CO	96	Ernie Fletcher, KY	84
Nathan Deal, GA	96	Ron Paul, TX	76
Buck McKeon, CA	92	Johnny Isakson, GA	72
Van Hilleary, TN	92	Michael Castle, DE	72
Matt Salmon, AZ	91	Marge Roukema, NJ	68
James Talent, MO	91	Vernon Ehlers, MI	64
Cass Ballenger, NC	91	Fred Upton, MI	60
Peter Hoekstra, MI	88	James Greenwood, PA	60
David McIntosh, IN	88		

Source: American Conservative Union, 2001

most relevant to the events of the ESEA reauthorization between 1998 and 2001 is that, overall, the committee's Democratic membership was composed of liberal Democrats, further to the left ideologically than President Clinton. Edward Kennedy (D-MA), long the committee's chair, was the ranking member, while liberal Democrats Tom Harkin (D-IA), Paul Wellstone (D-MN, now deceased), Jack Reed (D-RI), Christopher Dodd (D-CT), and Barbara Mikulski (D-MD) were senior members of the caucus. While some Democrats such as Jeff Bingaman (D-NM), and in the 107th, Hillary Clinton (D-NY) and John Edwards (D-NC), were identified more as centrists, the vocal and left-leaning Democratic composition rendered conditions ripe for a partisan battle.

A CLIMATE OF SKEPTICISM ABOUT SOCIAL PROGRAMS

As the two parties realigned demographically and ideologically, the alliance between northern moderate Republicans and moderate and liberal

Table 2.2. Rankings of Democratic Members of the House Committee on Education and the Workforce by Declining Levels of Conservatism

Tim Roemer, IN	37	Ron Kind, WI	8
Harold Ford, TN	24	Lynn Woolsey, CA	8
Carolyn McCarthy, NY	24	Ruben Hinojosa, TX	8
David Wu, OR	20	William Clay, MO	5
Robert Andrews, NJ	20	John Tierney, MA	4
Dale Kildee, MI	20	Robert Scott, VA	4
Loretta Sanchez, CA	17	Major Owens, NY	0
Patsy Mink, HI	16	Chaka Fattah, PA	0
Rush Holt, NJ	16	Donald Payne, NJ	0
Dennis Kuchinich, OH	16	Carlos Romero-Barcelo, PR	N/A
George Miller, CA	12		

Source: American Conservative Union, 2001

Democrats that had sustained support for Title I over the past thirty years, by 1999 was no longer assured of its continuation. When Democrats were predominant in Congress, their principal belief was that the federal government had a role to play in domestic affairs and that there should be federal aid distributed with an eye to promoting educational equity. That is, the debate in Congress focused on how to improve the education of economically and educationally disadvantaged children. As the next chapter describes, during the 1990s, President Bill Clinton succeeded in getting the 103rd Congress to pass both Goals 2000 and the Improving America's Schools Act immediately prior to the convening of the Gingrich Congress.

Members' skepticism about federal social programs bears directly on the question of why congressional Republicans proposed dramatic changes in federal education programs during the reauthorization process in the 106th and 107th Congresses. The origins of the recent attack on social programs are found in the 104th Congress. House Speaker Newt Gingrich's (R-GA) strategy for promoting the Contract with America was to highlight philosophical differences between the two parties, particularly about social programs. As historian Dan Carter notes, a central tenet of the Contract with America was that "federal programs begun in the 1960s had failed. The elimination of welfare as a federal entitlement, [Republican members] argued, would break the cycle of welfare dependency and restore individual 'initiative and dignity' to its recipients."[40] Further, Gingrich's strategy throughout the 1980s had been to create a so-called battleground between "godly Republicans" and the "secular antireligious view of the left" characterizing the Democratic party.[41]

Gingrich's mission to turn back the New Deal programs was supported by the election of a majority of Republican governors in 1994. The Republican strategists in 1995 favored highlighting the governors, and many in the new freshman class listened carefully to them. At the annual meeting of the National Governors Association in 1995, for instance, governors asked Congress to turn welfare over to them in the form of block grants.[42] In particular, Governor John Engler of Michigan was influential. He told the Senate Budget Committee about "a dizzying array of social programs that has destroyed families," and he advocated "getting rid of all the federal rules."[43] Testimony from governors like Engler brought about modifications in the Contract with America. The Contract originally had not called for turning welfare into a block grant; it had called for continued entitlements with "tougher strings."[44] But at the governors' meeting in Williamsburg, Gingrich saw an opportunity for meshing their agendas;

> When we were in the meeting with the governors and they said to us, "If you'll block-grant it and get the federal government out of the way, we don't need any more money." And my ears perked up and I said, you literally would accept a flat line for five years if you were in charge? And they said yes. But they all agreed they had to have a real freedom to manage the programs. And I said, "Fine. We're in charge, let's do it." So it was at Williamsburg that we had the really big jump toward something which, after all, Reagan had talked about in both 1976 and 1982.[45]

Devolution of programs to the states was thus revived by Gingrich and other congressional Republicans as an important part of their message and agenda. In education policy, it meant that the climate was ripe for the revival of certain Reagan-era proposals, such as educational choice and decentralization.

THE HEIGHTENED ROLE OF CONSERVATIVE THINK TANKS IN THE EDUCATION POLICY ARENA

The increasing polarization between parties created an opening for the rapid growth of conservative think tanks, as there was a new demand for the development of conservative policies. It is important to note, however, that the influence of think tanks on federal education policy extends back to the Reagan administration. Institutions such as the Heritage Foundation, the Hoover Institution at Stanford, and the American Enterprise Institute provided ideology and strategies that shaped the Reagan Education Department's "bully pulpit" in favor of cutting spending and program devolution.[46]

The 1990s were a period when conservative think tanks substantially built their political and fiscal capital. Data from 1997 collected by the National Committee for Responsive Philanthropy show that "spending by center-right and far-right think tanks continues to grow rapidly, suggesting that the 1990s has been a period of continued institution-building by political conservatives. Overall spending by these institutions between 1990 and 2000 is likely to top $1 billion. . . . Early generous support by conservative foundations and wealthy individuals has enabled many of these institutions to develop impressive fund raising apparatuses, allowing them to diversify their funding bases and attract even higher levels of donor support."[47] Many of these organizations were critical in ending the federal welfare entitlement in 1996.[48]

In spite of this influx of new monies in the 1990s, the success of conservative think tanks in the war of ideas cannot be attributed to their greater spending relative to those that are more centrist, neoconservative, or liberal; as Andrew Rich has written, these foundations have actually outspent conservative foundations in thinking about public policy. Instead, Rich finds, the power of the conservative advantage is *how* they have spent the money to shape public policy: "Conservative think tanks have quite successfully provided political leaders, journalists, and the public with concrete ideas about shrinking the role of the federal government, deregulation, and privatization."[49]

In education policy, the chief work of conservative think tanks such as Empower America, the American Enterprise Institute, the National Center for Policy Analysis, the Manhattan Institute, the Heritage Foundation, and the Hudson Institute has been "making the case for school vouchers, linking this issue with broader arguments about the superiority of market mechanisms over public institutions. In addition to using the education debate to promote market ideology, conservative think tanks have jumped into the controversies over national education standards and testing with an eye toward linking these issues with broader ideas about limiting the powers and reach of the federal government."[50] Not only have the larger conservative think tanks like Heritage developed education policy proposals; so have smaller and more specialized ones.

> Smaller conservative think tanks contributing to the education debate in the 1990s have included: the Reason Foundation, which produces work on school contracting and other aspects of privatization; Empower America, which gives

> an institutional home and staff support to William Bennett, Reagan's former Secretary of Education and a leading conservative spokesman on education; the National Center for Policy Analysis, which puts out policy briefs supporting school choices, attacking teachers' unions, and opposing new public spending on schools; and the Manhattan Institute, which provides analytical support in favor of vouchers.[51]

The growth of these conservative institutions has affected the access of other organizations to the policy process. Rather than trying to meet and deal with a plurality of interests, Republican lawmakers felt increasingly accountable to these newer, more ideologically aligned ones. Think tanks that released reports based on compilations of recommendations by university-based scholars, such as the Thomas B. Fordham Foundation's report on the ESEA, *New Directions: Federal Education Policy in the Twenty-First Century*,[52] were well-positioned to get the attention of Republican committee staff.

CONCLUSION

This chapter has argued that the context for understanding education policy across the two Congresses is polarization between parties and growing ideological coherence within parties, particularly over the past two decades. In light of these changes and divided party government in the 106th Congress, I argue, the stalemate of the 106th was far more predictable than the passage of No Child Left Behind in the 107th. President Clinton, however, moved both parties along the path of standards-based education reform during the 1990s, and this was to shape the eventual success of No Child Left Behind as much as changes within Congress itself.

Chapter 3

Federal Education Policy in the 1990s

Though the atmosphere in Congress during the 1990s was increasingly partisan, bipartisanship in producing education legislation survived until 1994. This chapter provides an overview of federal education policy in the 1990s, with an emphasis on how Title I was redesigned by the Clinton administration in 1994 as part of its overall strategy in elementary and secondary education to drive states to adopt standards-based reforms.

THE NATIONAL STANDARDS MOVEMENT

Although it is not my purpose here to provide a thorough history of the movement to create national standards in education, the legislative initiatives in the first Clinton administration were so heavily reliant on a standards-based strategy that some consideration is necessary.[1] The standards movement reached its high point following the 1989 Charlottesville governors' summit, at which six National Education Goals were adopted, and the National Education Goals Panel was created to monitor progress toward them. Various federal commissions, including the bipartisan National Commission on Education Standards and Testing (NCEST), recommended a federal role for helping states set benchmarks for what students should know and be able to do at different grade levels. "Standards-based, systemic reform"[2] was conceptualized as a strategy to change the way states governed their curricula and ensured access to the same kinds of teaching and learning by all students.

By 1993 the Office of Educational Research and Improvement (OERI) of the U.S. Department of Education had given grants to professional subject-matter organizations to develop standards in geography, civics, mathematics, history, science, the arts, and English/language arts. Thus the George H. W. Bush administration, led by Secretary of Education Lamar Alexander and Assistant Secretary Diane Ravitch of OERI, was a proponent of federally funded standards projects critical to their America 2000 initiative. There were no legislative mechanisms for federal enforcement of academic standards or curriculum of any kind; instead, America 2000 promoted the concept of states and local communities embracing the National Education Goals, and by extension, states' adoption of standards whose development the federal government had funded and disseminated. Thus the origins of the standards movement were bipartisan and had gained substantial momentum by the time Bill Clinton, the governor of Arkansas who had chaired the National Governors Association's education committee during the 1989 Charlottesville summit, was elected president.

Clinton's team of appointees at the Department of Education had a coherent plan from the start to pass education initiatives that supported a standards-based reform agenda. Title I, as the program with the largest pot of federal education dollars and thus the strongest incentive for states to change their policies, became the centerpiece of the administration's strategy.

ORIGINS OF CLINTON'S EDUCATION POLICY FRAMEWORK

Clinton appointed Richard W. Riley, a former governor of South Carolina which had passed a sales tax to support education, as his secretary of education. Riley would serve all eight years of Clinton's presidency, making him the longest-serving secretary of education. The internal 1992–93 Clinton education transition team—consisting of, among others, Marshall "Mike" Smith, Undersecretary of Education; Bill Demmert of the Office of Indian Education; and Terry Peterson and Michael Cohen, counselors to Secretary Riley—built its report's major recommendations around a standards-based agenda for Title I. Specifically, the group recommended the widespread adoption of schoolwide programs and legislation that emphasized that all children ought to be held to the same academic standards. The Commission on Chapter One (the Hornbeck Commission) also came to this conclusion, as did the National Assessment of Chapter I and the Title I Advisory Committee chaired by William L. Taylor of the Citizens' Commission for Civil Rights. Thus all these groups came to the same basic conclusions about the program: It should support standards-based reforms, and dual systems of academic standards and tests for different groups of students should be abolished. Further, a RAND report validating the same policy direction was released at the same time.

By 1994 forty-two states had developed or were developing content standards, and thirty were developing performance standards.[3] Undersecretary

Smith thought that Title I should be in the mainstream of states' standards-based reforms in two fundamental ways. First, the required standards and assessments in Title I should be uniform for all students. Academic expectations were supposed to be the same for different populations of students, which had not been the case when the program mainly supported remedial instruction. Second, Title I should not be an independent program within the school, but should be embedded in the school, and the achievement should be the responsibility of everyone in the school. These two concepts were linked and built directly into the Clinton K–12 transition team's report. "For children in high-poverty schools to meet high standards of performance, their entire instructional program—not just a separate Title I program—must be substantially improved. Schoolwide programs are the vehicle to do this."[4]

The legislative precursor to the 1994 IASA's schoolwide programs had been the Democrat-sponsored Neighborhood Schools Improvement Act, passed by both the House of Representatives and the Senate in 1992 (toward the end of the G. H. W. Bush administration). House Republicans sought to promote President G. H. W. Bush's initiative for choice for private schools, and the final bill was an $800 million school reform bill. It mainly authorized block grants to states (20 percent) and local education agencies (80 percent), with 90 percent of the latter to go to individual schools. However, in the conference of the final bill, Democrats rejected administration initiatives such as national testing, public school choice, and New American Schools.[5] The grants were to be used for teacher training, school construction, or other local priorities. The significance of the Neighborhood Schools Act was that it was the Democratic alternative to what President G. H. W. Bush proposed with choice. It emphasized whole-school reform and locally selected reform strategies, even though there was no federal mechanism besides funding to promote reform.

THE LEVERAGE OF GOALS 2000 AND THE 1994 REAUTHORIZATION

The 1994 reauthorization (also called the Improving America's Schools Act, or the IASA) represented a substantial shift in the accountability provisions and curricular policies in Title I. For the first time, policymakers shifted the program's emphasis from inputs to outcomes. The policies passed in the IASA were part of the Clinton administration's broader policy goals for elementary and secondary education. Within the Department of Education, the major legislative changes were overseen by Undersecretary Marshall Smith. During 1998 and 1999, Republicans in Congress claimed that *Prospects* showed that Title I had failed to do what it should have done: reduce the performance gap between students in poverty and others. Smith, however, accomplished a limited set of his original goals for redesigning the federal role in education via Title I over the course of six years, precisely what he had come to Washington to do. A professor of education at Stanford University and a former official in the Carter administration's Office of Health, Education, and Welfare, Smith used Title I to leverage Clinton's chief policy goal: setting a time frame for states' adoption of content and performance standards as well as assessments. The 1994 IASA bill marked the beginning of a standards-based focus for the program. These changes were based on the assumptions of the standards reform movement: Adoption of standards and tests, whatever a state might decide about their substance and use, was a major reform.

Of the two programs, Goals 2000 and Title I, the latter was a far more powerful lever for getting states to adopt standards-based reforms. Goals 2000 carried a funding appropriation which was meager by comparison; in its first fiscal year (FY 1995), the state grant program was authorized at $420 million. Still, in the administration's strategy, it was important because it was to serve as the framework for reform of other federal categorical programs for students with special needs, such as Title I.[6] As Jack Jennings, a long-time counsel to the House education and labor committee, explains, "in effect, the administration proposed a trade-off of more flexibility in the use of federal aid if a state adopted high education standards and measured student progress toward achieving that academic content."[7] Goals 2000 was seed money that would serve to redirect the $8.2 billion of Title I and provide leverage for state-level reform.

President Clinton advocated for the creation of a National Education Standards and Improvement Council (NESIC), and proposals for such a certifying board passed as part of Goals 2000. Undersecretary Marshall Smith recalls that the passage of Goals 2000 was "a little bit rocky, because a lot of the Democrats wanted a much splashier, original bill attached to more money."[8] The resources the administration could expend were very limited because the country was still in a recession. As Smith recounts, however, there was almost universal accord in Congress about changes in Title I:

> The agenda of the standards, state standards in Title I, and having the Title I curriculum and so on was never an issue: everybody was going to support it, the entire Congress, Republicans and Democrats . . . I don't know about the far-right Republicans and so on. The passage was overwhelming, but more important, the concept was never directly attacked. Nobody wanted the old way of doing it; everyone wanted the new way.[9]

As Smith later explained, "Goals 2000 was seen as a gnat. It could get battered, but [House Democratic aide] Jennings and other people were going to protect Title I."[10]

The conference committee for the IASA struggled over social issues such as withholding Title I funds from "schools that fail[ed] to expel for at least one year students who bring guns to school, that 'promote[d] homosexuality,' or that interfere[d] with 'constitutionally protected' prayer."[11] Still, the divisions were less between parties than between House and Senate;[12] the issues were ones on which traditional routes of compromise could be found. Congress made significant policy changes to the program in 1994, but they were agreed to by both parties; none of the amendments proposed changing the fundamental programmatic structure.

Thus the 1994 reauthorization changed Title I into a program that would drive the Clinton administration's standards-based reform agenda in education. The three major pieces of legislation passed between March and October 1994—the School-to-Work Opportunities Act, the Goals 2000: Educate America Act, and the IASA—shared several common themes. These were "coherence, high standards, and support for state and local reform efforts, rather than compliance with rigid procedures and regulations."[13] Said Clinton's Undersecretary of Education Marshall Smith,

> Title I was used to help drive the notion of having every state have standards, and [it] has driven the states to do that. . . . What Goals 2000 did was give enough money to states, to allow them to put together standards, so it facilitated it, and it provided a structure of sorts. But Title I with $8 billion drove it. . . .
>
> Once Congress has said there's going to be a time schedule on this thing, you're going to have standards-based reform in your states. . . . You lay out this agenda, and people follow agendas like that.[14]

The 1994 law also reduced rules and regulations in the ESEA by two-thirds.[15] The new law allowed for greater flexibility and some consolidation of funds across the different programmatic divisions. For instance, states were able to submit plans that allowed funds for bilingual education instruction (Title VII) to be merged with those of Title I. Thus the assistant secretary for elementary and secondary education, Thomas Payzant, oversaw the guidance to states about consolidation of their federal programs in ways that would assist whole-school change. The bill also put in place new requirements for measuring schools' progress toward meeting state academic standards, called "adequate yearly progress (AYP)," and specified time frames for making this progress, although states had wide latitude in deciding how to measure it.

The Clinton administration attempted to tighten the law to better target dollars to high-poverty schools.

TARGETING CHANGES

Promulgating standards through Title I was not the administration's only priority. It also focused on the targeting of dollars to the neediest students. While the formulas for directing federal dollars to the highest poverty districts did not change very much in 1994, the mechanism of allocating money did.

First, the Clinton administration shifted the allocation of funds within districts. Districts were required to rank schools and serve first those with 75 percent or more in poverty, without regard to grade span. This meant that the number of high-poverty secondary schools receiving aid should have increased. According to Smith, this was a very deliberate strategy to get money to secondary schools, which tended to receive low priority and a very small proportion of Title I funds. The provision, however, has not met its desired goal: the overall number of secondary schools getting Title I aid declined from 36 percent of all Title I–eligible schools in 1993–94 to 29 percent in 1997–98.[16]

Second, there was now to be a new formula for determining eligibility within districts that was based on the number of children in poverty. Superintendents had had discretion of how to allocate the local education agency's (LEA) share of funding. For instance, under the prior law, if two schools, A and B, had the same number of students, but School A had a better instructional program and a smaller proportion of students in poverty than School B, the superintendent could give School A more money. President Clinton and Undersecretary Smith changed the law to ensure that the money was allocated based on the number of students in poverty.

Finally, as a result of these changes, between 1993 and 1999, the proportion of low-poverty schools (less than 35 percent poor) receiving Title I funds declined from 49 to 36 percent—a significant reduction.[17] The Clinton administration touted as one of its achievements in education that by 1999, Title I funds reached 95 percent of the nation's highest-poverty schools (those with poverty rates of 75 percent or higher), up from 79 percent in 1993–94.[18]

CONGRESSIONAL REPUBLICANS ATTACK THE STANDARDS AGENDA

During the period from 1995 to 1998, Congressional Republicans mounted an offensive against Goals 2000 and Clinton's standards agenda.

As Jack Jennings has described, however, the conservative assault failed because Clinton, the governors, and the business community fought back.[19]

In 1994, Republicans gave a lower percentage of their votes for federal aid than they did at any time since 1965, as a result of pressure from the far right.[20] This support would erode even further, however, once the 104th Congress led by Representative Newt Gingrich (D-GA) came to power. Many Republicans campaigned in 1994 against Goals 2000 and the expansion of social programs, and the majority's attack on education programs, particularly national standards and testing, gained momentum. The party platform in the 1996 presidential election called for abolishing the Department of Education. Ideological opposition gained strength, with many Republicans claiming that the goals of the 1989 governors' summit had been corrupted.[21] Thus the former bipartisan coalition that had supported the development of national standards and Goals 2000 also rapidly disintegrated.

The congressional election of November 1994, following closely on the heels of the IASA and Goals 2000 signings in March, had the effect of hardening the opposition to the newly won victories for standards. As Jennings writes:

> The Republicans, whose leaders had sought to block Clinton's agenda, assumed power. The new congressional majority then proceeded in an attempt not only to undo Clinton's accomplishments but also to dismantle the traditional role of the federal government in education. . . .
>
> The new role of improving the quality of education was challenged as an item on the national agenda, as was the older and previously accepted purpose of encouraging equity. Thus, the battle to add a new national purpose focusing on improving the quality of education, which began in 1989 with President Bush, evolved into an assault during 1995 and 1996 on the traditional equity purpose of federal aid. The new conservatives wanted no federal role in education, whether to encourage equity or quality.[22]

The political context in which the U.S. Department of Education operated during 1995 and 1996 was one of survival. As Undersecretary Marshall Smith described the political struggle to save the agency, "We were fighting for our lives."[23] Secretary of Education Richard Riley and Smith had to do battle with the Republicans to preserve education programs. The top staff of the Department of Education and the White House invested large amounts of time trying to save the agency and its programs, a process described by Smith as "internecine warfare."[24] In the summer of 1995, during debates over the appropriations bill, the House voted to cut funding for the IASA and Goals 2000 by 15 percent, which was vociferously opposed by Clinton and the Democrats. The Senate appropriations committee, led by moderate Republican Arlen Specter, proposed cutbacks of 9 percent, but Clinton still threatened a veto and Senate Democrats threatened a filibuster.[25]

The 1996 presidential election accounts for the beginning of the sea change in the Republican's ideology. Following Bob Dole's defeat, party leaders increasingly realized that the public, particularly women voters, cared a great deal about education, and that the GOP platform, which included abolition of the Education Department, did not resonate with the electorate.[26]

CLINTON'S SECOND TERM: RISING BUDGETS, NEW INITIATIVES

A large part of Clinton's second-term strategy was to propose a variety of education initiatives in rapid-fire succession, from class-size reduction and hiring 100,000 new teachers to training a volunteer army of reading tutors composed of college work-study students and AmeriCorps members. Since Republican members of Congress feared being labeled as antieducation, the party pushed through a $6.5 billion increase in education funding between 1996 and 1999, presenting Clinton with successively larger appropriations bills.[27]

The proposal that met with the most political resistance during the 106th Congress's first session was instituting voluntary national tests in reading/language arts and math, which Clinton proposed in his February 1997 State of the Union address. Clinton explained the need for national tests: "To compete and win in the twenty-first century, we must have a high standard of excellence that all states agree on. That is why I called . . . for national standards of excellence in the basics—not federal government standards but national standards representing what all our students must know to succeed in a new century."[28] Most congressional Republicans had forgotten that President G. H. W. Bush in 1991 had proposed national tests as part of his America 2000 proposal.

Clinton's timing was strategic; if he had proposed the tests prior to the November election, congressional Republicans might well have criticized his wanting to exert excessive control over local school boards and used this as a rationale for cutting programs. Instead, in September the Republican Congress proposed major increases in Title I, special education, and Pell grants. The budget battles and the campaign had put him into a strong position. By the time he proposed the tests in the State of the Union address, he had already signed off on the Department of Education's internal plan to develop them based them on the fourth-grade reading portion of the National Assessment of Educational Progress and the eighth-grade math section of the Third International Mathematics and Science Study.[29] The administration hoped to circumvent Congress by paying for the tests' development out of the Department of Education's discretionary Fund for Innovation in Education. The President traveled across the country, looking for states and districts to sign onto the plan to administer the tests voluntarily beginning in 1999; by September of 1997 only seven states and fifteen large school districts had agreed to do so.

In the fall the Senate passed a measure 87 to 13 to allow the tests to be developed by the National Assessment Governing Board (NAGB), which is both independent of the department and bipartisan. House Education and Workforce chairman William Goodling (R-PA) strongly opposed the plan, however, and in September 1997 the House voted 295 to 125 to approve his measure prohibiting any federal money's expenditure on the tests. More than seventy Democrats joined the opposition, including many members of the Congressional Black Caucus, who "warned that the tests would unfairly stigmatize poor or minority students who have no choice but to attend disadvantaged schools."[30] The perennial objection to federal control of curriculum was voiced by Representative Frank Riggs (R-CA), who stated: "We already have plenty of testing. A lot of the states are already doing their own thing and worry about federal intervention. It is all well and good to say these are voluntary tests, but . . . what's voluntary today can be mandatory tomorrow."[31] Then-senator John Ashcroft (R-MO) led the fight in the Senate, proclaiming, "America cannot afford to destroy the educational success of our children through a dumbed-down national curriculum and a federal takeover of our schools."[32]

The 1998 appropriations bill prohibited any further expenditures on the initiative. In January 1998 Clinton's quest to get the policy rolling was thwarted when NAGB's 26 members voted unanimously to delay the tests' completion until 2001, stating that it would be technically impossible for them to be ready any sooner.[33]

ANOTHER CLINTON CENTRIST COUP: THE EDUCATION FLEXIBILITY PARTNERSHIPS ACT

The passage of the Education Flexibility Partnerships Act,[34] or "Ed-Flex," passed by the 106th Congress and signed into law by Clinton in April 1999, signified that the federal government was granting states unprecedented authority to approve waivers to localities to implement education reform. Ed-Flex was originally enacted in 1994 as a pilot program in twelve states, but the 1999 law extended to all fifty states the ability to apply to the Department of Education for the authority to grant waivers from regulations in Title I and many other ESEA programs.

The significance of Ed-Flex for the ESEA reauthorization was that it helped to build support, both inside and outside of Congress, for increased deregulation measures in federal education programs. In the 106th Congress Ed-Flex enjoyed broad bipartisan support. In the Senate only Paul Wellstone (D-MN) voted against it. At the time, James M. Jeffords (R-VT), chairman of the Health, Education, Labor, and Pensions Committee, said Ed-Flex offered "a deal no one can refuse."[35] However, by October 2000, only one state had applied to become an Ed-Flex state: Pennsylvania.

The major provision of the Ed-Flex legislation was to grant states greater waiver authority. As the *Congressional Quarterly Weekly* explained:

> The law gives states the power to approve waivers from federal regulations at the local level. Some regulations, such as those concerning health and safety and civil rights, cannot be waived. . . . Schools also will have to demonstrate that existing federal regulations are impeding their ability to raise student achievement, and will have to describe specific, measurable goals for students and schools affected by the waivers. States can terminate local waivers if performance declines for two consecutive years.[36]

But the legislation had a momentum of its own, as it spawned other working groups inside Congress that gave credence to the idea of state waiver authority. Most notably, Senators Mark Hatfield (R-OR) and Ron Wyden (D-OR) joined with Senators Slade Gorton (R-WA) and Bill Frist (R-TN) to work on questions of greater educational flexibility for states. The idea of increasing flexibility and decreasing red tape became, in the words of Frist's aide, "our education banner."[37] This was the beginning of the Republicans' attempt to fashion their new positions on education. While it began as an ad hoc task force of four senators working on technical details about the degree of regulation in education programs, rather than as a broad coalition, the group's activities sowed the seeds for what would become the central idea of their party's political agenda for the ESEA: block-granting categorical programs.

Senator Gorton already had a block-grant approach he had introduced in 1997 as an amendment to the Labor–Health and Human Services appropriations bill, whereby education allocations would go directly to local school districts. Gorton also served on the Frist task force, where he, Jeff Sessions (R-AL) and Tim Hutchinson (R-AR) tried to work out proposals for what entity should have oversight and control of the funds. The conclusion that Senators Gorton and Frist reached was that that entity ought to be the governor.

Gorton's amendment passed during the appropriation, but was dropped by the conference committee between House and Senate. Rather than give up on the idea, Senator Frist introduced his own bill, called "EdExpress" cosponsored with Pete Domenici (R-NM). Under this plan, it was the state's option to opt into the plan and consolidate funds. Working on a parallel track, Gorton had developed the "Straight A's" proposal from that Labor-HHS appropriations amendment. In September 1998, Senators Kay Bailey Hutchinson (R-TX) and Jeff Sessions (R-AL) sponsored the Dollars to the Classroom bill, which combined thirty-one programs into a $2.74 billion block grant. The groundwork was set for the block-granting proposals that would surface during the ESEA reauthorization process.

This background of the internal working group is critical for two reasons. First, one policy aspect of the Ed-Flex debate was used as a bargaining chip of sorts by House Democrats six months later in the debate over Title I. Democratic representatives George Miller (D-CA) and Dale Kildee (R-MI), during Ed-Flex debate on the House floor, proposed stronger accountability requirements for the performance of racial and ethnic subgroups of students, and their efforts failed. But in the course of that debate, Miller and Kildee's effort to secure tighter accountability provisions convinced many House Republican members that they did not want to be on the other side of the issue when Title I came to the floor.[38] Second, the internal Frist-Gorton-Hutchinson-Sessions coalition would negotiate with the National Governors Association, the Senate Health, Education, Labor, and Pensions (HELP) Committee chair, and internally among themselves. On the issue of greater administrative flexibility for states, the group's agenda-setting influence extended beyond the committee. By moving from specific education issues to basic federalism issues at a time when GOP governors led most large states, the process displaced education groups, with state officials as the key constituents.

CONCLUSION

By 1999, even though fundamental changes had been made with bipartisan support to the ESEA in 1994, Title I faced a history of weak program effectiveness. While a wide range of groups had reached consensus about how federal policy ought to be reengineered in support of a standards-based agenda and Clinton's standards-based reform agenda was very much alive in the states, the climate and tone had changed on Capitol Hill in the intervening five years. There were high levels of partisanship in a majority-Republican House and Senate, and members of the Gingrich Congress voiced skepticism about the value of federal categorical education programs.

Yet the Republicans had also begun to recognize that education was important to the public following Senator Bob Dole's failed presidential bid, especially as both the 1999 ESEA reauthorization and 2000 presidential election approached. The GOP needed to talk about education in constructive terms to enhance its appeal to the electorate, and the reauthorization would provide an opportunity to advance a new agenda. These were the conditions for that would underlie the volatility of the 106th Congress's second session.

PART II

THE 106TH CONGRESS, 1999–2000

How the GOP challenged the bipartisan consensus in education policy by transforming its long-held ideologies into an aggressive agenda.

Chapter 4

The Demise of the Clinton Administration's Proposal

By 1999 the climate of educational politics was ripe for partisan division. Because education had traditionally been the domain of the Democratic Party, developing policy proposals for ESEA programs was new for the GOP leadership. This chapter describes how Congress's external environment, both interest groups and think tanks, would prove a far greater influence on the range of Republican proposals than would Democratic committee members, not to mention the Clinton administration. Republican legislators would portray existing federal programs, particularly Title I, as failures, while asserting that the way to improve outcomes was to change the governance of the program and turn it over to the states. The Clinton administration sent its reauthorization proposal to Capitol Hill in 1999. The committee leadership, however, did not follow the Education Department's lead. Republicans sought to draw distinctions between their education proposals and the Democrats', hoping to create a clear political division in the 2000 presidential election.

Partisanship dominated the ESEA legislative process in the 106th Congress for several interrelated reasons which are described in this chapter and the next. First, as described in Chapter 2, the reforms of the 104th Congress had altered the composition of the education committees, laying the groundwork for ideological divisions. Second, the Republicans sought an opportunity to initiate and advance new education policy proposals. Third, outside interest groups were poised with attacks on categorical programs, that is, those targeted at specific populations of students or for a particular purpose. These outside groups devised new proposals to replace them. Fourth, the presidential election in which both major parties' candidates discussed education and Title I highlighted the dividing lines. Fifth, the Republican Party's dictum that there would be "no new programs" put into the ESEA bill resulted in further bad feeling and mistrust, especially in the committees.

The House of Representatives and the Senate considered the ESEA package differently (see Figure 4.1. for a time line of legislative events in the 106th Congress).

House Committee on Education and the Workforce chairman William Goodling (R-PA), hoping to pass the ESEA before he retired at the end of the 106th Congress, broke the omnibus bill up into smaller pieces. One of those pieces was Title I, which traveled through the House as HR2, passed in October 1999. In the House interparty negotiations over HR2, George Miller (D-CA), the second-most-senior Democrat (next to ranking member Bill Clay), and Goodling did compromise on some provisions such as how to hold states accountable for reporting student academic progress. Moderate Democrats joined Republicans in supporting strengthened provisions for students to transfer out of failing Title I schools to better public schools, while moderate Republicans thwarted efforts by members of their own party to turn Title I into a per-pupil entitlement that could be taken to either a public or private school.

The single largest point of contention in the House was the passage of the Academic Achievement for All, or Straight A's, bill, a pilot program that would allow fifteen states to enter into a five-year agreement with the Secretary of Education, specifying performance goals, but allowing governors freedom as to how to spend program funds. The funds of categorical programs could be mingled with other state programs. The Education Flexibility Partnerships Program (Ed-Flex) was the major legislative precursor to Straight A's. HR2 contained incremental changes to the law while preserving the basic infrastructure of state systems of standards, assessments, and accountability, although the separately passed block-grant pilot program was a large departure in terms of policy.

On the Senate side, as described in the next chapter, the Health, Education, Labor, and Pensions Committee chairman James Jeffords (R-VT) chose a different tack, which was to reauthorize the ESEA as a single package. The committee put together its proposal between November 1999 and March 2000. The committee was highly politically polarized. The gulf between Jeffords, a moderate Republican, and the other members of his committee made the majority's negotiations difficult, as all of the conservative members tried to find a way around the chair in order to get their proposals and amendments into the base bill. Jeffords ultimately yielded to pressure from the party caucus, so the committee bill, S2, included a pilot program not only for block grants to states, but also one allowing states and districts to convert Title I into a portable entitlement. President Clinton immediately threatened a veto should S2 pass the Senate.

Concurrent with these events was the presidential campaign between Republican governor George W. Bush and Democratic vice president Al Gore.

Figure 4.1. Reauthorization of the Elementary and Secondary Education Act and Related Legislation in the 106th Congress

---

January–September 1999

Hearings in both the House and the Senate

May–June 1999

Clinton administration and Department of Education introduce Educational Excellence for All Children Act, its reauthorization proposal, on Capitol Hill.

October 1999

Students Results Act (Title I reauthorization, apart from ESEA) passes in the House Education and Labor Committee, then passes in the full House.

Academic Achievement for All Act (Straight A's) passes as a separate measure in both committee and full House.

November 1999

Clinton's 100,000 new teachers initiative is approved

Clinton adds provision into Title I in budget negotiation that allocates $134 million to be used in school improvement/corrective action schools.

Senate HELP Committee chair James Jeffords circulates draft with proposed basic provisions for the ESEA; it is not based on the Clinton administration's proposal.

Senator Joseph Lieberman proposes the Public Education Reinvestment, Reinvention, and Responsibility Act (Three R's), calling for consolidation of sixty ESEA programs across five broad areas.

March 2000

Senate Health, Education, Labor, and Pensions Committee approves S2 along partisan lines. Amendments for portability and Straight A's are approved.

Secretary Riley denounces the Senate committee bill, while Clinton threatens to veto.

Lieberman introduces Three R's compromise on Senate floor

May 2000

Full Senate takes up S2, ESEA reauthorization bill as passed by the committee.

Democrats refuse to vote for closure on debate. ESEA bill dies.

The candidates' proposals for education, which had become key to both in the campaign, contributed to the unwillingness of senators to compromise or to consider passage of programs that had been Clinton's education initiatives. The full Senate debated S2 between May 3 and 9, 2000. Senator Joseph Lieberman (D-CT), a moderate "New Democrat," sponsored a compromise proposal designed to chart a third course for the ESEA between Republican proposals for block-granting and Democrats' calls for greater resources for existing categorical programs. This amendment was defeated on May 9. When Democrats refused to vote to bring closure to debate and bring S2 to a vote, the Senate leadership, under pressure to get a trade agreement with China, abandoned the bill for the rest of the session.

COMPETING CONCEPTIONS OF FEDERALISM

As the ideological divisions were particularly deep in the 106th Congress, a brief review of competing ideas of federalism is a useful framework for this story.

A central tenet of liberal ideology is that the connection between the federal and local levels of government is an important one, that federal policies can stimulate and guide local action. As Peterson, Wong, and Rabe write, "Federal categorical grants are said to be desirable whenever state and local governments do not provide a public service at a sufficient level unless the federal government assists."[1] In compensatory education policy this means that the federal investment in the education of children in high-poverty schools is one whose benefits, like those of other categorical programs, "transcend local boundaries. Otherwise, one would expect state and local governments to provide as much of this service as their citizens want."[2] A second central tenet of liberal ideology is that of leverage, the idea that the federal government, by spending strategically on certain priorities, can bring about desired changes over time at the other two levels of government. In the history of federal aid to education, an example of leverage was U.S. Office of Education Commissioner Harold Howe's efforts to enforce the requirement that southern school districts comply with civil rights laws and act to desegregate their schools in order to receive Title I funds.[3]

Conservative ideology, by contrast, emphasizes that the states are legitimate sources of policy, and may justify the devolution of social programs to the states, as did President Ronald Reagan. Some congressional Republicans have maintained that the U.S. Department of Education has no constitutional right to existence; the Contract with America of the 104th Congress called for the agency's abolition. The threat of federal interference in local educational decision making is one often invoked by Republicans, and it was one of the major reasons why passing a general aid-to-education bill had proven so difficult before 1965. Since 1965, however, congressional bipartisanship has supported a limited, targeted federal role in education.

Thus in the 106th Congress, members' views about the appropriate federal role in education ranged from a strong and targeted one to a weak and nondirective one.[4]

THE REPUBLICANS DEVELOP AN EDUCATION AGENDA

During 1998 and 1999 the Republican Party developed a series of education policy positions focused on block-granting, choice, and local control. The central ideological position of the Republicans throughout the legislative process was that states and communities needed to be given more power over educational decisions.

The Ed-Flex legislation had provided the occasion for Republican senators to form an internal task force to explore the issue of deregulation. At one meeting of this task force, the General Accounting Office brought in a chart (termed by staff the "spider web" chart) that showed several overlapping programs and their target populations.[5] The senators used this chart as a symbol of the overproliferation of categorical programs. As Senator Bill Frist's (R-TN) education aide Meredith Medley stated, this issue became politically useful for the party: "It became a big Republican thing, that we want to increase flexibility and cut through red tape . . . we waved it as our education banner for a while."[6] Thus Frist in particular promoted deregulation as a way to compete with the Democrats. That Title I had failed in its goal to close the achievement gap between disadvantaged students and others was a strong, frequently repeated criticism. And, of course, it was true. Sally Lovejoy, the top aide to Chairman Bill Goodling of the House committee, insisted that both Democrats and republicans agreed that Title I was a failure: "Even [Democratic Representative] George Miller has said over and over, what has $120 billion dollars gotten us since 1965? . . . Certainly money is part of the solution, but it certainly hasn't been the solution, because we have spent over $120 billion on Title I alone."[7]

House committee member Thomas Petri (R-WI) agreed:

> I'm not sure there was ever a time when Title I was unbroken, but it is certainly broken now. There may be some places where it works, including some in my own district, but on the whole, studies appear to show that the $120 billion we have spent on this program over the years has failed the children it was supposed to help. It's time to let the states try something different.[8]

Congressional committee staff from both parties acknowledged that the upcoming election was a major reason for the emergence of the Republicans' positions in education. Glen Chambers, an aide to Senator Sam Brownback (R-KS), a member of the Health, Education, Labor, and Pensions Committee, stated, "Republicans have started to really kind of cut their teeth on this issue . . . all of the sudden you have an aggressive, conservative education agenda as opposed to just a "let's-shut-down-the-Department of Education" agenda. And that's I think where the political rift is."[9] Jill Morningstar, education aide to the late Senator Paul Wellstone (D-MN) opined, "What [the Republicans] wanted originally was to abolish the Department of Education. They can't do that so they take all their power away by giving the states control of federal dollars."[10]

The coalition that had formed during the passage of Ed-Flex continued to develop its alternatives for giving states control of the money in exchange for results. Eleven months after the Ed-Flex law had passed, state leaders were not complaining about excessive regulations, as witness the number of applications to get Ed-Flex status. Only North Carolina had applied to the department during that period. In March 2000 the *Washington Post* reported that "the lukewarm response from states has raised questions about the political appeal of the central Republican message on education and, more fundamentally, the presumed demand among states and local school districts for relief from burdensome federal regulations."[11] House education committee chair Goodling said he was disappointed but not entirely surprised at the limited interest: "If you don't have any ingenuity, if you don't have any creativity, if you're just satisfied with the status quo, it's just much easier to do what the federal government says."[12]

The reality, though, was that there was no groundswell of protest from states about excessive federal regulation, nor were local districts pressuring states to apply for Ed-Flex. As Rhode Island's education commissioner Peter McWalters told the *Washington Post*, "I can get the flexibility I want under the current opportunities."[13] Elyse Wasch, a legislative assistant to Rhode Island senator Jack Reed (D-RI), said, "[Republicans'] claims that people are clamoring for flexibility, I don't think it is what the reality shows . . . [through] Ed-Flex, we've provided flexibility, and states by and large are not taking advantage of it. The twelve Ed-Flex states that have had this opportunity for several years, many of them have not really used it."[14]

Democrats, however, were not well equipped to counter the Republicans' claim that Title I had failed to meet its objective of narrowing the achievement gap between poor students and others. The best defenses could not be proven: neither that the program had provided a safety net that had prevented many poor students from falling further behind, nor that the 1994 reforms needed more time in order to produce results. By the time the department's proposal had been assembled, conservative think tanks were ready to promote a social policy agenda of their own, albeit one that No Child Left Behind would not fulfill.

PROPONENTS OF TIGHTENED ACCOUNTABILITY

Initially, it was Representative George Miller who argued for a new kind of Title I accountability, one in which each subgroup of students within a school would have to make adequate yearly progress by the state's definition. First elected to Congress in 1974, Miller had served on the education committee (then the Education and Labor Committee) for his entire career. He was the founding chairman of the House's Select Committee on Children, Youth, and Families, a nonlegislative panel that weighed in on education policy. What committee Republicans noted about him was his willingness to take positions that often were not backed by education interest groups. For instance, during the 1998 reauthorization of the Higher Education Act, he successfully championed a requirement that schools of education publicly report the pass rates on teacher licensure exams.

A bipartisan Title I working group in the 106th Congress began to meet in anticipation of the upcoming reauthorization, with the Center for Law and Education and the Education Trust as leading members. A paper by researchers Tammi Chun and Margaret Goertz, commissioned by the Civil Rights Project at Harvard University, examined Title I plans and concluded that the Texas system of holding schools accountable for the progress of student subgroups should be considered for state plans.[15]

The working group began to establish contacts with members of the House and Senate education committees. The Center for Law and Education worked particularly closely with the staff of Senator Jeff Bingaman (D-NM), while the Education Trust's lobbyist, Amy Wilkins, met with Representative George Miller (D-CA). As Charlie Barone, legislative director for Miller, the ranking Democrat on the House Committee on Education and the Workforce, said during a 1999 interview,

> The requirements, you have an accountability system in place, that were put in in '94, are just kicking in now. And it's clear that the department needed—we think, that's from Miller's perspective—tighter guidance around what an accountability system looks like, that measures the performance of all kids.[16]

The "tightening" idea made its way in not only from outside groups, but also during the hearings. Members of Congress and their staffs were dismayed when state education officials could not identify the characteristics of the students who were failing to achieve proficiency on their state tests.

Miller, who along with Kennedy had long-standing ties to the Education Trust, became an advocate of disaggregated data, and a bill based on his proposal passed the House in the fall of 1999. According to Christine Wolfe, who was then a professional staff member for the House Committee on Education and the Workforce's Subcommittee on Oversight and Investigations, many members who voted for the bill didn't understand the difference between simply requiring states to disaggregate data on student performance and the much more far-reaching requirement to make such disaggregated data the basis of their accountability systems. She recalled,

> People didn't even really talk about the Title I bill in those terms: "Hey, this is now requiring subgroup accountability at the school level!" But that was a major change in the Title I legislation. . . . A lot of people don't understand it! It's confusing to a certain degree because since 1994 Title I has required disaggregated data and the ability to examine test data by subgroups, but didn't require a state's accountability system to be built on that, and the achievement of all those groups.[17]

Even though subgroup accountability was very important to a few members, hearings on Title I in the 106th Congress divided its focus among disaggregating data by subgroups, increasing state and local flexibility in spending federal funds, and Title I portability.

As groups developed a variety of policy alternatives for Title I, from tightening to decentralization, officials in the Clinton Education Department had begun a strategy of basing their ESEA reauthorization proposal on complex research results. The expertise of staff inside the department, however, faced a strong disadvantage in an environment increasingly dominated by sweeping ideological statements.

THE EDUCATION DEPARTMENT'S STRATEGY

The U.S. Department of Education found itself in a strategic bind as the reauthorization process began. While the agency's leaders sought a bill that would preserve the basic structure of the program, strengthen accountability mechanisms, and add what Undersecretary Mike (Marshall) Smith called "opportunity-to-learn" provisions, the Republican leadership on the Hill was not much interested in the Clinton administration's priorities. Smith and his internal team, as they developed the Educational Excellence for All Children (EEAC) Act, were caught between the Clinton administration's ambitious accountability proposals and the demands for particular programs by outside interest groups accustomed to weighing in with their agendas.

The department's Planning and Evaluation Service's 1999 report, *Promising Results, Continuing Challenges*, argued that the 1994 changes to the law were beginning to effect improvements in achievement. The report reads: "The impact of standards-based reform is beginning to be seen in improved achievement among students in high-poverty schools and among low-performing students—who are the primary recipients of Title I services."[18] The difficulty the department had in making this case, however, was that its most recent indicator of student achievement was the 1998 National Assessment of Educational Progress (NAEP) reading test scores, and the 1996 NAEP math scores. For instance, the report indicates that the performance of nine-year-old public school students in the highest-poverty schools increased by 10 points on the NAEP mathematics tests between 1986 and 1996.[19] Lacking other kinds of data, the administration found it difficult to argue that there is a relationship between the 1994 reforms and such an achievement trend, particularly when the political climate was one of attack on the program's record of effectiveness over thirty-five years.

Undersecretary Smith knew that the changes to the 1994 law had not yet resulted in demonstrable gains in student achievement. In fact, the accountability mechanisms contained in the 1994 law requiring achievement growth by subgroups of students did not become effective until 2001. So his primary objective as the reauthorization approached was not only to keep standards in place, but also to push more aggressively for opportunity-to-learn measures that would support the implementation of Title I. As he recalled the administration's message for the reauthorization: "You stay the course on standards, you get as much attention paid to really increasing the quality across the board on things like professional development. You make clear and more focused attention to accountability issues, particularly on failing schools."[20] The administration also squarely placed adequacy of Title I resources and equity on the initial agenda. In one of its most ambitious proposals for equity, the EEAC proposal ventured to ensure "comparability" of state funding. One section called for "equal treatment for Title I schools by ensuring that they receive resources comparable to those received by other schools within a district, focusing on such factors as staff, quality, curriculum and course offerings, and safe school facilities."[21] The inadequacy of the program's funding was similarly emphasized by the Independent Review Panel of the Evaluation of Federal Education Legislation (1999), which recommended that Title I be fully funded, necessitating an increase in the appropriation from $8 billion to $24.3 billion.[22]

Smith emphasized to Department of Education staff that the proposal be defensible from a research angle. His primary charge to his internal team in the spring of 1998 was to look at evaluations and research. For Title I in particular, staff relied on the National Academy of Sciences report, *Preventing Reading Difficulties in Young Children*.[23] Based on this research, the department recommended earlier identification of children with reading difficulties and enhancing the quality of professional staff who taught reading.

Susan Wilhelm of the Office of Elementary and Secondary Education, a member of the team working internally to develop recommendations on Title I, said, "Our directions from Mike Smith were to look at the research and to say, what did the research show. And we basically weren't to put anything on the table that we couldn't go back and find the research finding for."[24]

The department's review of the Title I program revealed the need for other adjustments to the law. The department's proposal expanded adequate yearly progress to include overall growth in student achievement for lowest-performing students, and required that final assessments be put in place before placing schools in improvement status. These kinds of technical adjustments to the law, however, were not those that were front and center to the White House or the Republican Hill majorities. Another important piece of the Title I program which the department staff identified was moving states in the direction of a single accountability system for all students. State and district accountability systems sometimes had different measures for identification of low-performing schools, for instance, and in the department's view the 1994 statute needed clarification.

The White House staff, consisting of Bruce Reed and Michael Cohen, pushed the proposal in an added direction on Title I accountability: school improvement and corrective action. The question for them was how many years a school should be in school improvement before the state was required to intervene. Eventually, the number of years arrived at was three, which was the proposal Gore was using on the campaign trail.

Ann O'Leary, then Mike Smith's assistant, recalled that Smith was not as eager as were Reed and Cohen to devise interventions for schools in corrective action:

> From Smith's perspective, you didn't want to clamp down too much on a failing school, since they were still trying to implement their improvement plans . . . that was Smith's dilemma, meeting the White House's demand for getting tough on accountability while trying to do the right thing.[25]

As the Department of Education attempted to adjust the technical details in the bill, they dealt with the concerns and interests of outside organizations, as in past reauthorizations. For example, the department might have gone further on increasing requirements for Title I teacher credentials had it not been for the National Education Association and the American Federation of Teachers. As Ann O'Leary said, "It doesn't allow you to be as bold, because they can make or break a bill . . . we wanted to go much further than the unions wanted to go—but you want to make sure they don't overtly criticize you."[26]

Similarly, Undersecretary Smith and his aides met with the Progressive Policy Institute staff to discuss consolidation of programs. They were responsive to the PPI's proposals for greater consolidation and flexibility, "but our hands were tied in terms of the groups. We probably would have gone further, but internal politics and the groups prevented us," recalled O'Leary.[27] Civil rights organizations, such as the Civil Rights Project at Harvard University and the Citizens' Commission on Civil Rights, mobilized in opposition to the proposals that would require districts to end social promotion. Smith viewed it as an opportunity-to-learn provision: If local districts have received other resources, such as smaller class sizes and professional development, they should not be promoting students through the grades. Civil rights groups, however, claimed it would hurt economically disadvantaged students' educational attainment. Leaders Bill Taylor of the Citizens' Commission on Civil Rights and Wade Henderson of the Leadership Conference on Civil Rights, a coalition of more than two hundred organizations, expressed their disapproval forcefully; the department delayed sending the EEAC proposal to the Hill until they could work out their greatest differences. The department sent its proposal forward in spring of 1999, its top leadership anticipating that with Goodling, Kennedy, Jeffords, and Clinton all having electoral motivation to get a bill by spring, they would get one.

The department's influence on the Hill, however, was minimal. With the goal of preserving a program intact, there was no overhaul to propose, since that had been done in 1994. Since the department and the traditional interest groups were united in their agenda to keep the underlying structure of the bill intact, their negotiations were about individual "add-ons." A major reason for the weakness of the executive-congressional link was the divergence in ideology between the moderate Democrats in the Clinton administration (both the White House and the leadership of the department) and the comparatively liberal Democrats in the committees. Overall, the members of the Senate Health, Education, Labor, and Pensions Committee were far more liberal Democrats than those in the administration, as would be evidenced by their unanimous lack of support for the Lieberman compromise.

The policy agenda with the real momentum, however, was being formed by a fresh set of alliances in the education sphere. By the time the department's proposal had been assembled, this coalition was poised to promote an alternative agenda.

EARLY MOBILIZERS IN THE WAR OF IDEAS: THINK TANKS

The Fordham Foundation, the Progressive Policy Institute of the Democratic Leadership Council, and the Brookings Institution convened a meeting in April 1999 with the purpose of thinking differently about the ESEA. What united these groups was a deep frustration with what they perceived as entrenched interests, like unions, blocking reforms. Explained Fordham's education program director Kelly Amis: "We believe that the Democratic party in particular has been so closely tied to the teachers' unions that it is unable to look beyond the status quo and consider reforms to the ESEA that would create true accountability. . . . But at the federal level we need serious change. For one, we believe that the federal government should treat states more like charter schools: hold them strongly accountable for results while giving them significant flexibility in how they operate and achieve their performance goals."[28] These organizations' objective was to contribute substantively to the formation of the agenda. At the earliest stage of the reauthorization, a loose configuration of groups was sounding each other out for common policy and ideological ground. These were the Heritage Foundation, the Thomas B. Fordham Foundation, Empower America, and the Education Leaders Council.

At the center of the newly mobilized groups was the Heritage Foundation, a think tank "organized by congressional aides in 1973 as a Republican Party study group with conservative foundation support."[29] Heritage had historically not developed reform proposals for education programs, but rather recommended abolition of the entire Education Department. In 1994, for instance, after the Republicans won control of Congress, it wrote a guide for new members, calling for them to repeal "many of the harmful education programs of the last thirty years," including the Individuals with Disabilities Education Act. The same new members' guide called for the abolition of the Department of Education within five years.[30] But times had changed; now Heritage would advance ideas in favor of educational choice and ESEA program devolution to the states.

Chester Finn was a former assistant secretary of education during the Reagan administration and president of the Thomas B. Fordham Foundation (Fordham, an arm of the Manhattan Institute, is a think tank with a conservative political orientation focusing on education reform issues). Concurring with Engler, Finn contended that the 1960s paradigm of federal programs was outmoded, based on what he called the obsolete assumption that "change is always and properly dictated from on high."[31] In place of categorical, targeted programs, Finn proposed a different federal paradigm: "Resources would be entrusted to families and to general purpose governments (such as states and cities) rather than school systems. Market-style mechanisms rather than expert-driven 'central planning' would be embraced—and given maximum freedom and minimum constraint."[32]

In the House, Fordham and Heritage successfully promoted dissolution of categorical programs. Finn's language echoed that of the House committee report on Straight A's, which read as follows:

> It is the committee's view that the time is now to take bold reforms and encourage reform-minded States to continue their successes. Federal funds should be focused on helping children and their schools, not on preserving separate funding streams and maintaining separate categorical Federal programs.[33]

Senator Slade Gorton (R-WA) worked closely with Heritage, Fordham, and Empower America to develop the Straight A's proposal. Charles Barone, the legislative director for Representative George Miller (D-CA), recalled that "Straight A's seemed to come down from the leadership. I think it was essentially the Heritage Foundation and the Fordham Foundation."[34]

Scholars in think tanks also developed the concept of "portability," a major proposed administrative change in Title I that would tie program dollars to the backs of eligible children. The Fordham foundation collection of papers, *New Directions: Federal Education Policy in the Twenty-First Century*, brought together the ideas of several scholars, including Diane Ravitch of New York University and Paul Hill of the University of Washington. Ravitch, a former assistant secretary under President George H. W. Bush, argued that Title I had come to fund administrators and local bureaucracies. Ravitch and Hill contended that money in Title I did not reach students in poverty; many dollars were absorbed by the state and local officials and could not meet the educational needs of the child. Therefore, dollars should follow the child in the form of a per-pupil allocation.[35] The idea, when translated into policy proposals, was termed a "child-centered" strategy, or "portability," in reference to dollars following students. House Education and the Workforce Committee member Thomas Petri (R-WI) would unsuccessfully propose legislation to make Title I a portable entitlement in HR2, while Judd Gregg (R-NH) would enjoy greater success with it in S2.

THE EXPECT COALITION

One of the strongest examples of the conservative coalitions that emerged during this period was the Excellence for Parents, Children, and Teachers (EXPECT) Coalition, founded in 1998 to organize both education policy groups and family groups whose positions had not been heeded by the Democrats when they controlled Congress. The coalition's steering committee consisted of a representative from each of the following groups: the Education Policy Institute, Concerned Women for America, the Traditional Values Coalition, the Republican Jewish Coalition, the Home School Legal Defense Association, the Christian Coalition, the Jewish Policy Center, the American Association of Christian Schools, Empower America, the Family Research Council, and the Lexington Institute. The coalition's success in forging a coherent set of positions and working closely with the Republican leadership in the House illustrates the emergence of an alternative configuration of interest groups.

One of its founders, Charlene K. Haar of the Education Policy Institute (a group founded by parental choice advocate Myron Lieberman), said that for many years, these groups had necessarily taken "reactionary" stances in education policy.[36] At first, about forty organizations signed onto the core principles, but there might now be as many as sixty, according to Haar. The Heritage Foundation's representative to the coalition, Nina Rees, explained that it was time to form an active coalition because the groups were tired of merely going on the defensive when a Democratic initiative had upset them:

> We have all these groups that sort of marginally weigh in on education issues, they get together whenever there's a threat of national testing, especially the Home School Legal Defense, whenever something really bad is going to happen; they're very useful to mobilize, to stop things from happening. Why not get everyone together, for them to work as a team, the same way that the education establishment works in unison when they want to push through something?[37]

The Heritage Foundation positioned itself in two networks: It was not only a member of the EXPECT Coalition, but also a member of one that included the Heritage and Fordham Foundations, Empower America, and the Education Leaders Council, formed after an initial meeting to discuss their positions on ESEA.

According to Haar, the groups in EXPECT did not always reach consensus easily. However, the core membership of the coalition agreed that they must counter the power of teacher unions:

> One of the things that brought us together, about which virtually all of the groups could agree, was that the role of the teacher unions as a special interest group was inordinately effective . . . oftentimes to the detriment of the issues that were of major concern to these groups in the EXPECT Coalition.[38]

A further clear commonality of most groups in EXPECT was that their constituent base was in the suburbs. They did not focus their resources on students in poverty or urban education and thus had little or no interest in protecting categorical programs for the children of the poor. While these groups were not unified on all issues, they were all champions of local control and were energized by the idea of diminishing the federal role in education. Consequently, another common ground became the advocacy of increased state control of funds, through deregulation, block grants, or the reduction of federal programs.

Many conservative groups had worked closely with Chairman Bill Goodling (R-PA) when it had been time to defeat the Clinton administration's voluntary national testing proposal. So Goodling's staff suggested that the EXPECT Coalition come meet with them monthly. Over the course of these meetings with the majority staff of the committee, Goodling asked the group to draft a proposal for state flexibility for results in student achievement. This eventually became the Academic Achievement for All (Straight A's) Act, a pilot program block-granting categorical education funds to governors, that passed in the House alongside the major reauthorization bill (HR2).

EXPECT's steering committee met for breakfast once a week with staff representing the House Republican leadership. The party leadership offered them a sense of what proposals they should push for in their monthly meetings with the committee, Rees recalled:

> What the meeting with the leadership staffers did was basically reinforce what we could and couldn't do . . . if [Hastert's and Armey's staff] felt that we were right in pressuring for something, we would take it into account and take it back to the larger group.[39]

For instance, when Straight A's was proposed in the 106th, Representative Michael Castle (DE), a moderate Republican, wanted to remove Title I from the list of programs that could be block-granted. At that point, Majority Leader Armey negotiated to keep Title I in but to limit the pilot program to ten states. This was an example of the alliance formed between outside groups and party leadership, which took a more active role than in the past in shaping and determining the direction of policy positions.

The EXPECT Coalition exemplifies part of the new conservative education issue network: suburban in terms of its member groups' constituents, savvy at gaining access to both committee staff and party leadership's staff, and clear in their political and organizational goal of challenging what they viewed as the teacher unions' past power.

GOVERNORS AND THE EDUCATION LEADERS COUNCIL

Governors and the Education Leaders Council, a coalition of conservative-leaning state education leaders formed in 1995, further reinforced the idea of giving control over federal programs to the states. Founding members of the Education Leaders Council included Republican state superintendents Lisa Graham Keegan of Arizona, Linda Schrenko of Georgia, and Eugene Hickok of Pennsylvania. Schrenko and Graham Keegan both quit their membership in the Council of Chief State School Officers. The new coalition had numerous objections to the traditional structure of federal categorical programs. First, these programs did not allow choice into alternative sectors, and thus were said to prevent innovation. Second, they promulgated an intergovernmental bureaucracy that was inefficient, preventing monies from reaching students. Finally, they allegedly did not let states set their own goals and spend money as they saw fit; the monies in categorical programs went to state agencies, not governors.

Governors and new groups like the Education Leaders Council helped the committee Republicans in both houses justify the dismantling of the categorical structure of federal education programs. When Governor John Engler (R-MI) testified to the Senate committee in 1999, he called for them to do with the ESEA what they had done with welfare reform: give all monies to the states and allow governors to set the policies. Noting that President Clinton had just asked states to turn around the worst-performing schools or shut them down, Engler continued: "The Governors accept the President's challenge. This morning, we ask you to help us. Specifically, here is how you could help. Block-grant funds to the States and hold us accountable."[40] Block-granting dollars to the local level would not be an effective strategy, said Engler, "if that were to be the decision, I would even go so far as to suggest that if Washington wants to do that, then get the States right out of the middle and have every school district in the country report directly to a federal bureaucrat."[41] As described in the next chapter, the National Governors Association (NGA) was the organization that most successfully pressed its interests in the Senate.

THE PROGRESSIVE POLICY INSTITUTE: AN IDEA-BROKER

If one group enjoyed some fluidity in staking out its positions in this relatively frozen ideological landscape, it was the Progressive Policy Institute (PPI), the think-tank arm of the Democratic Leadership Council. The genesis of the PPI followed Walter Mondale's staggering defeat to Ronald Reagan in the 1984 presidential election. The institute was "established to serve as a source for new policy ideas, based on the principle that activist government could be a force for good, but was not itself good."[42] Other observers have noted that as much as developing new policies, the PPI founders sought to change the negative image of Democrats in national electoral politics.[43]

The PPI's ESEA proposal, advanced on the Hill by Joseph Lieberman in his compromise bill in the Senate, attracted attention from across the political spectrum because it proposed changes, though mostly not to the basic structures of Title I. While the PPI favored keeping Title I intact as a categorical program and increasing its funding, it was able to interact easily with more conservative groups because it embraced "reinvention" of the federal role. What this meant was that the PPI and Lieberman engaged in policy entrepreneurship,[44] testing the limits of what both sides of the ideological spectrum would accept. "We put out an idea here of what ought to be done. Michele [Stockwell, Lieberman's education aide] deserves a lot of credit for shepherding it through and getting it into legislation," explained Andrew Rotherham, the proposal's chief architect and director of the 21st Century Schools Project at the PPI.[45]

Unlike Heritage and Fordham, which settled early on choice and Straight A's, the Progressive Policy Institute did not lobby for discrete programs or ideas. Instead, it rethought the entire federal role in elementary and secondary education, and these ideas were transformed into a new bill. Its sponsors were most interested in how the stalemate between Democratic advocacy for specific programs and Republican determination to block-grant could eventually be broken, whether in this Congress or a future one.

The PPI staff wanted to use the legislative process in the 106th Congress to build its idea base and possibly to identify common ground. For instance, Lieberman convened an unofficial hearing to discuss the ideas with William Bennett of Empower America, the Education Trust, Achieve, Inc. (a standards group), and Joseph Olschefske, the superintendent of Seattle Public Schools. In one sense, the PPI was the group that got the outcome it sought, because what it wanted was to test new ideas.

THE PASSAGE OF STRAIGHT A'S, HR2, AND THE "TEACHER BILL"

Especially when compared with the sweeping changes of No Child Left Behind, the House's Student Results Act (HR2), passed in October of 1999, was not an overhaul of Title I. The legislation was largely built on the 1994 Improving America's Schools Act. The assessments for Title I in reading and math were not expanded beyond the three required grades, though Representative Vernon Ehlers (R-MI) did add science as another required subject that states would have to assess by 2004.

Bipartisan compromise was hammered out on Clinton's 100,000 new teachers plan as part of the Labor, Health, and Human Services spending bill for fiscal 2000. Although Congress in 1998 had enacted Clinton's program to hire the new teachers and reduce class size in public schools, by 1999 Republicans were attacking the measure as too inflexible for local needs and objecting to the mandatory use of funds to hire new teachers, instead of allowing the funds to be spent in some districts for teacher training. The compromise, worked out in the November 1999 budget negotiations, combined Clinton's class-size reduction funds with other programs into a more flexible spending pool while adding requirements for teacher quality. Twenty-five percent of the money could be spent on training teachers rather than hiring them, and a school could use all of the money for teacher training if 10 percent or more of the staff was uncertified.[46] Republicans dropped a demand that school districts be allowed to spend money on "any other local need." The Clinton administration and the National Education Association claimed that provision could be used as a loophole to use federal money for vouchers.[47]

One of the last and most contentious issues in the House was the mandatory parental "opt-in" for bilingual education. Federal policy had always been that parents had the right to "opt out," or ask the school to remove their child from bilingual instruction, but this proposal instead would have required Title I schools to notify all parents, who likely were not English speakers themselves, of their right to "opt into" such programs. The debate was heated, with the congressional Hispanic caucus and civil rights groups opposing the measure, which nevertheless eventually passed with HR2. The final vote tally shows that many members of the Hispanic caucus voted "no" on HR2 because of the opt-in provision. One aide claimed that more Democratic votes had been lost over that one issue than any other. Certainly, this would have been a significant change for Title I policy.[48]

DEMOCRATIC RESPONSE TO STRAIGHT A'S

House Democrats were decidedly on the defensive when the Straight A's pilot proposal passed in the House of Representatives in October 1999. Their response fell into three broad kinds. First, grants given to governors were not tantamount to local control. Second, Title I had already been block-granted, and with very little to show in the way of results; governors had not shown leadership and there was little reason to trust them with these reforms. Third, categorical programs had come into existence for specific purposes. They should not be dismantled, because they represented a national commitment to specific populations of students.

Democratic House committee members were the first to point out the philosophical inconsistency in the Republicans' position. Straight A's, as a measure that gave complete fiscal and policy discretion to governors, was inconsistent with their rhetorical support for local control. The late representative Patsy Mink (D-HI) expressed bewilderment that the committee had spent four days in markup, trying to improve accountability in Title I, only to encounter Straight A's.

> For the life of me, I cannot understand why we spent four days debating and marking-up an ESEA bill if we are going to pass a bill which will do away with all of these federal requirements! . . . Waiving targeting requirements for the disadvantaged is not "academic achievement for all." It is academic achievement for whomever the governors deem worthy. It is mind-boggling that the Majority preaches accountability for federal tax dollars, yet they are willing to hand over billions of dollars to the states with hardly any accountability.[49]

Representative Tim Roemer (D-IN) compared the committee's back-to-back passage of the Title I and Straight A's bills to the Greek myth of Sisyphus, a king who is doomed for eternity to roll a boulder up a hill, only to have it roll back down again. He said, "We've just blown up the rock and the mountain. . . . There's no moral to this story."[50] Representative Mink also called Straight A's "the first step in eliminating the federal role in education."[51]

Representative George Miller's legislative director, Charles Barone, emphasized that the Republicans' claims of too much regulation in Title I were inconsistent with the kinds of waiver requests that states had actually made to the department since 1994: The three most common requests were lowering the threshold for schoolwide projects, circumventing within-district targeting provisions, and switching Eisenhower Math and Science Program funds to reading.[52]

LIMITS OF THE GOP'S IDEOLOGICAL UNITY

Drawing on what he saw as success in Wisconsin's voucher program in Milwaukee, Representative Thomas Petri (R-WI) argued that Title I dollars should go to a public or private school. Contending that "consumer choice produces better products," Petri proposed that states should have the option of turning Title I into a "portable" program, under which funds would follow students to the public or private school of their choice.[53] In his radio address to Wisconsin constituents, he appealed to what he saw as the homegrown success of the Milwaukee choice experiment: "I sugges[t] we allow up to ten states to develop test programs to see if providing education vouchers for disadvantaged children—as we already have in Milwaukee—could open up some educational alternatives, and stimulate some competition in providing educational services."[54] In his appeal for support the week before, he wrote in favor of making Title I more market driven: "Why not give parents the power to purchase the services they think will help their children? In all other markets, consumer choice produces better products and service. Why not let some states try it in education? What have we got to lose?"[55]

Petri's portability amendment was unsuccessful both in committee and on the floor. In the committee, it was defeated 13–28. "This amendment provides real power to the people and one of the strongest kinds—real purchasing power," said Petri.[56] Tim Roemer (D-Indiana), considered a moderate Democrat, countered that portability was a "90s focus group phrase for vouchers."[57]

In response, Petri scaled his proposal back to a ten-state demonstration program, requiring the approval of governor and legislature—but it still did not pass in committee. Congressman Michael Castle (R-DE), chair of the House Subcommittee on Early Childhood, Youth, and Families, was instrumental in opposing Petri. As his aide, Kara Haas, explained, Castle was not ready to legislate about choice: "The Congressman, personally, isn't ready to make that next step to private school choice. He's not sure how exactly that works. He thinks it's something that maybe the courts have to wrestle with a little more before we start legislating it."[58]

Representative Castle was joined by House Committee on Education and the Workforce chairman Bill Goodling in opposing Petri's version of portability extending to private schools.[59] In the end, it only took the defection of several moderate committee Republicans to defeat the measure. On the House floor, Petri again offered the ten-state pilot as an amendment, but it failed 153–271.

Majority Leader Richard Armey offered a voucher amendment on the floor, the Pupil Safety, Academic Emergency Act. The measure would have provided up to $3,500 in "academic emergency relief" funds (a total of $500 million over five years) to the parents of participating eligible children in consistently failing Title I schools, redeemable at private schools. The amendment was defeated by a vote of 166–257, a vote tally that included fifty-two Republicans opposed and three Democrats in favor.[60] This vote signified that Republican support in the House for sending dollars to private schools had dwindled since 1997, when a voucher proposal had been defeated 191–228.[61]

The defeat of both the Armey and Petri amendments raises a central question: Why were Republicans reluctant to vote to pass measures that would give federal aid to private schools? The main explanation is an electoral one: Members were aware that public opinion at that time was not supportive of vouchers for private schools. The House voted on HR2 in October 2000, when polls in both Michigan and California showed that voucher initiatives on the November ballots there were unpopular with roughly two-thirds of voters. For instance, leading up to the November election, a *Detroit News* poll found that Proposal 1, which would have given vouchers for private schools to parents of children in seven failing Michigan school districts, was trailing in the polls by 56–29 percent.[62] A *Los Angeles Times* poll on October 26, 2000, found that two-thirds of voters said they planned to vote against Proposition 38, a measure that would have provided a $4,000 voucher for every California schoolchild to attend a private or religious school.[63] (Fully 70 percent of California voters rejected a similar ballot initiative in 1993).[64] The poll predictions were accurate: the measures were defeated by a 2 to 1 ratio in both states.[65] Thus, while the Republican leadership in the House throughout the 1990s proposed voucher amendments, many Republican members perceived that a vote in favor of vouchers was taking a risk with their constituents. They could safely support ideological positions such as block-granting without fear of disrupting their constituent base, but their support of vouchers would potentially upset their suburban constituents who were largely content with their public schools. It was safe for conservative activists to attack federal education policy in general. But with 90 percent of American students still in public schools and most still having very positive attitudes toward their own schools,[66] Republicans perceived that supporting vouchers was an electoral risk they would not take.

Public school choice emerged as a critical issue on which both committee and floor could reach a bipartisan agreement, however fragile. This signaled that school choice within the public system had become embraced by coalitions on the left and the right. In 1994 the IASA had mentioned public school choice as one possible option after three years of a school's having been designated as "low-performing." The initial designation would be "school improvement," meaning a school receiving Title I funds had not made adequate yearly progress on its assessments. After that period, choice could be part of a state or LEA's interventions for "corrective action." This time, though, the House's moderate committee Democrats agreed that students should be able to transfer out of a failing public school, and that parents should be notified within eighteen months of a school's being designated in "school improvement." Representative Robert Schaffer's (R-CO) amendment introduced provisions allowing students to transfer out of unsafe schools that were also in "school improvement" status in Title I. Under this new policy, when a Title I school is initially designated "low-performing" by the state, parents automatically have the right of choice. Moderate Democrats in both houses supported a faster timeline for public school choice as an accountability measure for failing schools, which assured its victory in both the House bill and the Senate committee bill. As Terry Moe has written, public school choice is an alternative to private school vouchers on which liberal opponents and conservative supporters have increasingly agreed.[67] Clinton's endorsement of choice within the public system, including charters, had heightened the acceptance of support for the concept among moderate to liberal congressional Democrats.

As the Senate committee began its work, the presidential election was already gearing up, leaving uncertain the reauthorization's chances for completion.

Chapter 5

Election Year and Stalemate in the Senate

The debate on the Senate floor featured the parties' competing ideologies over categorical programs. It was this philosophical chasm that Senator Joseph Lieberman would attempt to bridge. The partisanship in the Committee on Health, Education, Labor, and Pensions contributed to the Democratic leadership's decision to not bring closure to debate after four days of floor debate on S2 in May 2000. The unwillingness of the HELP Committee Republicans to compromise at all on new programs, along with the gaining momentum of the presidential campaign, sent S2 into a downward spiral.

THE CAMPAIGN

Prior to the introduction of the committee bill in the Senate, both presidential candidates, George W. Bush and Al Gore, outlined their proposals for elementary and secondary education, and for Title I in particular. The campaign had two major consequences for the reauthorization. First, it heightened partisan tensions, where a mirroring effect occurred: The more Bush emphasized choice in Title I proposals, the more committee Republicans did. Second, both presidential candidates' messages supported the idea that after a fixed period of time, federal funds should not go to chronically low-performing schools. This in and of itself represented a philosophical challenge to what compensatory education had long meant.

The Republican Party platform was updated to reflect that the GOP no longer supported abolishing the U.S. Department of Education. Thus, even as candidates Bush and Gore sought to compete on education, their proposals, with an emphasis on Title I accountability, were not radically dissimilar.

Choice played prominently in Governor George W. Bush's proposals for Title I reform. If schools receiving Title I funds were "persistently failing," the funds could be used to send students to private or charter schools: "[Bush] would pull Title I money from individual schools that fail to improve, giving the money over to parents in $1,500 vouchers that could be used for students to attend private schools."[1] The source of the $1,500 voucher amount was unclear, as Title I, in policy terms, had never been conceived as a per-pupil entitlement. Bush stated, "The federal government will no longer pay schools to cheat poor children."[2] According to his plan, Title I funds would be converted to vouchers when low-performing schools failed to make progress for three years.[3]

Bush highlighted reading, proposing that all states would have to adopt a reading diagnostics program to test the reading skills of children in all schools receiving Title I money. As the *Washington Post* reported, "teachers in those [Title I] schools would have to attend special classes instructing them in how to teach reading. School systems would have to adopt intervention programs, such as tutoring, after-school programs, and summer school programs."[4] He proposed $1 billion a year for five years under Title I for the categorical purpose of training reading teachers to diagnose reading problems in young children.

In addition, Bush's accountability proposals called for establishing a $500 million fund for rewards for high-performing districts, while low-performing schools would face losing part of their federal funds.

Vice President Al Gore opposed such a use of Title I funds, and school vouchers overall. Gore's proposals also included a variant of school reconstitution. Under federal policy in general, states would be required to set standards and identify failing schools (something the department did not require of states and Senator Jack Reed offered an amendment in committee to change). If these schools did not improve within two years, they would be closed, then reopened under new leadership. Presumably prior to this sanction, however, to help implement reform plans in low-performing schools trying to turn around, Gore would make available a $500 million fund. Federal monies withdrawn from failing schools not making improvement would be redirected to the fund.[5]

Both candidates' rhetoric claimed that federal monies should be employed to "narrow the achievement gap." Sometimes they linked this idea to the gap between minority students and others, sometimes they used it to mean just Title I recipients and their nonrecipient counterparts. In April 2000 Gore told the National Conference of Black Mayors,: "I propose a plan with clear financial incentives for states and school districts that successfully narrow the achievement gap, and there will be clear financial consequences for those that don't."[6] Both candidates asserted that it was time to take away part of compensatory funding from poor schools that did not improve.

Thus the election affected the substance of congressional proposals, as Gore and Bush talked about "fixing failing schools" or withdrawing funds in Title I. Congressional Republicans would not have been unhappy if Clinton vetoed a Senate bill; as one Republican aide said before the Senate committee bill went to the floor, a Clinton veto of an education bill might possibly be a gain for Bush: "If the President vetoes it, I think that helps. I mean, I think that Republicans could spin that such, and I think particularly on the presidential level, all of a sudden you've got a guy who really kind of understands education policy at the top of the ticket."[7]

THE PARTISAN LINES ARE DRAWN

When the Clinton administration's ESEA proposal reached the Senate in January of 2000, it was quickly apparent that it was not destined to garner much political support. The late Senator Paul Wellstone's (D-MN) legislative assistant Jill Morningstar said of the committee process: "It started out with the assumption that the administration's proposal would be the one that Jeffords would work off of. And then Jeffords did not, Jeffords worked off the existing law. And so I think [the administration] has been displaced in a big way."[8]

Between January and March, Jeffords attempted to bring together the members of the HELP Committee. By the time the Senate committee began its work, Republicans were actively drawing lines in the sand with the Clinton administration, emphasizing that they were the party of local control. In the Republican response to President Clinton's January 2000 State of the Union address, Senator Susan Collins (R-ME) made the following statements:

> The debate in Washington is not about money. It's about who makes the decisions. We need a change of approach—one that recognizes that local schools, not Washington offices, are the heart and home of education. We will empower states and communities to use federal education dollars in the ways children need most.[9]

The Senate HELP Committee: "No New Programs"

In the Senate committee, virtually every Democratic amendment was voted down on the grounds that it constituted a new program. What drove the opposition was that many amendments had had a first run as Clinton initiatives, such as class-size reduction and set-asides for new teachers in Title II, both of which Chairman Jeffords block-granted. Examples of proposed programs rejected on this basis were Senator Jack Reed's amendments for creating parental compacts in Title I and setting aside monies for school libraries, Senator Wellstone's for community involvement centers in Title I, and Senator Tom Harkin's for school construction. One of Senator Edward Kennedy's aides, Laura Chow, recalled another example:

> [Senator Wellstone] advocated strongly for children who witness domestic violence at home; this particular amendment would allow those children to have counseling or to have special programs set up in schools to help children deal with those kinds of serious issues. . . . And one of the Republican senators said, "You know, your program sounds good, I believe in just the core notion or the ideas behind it, but it's a new program, therefore I'm voting against it." . . . It was almost like a slap in the face.[10]

In fact, said Chow, the Republicans violated their own rhetoric in committee by approving several new programs introduced by Republican senators. For instance, Senator Judd Gregg's (R-NH) amendment establishing a fifteen-state pilot program for Straight A's constituted a new program, as did Chuck Hagel's (R-NE) Rural Flexibility Program.

Supplemental Services as an Alternative to Vouchers

Choice provisions were presented with a variety of rationales. Senator Judd Gregg's (R-NH) proposal was called the "Child-Centered Education Act." The problem, as Gregg defined it, was the structure of money going to schools and districts, rather than to eligible children. The proposal, circulated in late October, alleged "program creep" in Title I, meaning that the way funds were administered had made it difficult to focus on students' educational needs.[11] "This process of sending dollars to districts and schools rather than students has a serious unintended consequence—millions of eligible children never receive the educational services promised them by this program," read Gregg's literature.[12] The senator claimed that using the money to purchase supplemental services would serve as an incentive for schools to improve their overall instructional programs.

Gregg and his staff denied that portability was a "back door" to vouchers. While the bill technically did not allow money to flow directly to private schools, it was close. It was a pilot program limited to ten states and twenty districts. A state or local educational agency would apply to the Department of Education to participate in the pilot program for five years. Allocations of Title I funding would flow through districts to a child's public school, where parents would then have a choice of how to use the allocation. Once the state or LEA made available a per pupil allocation, parents could use it to help purchase instructional services at a wide array of locations. It is important to note that unlike George W. Bush's later proposals for choice, Gregg's portability proposals were not just for nonimproving Title I schools. Instead, if a state applied to the Department of Education to participate in the ten-state pilot program, potentially parents in *any* Title I school in that state could participate.

Gregg's amendment passed in committee, though the chair, Jim Jeffords, voted "present." Along with Democrats, his concern was that portability would disrupt the concentration of limited Title I dollars to the highest-poverty schools. As the minority view of the Senate committee report read:

> Title I grants have been historically concentrated on higher poverty schools, and they should continue to be targeted this way if they are going to address the greatest needs. If Title I funds are dispersed among public schools regardless of need, or to numerous private outside providers, the program will not be able to function as intended.[13]

But from the perspective of the Heritage Foundation, Gregg's pilot program did not go far enough in allowing Title I money to go to private schools. Said Nina Rees, then the education program director there, "When people called it a voucher, to most of us, this was not the vouchers that we always advocated for."[14]

THE NATIONAL GOVERNORS ASSOCIATION ENTERS THE SENATE NEGOTIATIONS

Both individual governors and the National Governors Association (NGA) shaped the reauthorization process in the 106th. It is important, however, to distinguish the political power of the position of an individual governor from that of an NGA policy position. While an individual Republican governor might be a strong advocate for easing requirements of federal education programs, it is the organizational clout of the NGA that had made governors truly influential on the Hill, especially in the Senate.

Several governors on their own had presented committees with specific demands in the House and Senate hearings in 1999. In February 1999 governors Parris Glendening (D-MD) and John Engler (R-MI) testified at a hearing before the HELP Committee. It was there that Engler asked the committee to "put the responsibility squarely on the shoulders of America's governors."[15] Glendening, however, urged a continuation of the 1994 policies, schoolwide programs and standards.

While individual Republican governors at hearings requested that ESEA money be block-granted to states, the National Governors Association's internal politics led the process in a somewhat different direction. Since the late 1980s governors had begun to play a role in the legislative arena,[16] and the NGA offered them a means to formulate and promulgate their positions. Southern education governors, like Lamar Alexander (R-TN) and Bill Clinton

(D-AR), were chairs of the education working groups that had been central to developing the National Education Goals.

By 1999 NGA's policy positions had become increasingly influential with lawmakers. Kent Weaver noted in his study of the shift in welfare policy that "intergovernmental groups generally have good access to federal policy-makers."[17] This was because governors were seen as both having good links to constituents and being knowledgeable about what programs and policies could do at the ground level. As Fuhrman and Elmore note, "NGA's positions carry high visibility; they draw authority not only from their own validity but from the political power they represent."[18] Indeed, the political activism of governors in education was at an all-time high.

The organization can only be influential, however, to the extent it adopts organizational policy positions. In the NGA this requires approval by a "supermajority," or two-thirds of membership vote, to adopt a position with a sunset period of two years.[19] This supermajority approval is designed to encourage bipartisanship in working out agreements on policy positions. At the time of the reauthorization, the NGA was comprised of thirty-one Republicans and nineteen Democrats, with James Hunt (D-NC) as the chair of the education committee. The development of a policy position on the ESEA was dependent on the leadership of Hunt, but also on the consensus-building skill of Patricia Sullivan, the director of NGA's Human Resources Committee, the one that hammered out compromises on education and that ultimately drove policy.

Sullivan said that the organization wielded more political influence than did many Senate HELP Committee members.[20] Getting all of the governors to come to a single bipartisan agreement was Sullivan's job. Once an agreement was reached, she said, it was usually politically powerful:

> The way that NGA is effective is that we cut out the center first; we get governors to sit down and come to a bipartisan agreement. . . .
>
> But once you did that, you had this very solid agreement, it was bipartisan. And it was hard for either the Congress or the administration to discount it, because it was moderate, it was bipartisan, it was usually pretty flexible. And it was also put together by these incredibly popular governors.[21]

In developing an NGA policy on Elementary and Secondary Education in 1999, there were several factors that drove the process internally. A number of governors were starting to run for vice president; for instance, Tom Ridge (R-PA), who chaired Sullivan's Human Resources Committee, was being considered by George W. Bush as a potential running mate. The House Education and the Workforce Committee Chairman Bill Goodling, who represented Pennsylvania, consulted regularly with his state's education chief, Eugene Hickock (who would later become Bush's Undersecretary of Education). Hickock, meanwhile, was active with the Education Leaders Council, which advocated for Straight A's block grants. Sullivan found that her job of trying to get the governors to reach consensus was immensely difficult. The eventual position, once it was hammered out, was to keep the basic 1994 IASA framework in place. As Sullivan put it, the federal role should be to "fix some of the obvious errors, and stay out of the way."[22]

The NGA wanted the Title I formula between districts and schools left intact. This compromise is what became known as "performance partnerships," which would have required that a state negotiate an agreement with the secretary of education about the funding flexibility. If a state used Title I money, it had to keep it targeted on those schools receiving funds under current law. The Democratic governors would not give that up; in particular, James Hunt, vice chair of the Human Resources Committee, voiced his philosophical opposition to taking money away from poor kids. In an election year, no governor wanted to be seen as doing that either. The Republican governors, for their part, secured in the agreement greater flexibility in Clinton's many specific education initiatives, such as hiring teachers and class-size reduction, and promoting some of the same issues George W. Bush would emphasize in his campaign. Following organizational procedure, the policy paper was approved by all of the governors.

The irony of NGA's involvement on the Hill was that while the organization was approached to be a broker, it made neither Democrats nor Republicans happy. Both sides questioned NGA's role in the process. Committee Democrats perceived that its influence was eclipsing their own, while committee Republicans saw that Jeffords was relying more on NGA's legislative proposal than on anything they had drafted for him.

When Jeffords approached NGA for draft language on the bill, it surprised his fellow committee Republicans. Sullivan recalled,

> What [Jeffords] did, to the dismay of people on the left and on the right, was come to NGA, and say, "We like your policy; but it's not detailed enough." . . . It was very interesting, and also a little bit awkward. Because instead of going through the regular process, what happened, ultimately, was Jeffords took our stuff. We had a series of meetings, again internally, we put much more meat on the proposal, and then we sent that to the Hill.[23]

As Sullivan said, "On the Democratic side they were just furious, they were so angry. Because for example, I would see drafts of the bills before the Democratic staff would. And I was much more involved in drafting than they were." As for the Republicans, "they were angry; Gregg, and some of the other conservatives were angry because they didn't feel our bill went far enough."[24] Specifically, Gregg and others wanted to have the categorical formulae lifted so the states would get legal autonomy to spend the funds.

Conservative groups did not approve of the NGA's performance partnerships proposal. They opposed its preservation of the within-district targeting mechanisms in Title I. Nina Rees of the Heritage Foundation criticized performance partnerships for not allowing a district to spend money on either choice initiatives or charter schools.[25] In a policy brief entitled *The NGA's Phony Education Reform Plan*, Rees wrote, "By keeping the rigid strings on Title I intact, the NGA plan would seriously limit a state's ability to use federal funding to implement systemic reform."[26] Other conservative Republicans thought that the NGA proposal offered too much power to the Secretary of Education to negotiate the terms of states' performance contracts. Jeffords resisted putting Straight A's into the base bill, but finally both Straight A's and performance partnerships passed in committee. Jeffords believed this ensured that he would have more options to negotiate on the floor.

It was the party leadership that exerted tremendous pressure on him to vote to include Straight A's. Patricia Sullivan recalled the markup and the vote:

> I think what happened, frankly, was that the leadership came in and said, "Jeffords, you will put this in your bill. And you will vote this out of your committee." Now Jeffords didn't vote for it. . . . And it was the only time where Lott's staff guy came and stood in the room behind Jeffords on the dais, standing up with his arms folded across the chest, until the vote was taken, and then he left.[27]

Jeffords voted "present" on Straight A's while the committee approved it along party lines.

After S2 left the committee, however, other moderate Republicans also sought assurance that Straight A's funds would not be used by a governor to support programs channeling funds to private schools. Senator Susan Collins (R-ME) raised the question while the bill was on the floor, and the Gorton amendment that passed 98–0 on May 3 clarified that Straight A's funds would not go to private schools.[28] Collins's and Jeffords's position was an indication that not all Republicans were ready to embrace privatization.

The NGA itself, Sullivan said, ended up pleasing very few constituencies with the negotiated policy: "We got hammered unbelievably because of this deal from both sides."[29] Groups such as the Council of Chief State School Officers were not accustomed to the NGA having more influence on an ESEA bill than they did. Individual governors were criticized back in their home states by education groups and state boards about the agreement, Democrats for not preserving initiatives targeted by Clinton, like class-size reduction, and Republicans for not going far enough to a Straight A's proposal. Sullivan recalled telling her boss, "It's the only time in my life when I've had editorials in both the *Post* and the *Times* attacking what we're doing."[30]

ACCOUNTABILITY PROPOSALS: INTERVENTION IN FAILING SCHOOLS

Just as Representative George Miller had done in the House, Senator Jeff Bingaman (D-NM) proposed interventions for failing schools that were quite specific. If a Title I school was chronically low-performing—in "corrective action" status—Bingaman asserted there should be a required change in its governance. Therefore, his amendment strengthened the LEA and state mandate from 1994 for intervention in low-performing schools. Based on recommendations from the staff of the Center for Law and Education, Bingaman's position was that states would have to make direct interventions to aid schools in "improvement" or "corrective action" status, and he offered language that was very specific about what some of those interventions had to be. The senator drew on governance ideas that had been supported by the Clinton administration, such as charter schools, creation of smaller schools, and reconstitution of failing schools (a sanction employed by a few states and districts involving partial or full replacement of staff). All of these were policy alternatives that had gained increased national attention since the 1994 reauthorization.

Bingaman's accountability amendment specified that if a LEA was providing technical assistance to its schools in school improvement, it could take such corrective actions without waiting for the end of three years for a judgment about whether or not the school had improved. This was important, as it spelled out in far greater detail the powers of a district with respect to failing schools. The senator's proposal, which Senator Kennedy's staff also helped draft, specified what governance changes the LEA could undertake before three years had elapsed. Once a school entered "school improvement" status, the district could intervene by reconstituting part or all of the staff, creating a charter school, creating schools within schools or other small learning environments, reducing or withholding Title I funds, implementing an evidence-based program, or closing the school. It could also mandate intensive professional development aligned with the state's content and performance standards.

In the case of a school where three years had gone by without its making the gains needed under the state's definition of adequate yearly progress, the Bingaman amendment specified that the corrective action had to do two things. First, it had to change the school's administration or governance by the means described above (i.e., reconstitution or creation of a charter school). Second, the corrective action had to provide for all staff professional development that was supported by reliable evidence of effectiveness and was related to the state's content and performance standards. Even though this Bingaman amendment failed in committee, Republicans took its contents wholesale, but removed the two mandatory requirements (i.e., one governance intervention plus professional development). Instead, districts would be required to pick just one intervention from the list; the HELP Committee approved that version. Thus, despite the defeat of his own amendment, it really was Senator Bingaman who succeeded in advancing the idea that the 1994 accountability requirements for low-performing schools needed to be tightened and more specifically define what kinds of intervention states and districts should take. His policy proposals would survive into the 107th Congress and become the foundation for the accountability provisions in No Child Left Behind.

DUELING THEORIES OF FEDERALISM: RHETORIC ON THE FLOOR

During the floor debate, Republicans characterized the federal role in education as serving the interests of a bureaucratic system. They called for a nondirective federal role, asserting that the federal government had become an obstacle to school improvement. Senator Bill Frist (R-TN) characterized the federal government's involvement in education as a barrier to innovation: "Mired in bureaucratic mediocrity, government today has become almost an obstacle, a barrier, not an ally, and it is time for us in Washington to acknowledge that the federal role in education is not just to serve the system, but to actually serve the child."[31]

Democrats' opposing ideology supported a federal partnership with states and localities that would keep categorical programs in the ESEA targeted on the most economically disadvantaged students. Senator Wellstone, in his floor speech, protested the Republicans' attack on categorical programs, articulating that Congress had committed to the programs for legitimate reasons:

> Madame Chair, this bill is fundamentally flawed because of the programs that it block grants. There's a reason why we made a commitment to migrant education, there's a reason why we made a commitment to homeless children, there's a reason why we make a specific commitment with accountability standards to make sure that Title I works for children that are disadvantaged, and that they can do better in school. There's a reason why these are categorical programs, there's a reason why we've set some standards. And the reason is, that the United States House of Representatives and the United States Senate decided that we are a national community as well as states, and as a national community, we make a commitment in the House and in the Senate that no child, no matter how poor or how vulnerable, no matter the son or daughter of migrant farm workers, or a child that's homeless, or a child that's living in an inner city or a rural neighborhood that's poor, it doesn't make any difference, those children will also receive assistance. And there will be standards, and that's a national

> decision, 'cause we are a national community. And this piece of legislation throws that out.[32]

Similarly, Senator Byron Dorgan (D-ND) defended the federal direction of education dollars: "There is almost a boast here in the Senate by some that we don't want to have any national aspirations or goals for our education system. And I don't know why people do that."[33] Using school renovation and repair as an example, he argued that the federal government should target its funds to assist the most disadvantaged students:

> Some of the same folks who stand up in this chamber and say, Well, we can not commit any federal money to improve America's schools, [are] saying [they] want to commit federal money to help state and local governments improve their jails. . . .
>
> Jails and prisons take priority over schools? I don't think so. It seems to me there's a contradiction here. Now all of us have been around to school districts all around this country and we've seen young children walk into classrooms that we know are in desperate need of remodeling and repair. Forty, fifty, sixty, eighty years old, I was in one the other day that was ninety years old. And the school is in desperate disrepair, and the school district has no money with which to repair it. Now what are we going to do about that? It's a school district next to an Indian reservation. Are we just gonna say those kids don't matter? Or are we going to say, by the way, if we're going to commit federal dollars, we don't want to know where those dollars are going and we don't want to direct it to deal with the issues we know are important, such as school renovation and repair, and dealing with crumbling schools, or decreasing classroom size by adding more teachers? We don't want to know about that. We don't want to direct investment in order to reach some sort of national goals, or have an aspiration of what we want to get out of this school system, because we're worried someone will mistake that for federal control of local schools.[34]

By contrast, Senator Judd Gregg described a completely opposite vision for the federal role, in which states are given the option of participating in federal programs that appeal to them:

> We don't know what the states need and what they want, so we're going to give the states an optional approach. . . . We don't say you have to take any specific program. We don't say in order to get a new teacher, you have to take classroom-size dollars, and if you take classroom-size dollars, you can't do anything but get new teachers. We don't say that. We say you the state can go down this cafeteria line, and if you like this program, if you like Straight A's, or you like portability, or you like public school choice, you can just take that program. And try it out in the context of an accountability system where you have to prove that you achieve the results of improving the quality of education for the low-income child.[35]

Thus the ideological lines were drawn in the Senate debate in May 2000. While Senator Joseph Lieberman (D-CT) attempted to bridge this divide with his compromise proposal, he was unable to do so in this political environment where the differences were basically philosophical.

LIEBERMAN'S "THIRD WAY"

After the block-granting pilot program had passed the House, there was still optimism on the Democrats' part that the Senate would behave more moderately because of Jeffords's leadership. The lines were not drawn in the sand in the Senate for several more months. It was during this time that Senator Lieberman advanced a set of policy ideas that attempted to find a "Third Way" between Democrats' programs and Republicans' block grants. To understand why the amendment failed on the Senate floor in May, it is important to know two things: first, what the substance of the proposal meant; and second, what Lieberman was trying to accomplish politically.

Lieberman had unveiled his Public Education Reinvestment, Reinvention, and Responsibility (or "3 R's") plan in November 1999, while the House was debating HR2. The bill was based on a policy paper that had been written by Andrew Rotherham of the Progressive Policy Institute entitled *Toward Performance-Based Federal Education Funding.*[36] In introducing the legislation, Lieberman stated that Congress's way of doing education policy represented "a false choice between a Democratic agenda of more spending and a Republican agenda of more block grants and vouchers."[37] Among other measures, the plan would allow the Department of Education to "get tougher on low-performing schools."[38] The senator's proposal also addressed the problem of resources for high-poverty schools, calling for increase in funding in Title I by 50 percent, up to $12 billion, while targeting far more of the money to high-poverty schools.

The main problem to be addressed in Title I, as Lieberman defined it, was concentration of the program funds to the neediest students. "The truth is that this well-intentioned program is not nearly as focused on serving poor communities as it is perceived to be, leaving many poor children without any aid or hope whatsoever. . . . We simply must do a better job of driving Title I, along with other federal education aid, down to those schools and those children who need it most. New money alone won't fix all that ails these schools, but it is a critical piece of the puzzle."[39]

The plan would achieve this targeting goal by first increasing the authorization by $4 billion, to $12 billion a year. The new dollars would be tightly targeted so that states and districts with the highest concentrations of poor children would receive a significant increase in their Title I funding. There would be a gradual phaseout of the "hold-harmless" provisions, that is, those that guaranteed states and districts the same amount of funding as in the previous year. Lieberman knew that it was politically difficult to get members to vote for any immediate phaseout of hold-harmless provisions, so he began with changing funding allocations within the state first.

The three other major provisions would affect the many categorical programs in ESEA besides Title I. The programs would be consolidated into funding streams. These were Teacher Quality; Fostering English Proficiency; and High Performance Initiatives. Each performance initiative would become its own title, and the whole bill would thus consolidate about twenty ESEA programs, including school safety, literacy technology, and summer and after-school programs.

Lieberman incorporated selected ideas of other Democrats, such as Bingaman's accountability provisions for schools in "corrective action" (designated low-performing in Title I), and some of Kennedy's on teacher quality from Title II. The bill's major aim was to streamline federal education programs and target limited federal resources. Andrew Rotherham explained that encouraging state experimentation was another underlying principle:

> The states are moving forward on education, rapidly. On every front—choice, charter schools and so forth, what they've done on standards. . . . In that context, should we not rethink the federal role? Why should we have this static federal role?[40]

Rotherham further explained that both the 1994 reauthorization and the "Three R's" were very controversial with Republicans because while they included programmatic devolution, they also increased programmatic accountability. Thus Lieberman's proposal did not involve GOP-style devolution per se, but a hybrid approach.

The New Democrats' reason for introducing the bill was that they were concerned over the lack of accountability of schools for academic performance and the failure of a dispersed federal system of funding and programs to close the achievement gaps in the country; they were equally frustrated by the polarization in the Senate that blocked major education reforms. Lieberman was willing to risk criticism from within his own party if it meant achieving progress toward a real compromise; as his aide Michele Stockwell acknowledged, "We probably are asking for more streamlining and consolidation than most people on the Democratic side would be willing to jump onto at this stage."[41] When the bill was introduced in the Senate on March 31, 2000, there were eight "New Democratic" sponsors.[42] Five were from increasingly conservative southern states, like Blanche Lincoln of Arkansas and Mary Landrieu of Louisiana. John Breaux (D-LA), considered the Senate's most conservative Democrat, was among them, as was Charles Robb

(D-VA), who would go on to lose his seat to Republican Governor George Allen in November. Another was Evan Bayh (D-IN), who had long been active in the Democratic Leadership Council and had been mentioned as a potential Gore running mate. It is plausible that Lieberman, too, was motivated by the prospect of becoming the running mate. His promise to "restructure a thirty-year-old system" matched David Mayhew's observation that Senators looking to advance often take positions with the theme, "We can do better."[43]

Yet as Glen Chambers, an aide to Senator Sam Brownback (R-KS) observed, Lieberman's proposal became an explicit challenge to other Democrats: "[The Democrats] have to deal with him, they have to deal with his policy, and should they take back the House and Senate, Lieberman is in a good position to push this kind of an agenda. It's creating a lot of excitement. You have a real reform and a recognition that what we've been doing for the past thirty years is not the way to go."[44] The Democrats did, in fact, have to contend with Lieberman's ideas. His middle ground of targeting Title I funds but allowing an easing of regulations and "performance partnerships" was a major departure from the policies supported by the more liberal HELP Committee Democrats, who were already grappling with their responses to Lieberman's proposal.

Even before Lieberman introduced the bill in the Senate, Republican aides saw that it had the potential to divide the Democrats politically. Senator Brownback's aide (R-KS) said, "If I were in the Democratic leadership, I would be really putting the screws to Lieberman on this. Because if the Republicans embrace this thing, then it puts the Democrats in a very awkward position because they're fractured."[45]

Some committee Democrats did not like Lieberman's emphasis on expansion of public school choice. But the chief objections of committee Democrats was to the fact that the bill required districts not making adequate yearly progress to redirect funds away from programs such as Safe and Drug Free Schools and After-School Programs to Title I. As Wellstone's aide, Jill Morningstar, explained: "Even if you are making adequate yearly progress, does that mean you don't need Safe and Drug Free Schools? Does that mean you don't need after-school [programs]? Does that mean you don't need ed tech? Of course it doesn't. And does that make them lower priorities because your standardized test scores are going up? No. Wellstone would never support that. . . . There's no way a single committee Democrat would support what they're doing."[46] She was correct in her assessment. The HELP Committee Democrats did not embrace the 3R's proposal. Not a single Republican voted for it on the Senate floor on May 9, only the bloc of 13 New Democrats. The presidential election had precluded a Democratic legislative success.

Even though formation of a coalition to bridge ideologies proved impossible, Lieberman's proposal put onto the table specific policy ideas and alternatives that other senators, particularly other New Democrats, would borrow. Following the May 2000 defeat, for instance, New Democratic senator Mary Landrieu (D-LA) offered a measure in the July appropriations process to fund Title I targeted grants. This measure received the votes of twenty-six senators, including some Republicans.

Andrew Rotherham and other New Democrats viewed it as inevitable that the ESEA would have to become more flexible, efficient, and effective; in October 2000, both Rotherham and Lieberman's staff predicted that the 3R's bill would have a political renaissance in a new Congress.[47]

CONCLUSION

There are several political elements manifest in the 106th Congress that would be critical to the passage of No Child Left Behind in the 107th.

First, the Democrats fought the Straight A's block grant, arguing that giving money to the governors to spend as they chose was not an act of support for "local control," as Republican rhetoric claimed, but an abdication of federal responsibilities to serve the most disadvantaged students. Democrats would not step away from what they viewed as a historic commitment to the neediest students. This fundamental schism would continue into the 107th Congress, though President Bush would ultimately have to resolve it himself in order for No Child Left Behind to pass.

Second, the profound divisions between parties and within the politically polarized HELP Committee led New Democrats to introduce a bill that represented a "Third Way," one that incorporated Senator Bingaman's and Representative Miller's proposals for accountability. This proposal would lead the way directly to the No Child Left Behind Act in the 107th Congress, both substantively and politically. Lieberman's proposal ensured that the subgroup accountability model remained alive in the policy stream, having won support from both parties in the House. The presidential campaign, too, reinforced the idea that accountability, whether through choice or intervention in failing schools, needed to be strengthened in Title I.

Third, interest groups representing the former education establishment saw their influence diminished. While the HELP Committee liberal Democrats' staff did reach out to outside groups for technical assistance on the substance of the bill, such contacts took place in a fairly limited sphere and they failed to have a broader impact. One instance of their indirect influence is that the Center for Law and Education and the Education Trust were instrumental in advising Bingaman's aides as they drafted language about mandated interventions for failing schools. Although Bingaman's amendment failed, these policy alternatives would resurface.

The groups that were most influential in policy development, however, were invited to strategy sessions with Republican aides on a selective basis. The chief external sources of influence on policy proposals during the 106th were those of conservative think tanks, the National Governors Association, and the EXPECT Coalition. In the Senate, the moderate Republican committee chair, Jeffords, did not seek the input of think tanks, but chose the NGA instead. On the other hand, the Department of Education, whose primary agenda was preservation of the structure of the IASA, was not consulted by the Republicans. The department, meanwhile, negotiated with many of the traditionally liberal interest groups, as well as with White House staff, to ensure that Clinton's priorities were reflected in the bill.

Because education had traditionally been the political domain of the Democratic Party, developing policy proposals for ESEA programs was new for the Republican leadership. Consequently, the Republican Party leadership perceived a strong impetus for change in federal education policy. In this political context, many Republican education staff labeled liberal-leaning education interest groups as the "status quo" establishment and associated these groups with the failure of compensatory education programs. The education lobby groups representing practitioners, for so long allied with the Democrats in the majority, faced new and more conservative competitors. Under such conditions, the expertise itself became contingent on ideology.

Part III

THE 107TH CONGRESS, 2001: PARTISAN LOYALTY AND IDEOLOGICAL DEFECTION

How President G. W. Bush was able to move his party to the center and encourage Congress to pass the largest expansion of the federal role in education since 1965.

Chapter 6

Bush, Kennedy, and the New Democrats Play Alliance Politics

The centrist Democratic proposals of the Progressive Policy Institute, introduced by Senator Lieberman without success in the 106th Congress, would be merged with the Bush administration's proposals through a process of negotiation among a small group of senators to produce the No Child Left Behind Act of 2001. In contrast to the stalemate of the previous Congress, there was a return to more typical patterns of bargaining and negotiation between the two parties over specific policies and programs, such as testing, choice, and funding levels. Changes in the leadership of the education committees and the Senate as a whole allowed the Democratic Party greater leverage, counterbalancing the new Republican administration. President Bush would play an active, agenda-setting role, publicly and privately charging the committee leadership to pass an education bill. The four leading negotiators, the two chairmen and two ranking members of the House and Senate education committees, continued to be willing to seek common ground. In the aftermath of the September terrorist attacks, President Bush urged Congress to act quickly to pass the bill in order to demonstrate that it was not immobilized and could still tend to the nation's needs. In this, he and Secretary of Education Roderick Paige were successful. The Republican Party leadership, notably Majority Leader Trent Lott, also exerted pressure on members to reach agreement and produce a bill.

THE POLITICS OF ENACTMENT

President Bush and the Republican Senate leadership saw that circumventing the HELP Committee in favor of dealing with the New Democrats was necessary for the development of its message on education as well as the policies. After all, the 106th Congress had made it apparent that Bush needed the thirteen New Democrats to join the Republican majority in order to get the bill. It has become more frequent in recent Congresses for the party leadership to affect the agenda setting and content of a bill in committee or to circumvent the committee entirely. "In contrast to committee chairs," writes Larry Evans, "party leaders are able to expand the range of feasible bargains and side-payments beyond the jurisdiction of one or two panels, facilitating efforts to broker disagreements among warring factions."[1]

Because the House and Senate did their work and passed their respective bills simultaneously (see Figure 6.1. below for legislative time line), the substantive issues were highly interdependent. While there were differences in the ways in which the two chambers developed and managed their bills, the chapters that follow emphasize the common patterns of inter- and intraparty divisions on particular issues across chambers, as well as how the executive and interest groups positioned themselves relative to the Congress. While the House presented some challenges, the president's challenge throughout was to break the partisan division of the Senate. To do so, he and his advisors would have to circumvent the HELP Committee.

Changes in Leadership in the New Congress

The 2000 Congressional election gave Republicans a margin of control of seven votes in the House: there were 221 Republicans, 212 Democrats, and 2 Independents, a net loss of only 2 Republican seats from the 106th. In the Senate, however, there was a 50–50 split between Democrats and Republicans (with Vice President Cheney the tiebreaker), and Republicans retained control of the committees. When House Education and Workforce Committee Chair Bill Goodling retired at the end of the 106th Congress, both Thomas Petri (R-WI) and Peter Hoekstra (R-MI) vied to become his replacement. Petri claimed that as a more centrist Republican, he had a better chance of being able to negotiate a bipartisan bill.[2] The party leadership, however, favored John Boehner of Ohio, a conservative member who won election to the House in 1991 and who had been a loyal supporter of Gingrich. Boehner was among 132 representatives to oppose the 1994 reauthorization of the ESEA, though he had succeeded in attaching a public school choice amendment to the bill. He had voted in the past in favor of both private school vouchers and the repeal of bilingual education programs.[3] Boehner got the chairmanship.

While Goodling had a record of working on legislation in a bipartisan way, at least one staff member says that it would have been politically difficult for Goodling to have supported many of Bush's key proposals. In contrast, Boehner had worked mostly on labor and workforce issues and had

Figure 6.1. Chronology of Passage of No Child Left Behind Act in 107th Congress

December 2000: President-elect Bush invites Congressional leaders, including selected New Democrats, to Austin during transition to encourage bipartisan work on education bill.

January 2001: Bush sends his No Child Left Behind blueprint proposal to the Hill.

March 2001: House Committee on Education and the Workforce approves HR1.

March 8, 2001: Senate Health, Education, Labor, and Pensions Committee approves S1, the Better Education for Students and Teachers (BEST) Act of 2001.

March and April 2001: Senate negotiating group, consisting of New Democrats, Republicans, and later Edward Kennedy, meets separately from the HELP Committee to draft an alternative bill, which will become the base package for the Senate floor (instead of the HELP Committee–reported bill).

May 9, 2001: HR1 goes to House floor.

May 23, 2001: House approves HR1 by vote of 384–45.

May 24, 2001: Senate HELP Committee Chair James Jeffords switches parties while S1 is on the floor; chairmanship passes to Edward Kennedy.

June 14, 2001: Senate approves S1 by vote of 91–8.

June–December 2001: Conference committee, or "Third House," convenes to reconcile differences between two bills.

December 13, 2001: House approves conference report.

December 18, 2001: Senate approves conference report.

January 8, 2002: President Bush signs No Child Left Behind Act in Hamilton, Ohio.

not been very involved in education issues on the committee. Republican aide Sally Lovejoy of the House Education and Workforce Committee noted, "Mr. Boehner's vision was, I'm here to push the president's agenda. . . . And for someone that didn't have much of an agenda on education it was easier for him to do that, because he didn't have a background on that, he didn't have any set views on how he felt."[4] Lovejoy added that Boehner had always had a conservative voting record on education, joining with the Gingrich Congress's proposal to abolish the Department of Education, "but I think he realized that that didn't help us at all and actually we lost seats."[5]

Alex Nock, Democratic aide to Representative Dale Kildee (D-MI) on the House Education and Workforce Committee, agreed:

> Boehner was much less entrenched in terms of a firm ideology, having not been the lead on a lot of education legislation in previous Congresses. This contrasts with someone like Goodling. Chairman Goodling had seen it all before. From being a teacher, a superintendent, a principal, a member of Congress on the committee for twenty-some odd years, he had seen it all before. But Boehner, having never been heavily involved with education issues, didn't come to the table with a whole lot of preconceived notions. This was useful in being able to fashion a bill.[6]

On December 29, 2000, President-elect Bush nominated Dr. Roderick Paige to serve as Secretary of Education. A superintendent of the Houston Independent School District since 1994, Paige was not only the first African American to serve as U.S. Secretary of Education, but also the first to have led a big-city district.

A Team Emerges from the Campaign

As described in the previous chapter, Bush placed education at the forefront of his presidential campaign. Using the slogan "Leave No Child Behind," a decade-old motto of the Children's Defense Fund, he emphasized annual testing, accountability, and private school vouchers. To distinguish his agenda from Gore's, however, he also talked about "character education" and bilingual education that favored English immersion, and proposed to spend $1 billion a year for five years on programs to diagnose reading problems in young children.

Rhetorically, Bush emphasized "the soft bigotry of low expectations" and the failure of poor schools to educate children. Bush presented himself as a leader who was able to work with both Democrats and Republicans, pointing to his record in Texas of supporting education reform. As for the plank still in the Republican Party 2000 platform supporting abolition of the Department of Education, Bush lobbied to have it stricken.[7] Thus Bush's vision of the federal role, as it emerged on the campaign trail, was one that stressed local control as well as federal assistance to the most economically disadvantaged students. As he stated within days of taking office,

> Change will not come by disdaining or dismantling the federal role in education. I believe strongly in local control of schools. I trust local folks to chart the

path to excellence. But educational excellence is a national issue, and at the moment is a presidential priority.[8]

The substance of the education proposals on the campaign trail were largely crafted by Barnett A. "Sandy" Kress, an attorney, a former Dallas school board president, and member of the centrist Democratic Leadership Council; Margaret LaMontagne, Bush's chief education policy adviser in Austin; and Sarah Yousseff, a former staff member from the Heritage Foundation. As a former chairman of the Dallas County Democratic Party, Sandy Kress was a somewhat unlikely Bush associate, but ever since the governor had contacted him in 1993 about his work on an education accountability task force, the two had worked together on Texas's package of testing and accountability reforms.

COURTING KEY LEGISLATORS AND GOVERNORS IN TEXAS

Meanwhile, during the period of transition to a new administration, President-elect Bush invited a select group of congressional leaders down to Austin on December 21 to discuss education reform.

The group was comprised of both Republicans and moderate Democrats like Representative Rob Andrews (D-NJ) and Senator Evan Bayh (D-IN). There he asked them to dedicate themselves over the coming months to passing a bill in a bipartisan fashion. There was one key Democratic member of this delegation who was initially not on the invitation list until John Boehner insisted on his inclusion: George Miller.

With the retirement of William Clay (D-MO) after the 106th, Representative Miller became the ranking Democratic member of the House Committee on Education and the Workforce. This, too, would make a difference in the tenor of negotiations in the 107th. As one Democratic aide in the House said, "I've heard that [Clay] was just too beholden, maybe, to some of the interest groups, to some of the teachers unions, different things like that. A little inflexible."[9] The Republicans, though, knew that Miller was one of the most important Democrats to have on their side. He had shown willingness to negotiate and occasionally cross party lines, particularly on accountability and teacher qualifications. During the reauthorization process of the ESEA in the 106th, for instance, he had voted in favor of the Republican-sponsored Teacher Empowerment Act.[10]

Thus when Boehner learned that Miller was not on the invitation list for the Austin meeting, as he later recalled, "I told the Bush staff that if I became chairman of the committee, this is the last meeting I go to without Miller. So they invited him."[11] While Boehner and Miller had been former adversaries, respectively anchoring the right and left wings of their committee, Miller realized they had common ground if Bush wanted to focus on the achievement of the poorest students. Further, they shared a history of having been through the House ESEA reauthorization process in 1999 and knew that the two parties had been able to find common ground. It was in the Senate where ideological divisions had been the strongest in the 106th Congress and where a compromise had to be found in order for there to be an education bill in the 107th.

The House Republican leaders, Majority Leader Richard Armey (R-TX), Speaker Dennis Hastert (R-IL), and Whip Tom DeLay (R-TX), did not share President Bush's predilection for a centrist education bill. Nor did Senate Majority Leader Trent Lott (R-MS), who consistently opposed Democrats' efforts to secure funding increases for Title I. When the House Republican leadership appointed Boehner as their education committee chair, they could not foresee how far to the center he would be willing to move for President Bush's sake.

Shortly after New Year's Day 2001, Bush convened nineteen Republican governors at his Texas ranch and stated his support for annual testing as a nonnegotiable part of any education reform plan, while promising them greater flexibility in the use of federal dollars.[12]

PRESENTING THE BLUEPRINT TO THE HILL

Rather than sending the President's program as a bill to Congress in January, the administration opted for a strategy of proposing broad principles and allowing members and their staff to develop legislation. Bush appointed Kress to be his chief negotiator on the bill. Sarah Youssef, who joined the staff of the Domestic Policy Council, was assigned to work as Kress's assistant. Youssef recalled that unlike the Clinton administration, which sent a proposal up to the Hill in 1999, the White House was glad to let congressional leaders take the lead role in putting the legislative "meat" onto the bones of the President's plan:

> I think the way we approached it was very smart because we knew that people already had their minds made up about certain things. There was already consensus around certain issues, like the teacher bill for example. . . . It was actually very similar to what the President proposed during the campaign. . . . We knew if we could be that unifying factor, that we could get the House and the Senate to work on something that was conferenceable.[13]

Kress agreed; the President wanted "to let the legislative process take place within the Congress."[14] That way, Congress, and likely the Democrats, would have to shoulder the blame for any breakdowns in the process.[15]

Though Education Secretary Roderick Paige testified once before the HELP Committee, the Education Department was not actively involved on the Hill in the development of new policies the way that Bush's White House staff was. The Assistant Secretary for Legislation and Congressional Affairs, Rebecca Campoverde, was not even nominated until July, months after both bills had already passed. Bush's strategy was to first lay out a thirty-page legislative blueprint and then let the committees draft the bill.

A legislative aide to the majority on the House Education and the Workforce Committee confirmed that the department and Secretary Paige played less of a role in the legislative process than did the committee:

> Secretary Paige had a somewhat limited role because he was just coming on board. And the plan had essentially been formulated by the Bush administration prior to his getting into the position. He certainly was an advocate, and he was helpful but a lot of the policy decisions were being driven by the White House and this committee.[16]

Alex Nock, a legislative aide to the Democratic side of the House committee, agreed: "In terms of framing the proposals, a lot of that was done before the department and Paige had a chance to influence it." He added that the White House played more of a role when the two bodies were forming the bills, rather than in the conference.[17] With the legislative agenda being so definitively set by the White House and the Domestic Policy Council, most education interest groups had a diminished role in affecting the legislative process in the 107th Congress. Sarah Youssef of the Domestic Policy Council recalled that she could not "ever remember really hitting snags with interest groups. . . . We weren't persuaded or pressured by them, and I think that's partly because they were already on board with what we wanted to do or they were willing to go along with it."[18] She added, "The message of accountability, the message of reform in the system, was something that I think people either had been won over to, or were winnable over to."[19]

Bush's legislative blueprint reflected his campaign proposals. It proposed consolidation of categorical grant programs; annual testing in Grades 3 through 8; annual participation by all states in the National Assessment of Educational Progress in fourth and eighth grades; and when schools failed to make progress for three consecutive years (termed "corrective action" status in Title I), both public school choice and "exit vouchers" to private school tuition or supplemental services. "Closing the achievement gap" was also a stated goal, as set forth during his campaign. States and schools that "closed the gap" under Title I would receive federal bonuses, while those that did not would be subject to losing a portion of their administrative funding. State and school report cards with disaggregated racial achievement data, a feature of both the Texas accountability system and the House bill in the

106th Congress, were included. Finally, the blueprint included a proposal called "charter states," modeled on the Straight A's block-grant proposal from the 106th Congress, by which states could consolidate categorical programs in exchange for results.

The process of legislative development in the House was less complex than that in the Senate because Representatives Boehner and Miller led a "working group" drawn from the membership of the Education and Workforce Committee. The negotiations in the Senate, by contrast, were elaborate because there were, in fact, two separate sets of negotiations occurring simultaneously: one in the committee and one outside of it. A second major difference was that the House, by a narrow vote of 219–201, adopted rules that barred Democrats from offering a range of amendments, many directed at school construction and class-size reduction. Democrats did not face that particular barrier in the Senate and thus had the chance to make the case for their priorities.

In many respects, Bush's blueprint closely reflected the New Democrats' priorities. The White House's negotiations with Senate Democrats not on the education committee, including Lieberman and Bayh, would prove crucial to getting many of Bush's proposals enacted, and Kress led the way in courting them. One of the consequences, though, was the growing alienation of the committee chairman, James Jeffords (R-VT).

THE RETURN OF THE "NEW DEMOCRATIC" AGENDA TO THE FORE

From the time that Bush invited Senators Evan Bayh and Jeff Bingaman, Representatives Tim Roemer, Michael Castle, George Miller, and Rob Andrews, along with other Congressional Democrats to Austin in January to talk about education but excluded Kennedy, it was clear that Bush was courting moderate Democrats. (Bush did not invite Senator Joseph Lieberman because of the obvious awkwardness; the Supreme Court had just ruled on the election.) This meeting set the tone for the administration's focus on getting a bipartisan consensus on education. Bush even told a group of New Democrats in a meeting that "imitation is the sincerest form of flattery," referring to the Progressive Policy Institute's education proposals from which he drew many ideas.[20] As soon as Bush revealed his legislative blueprint, the New Democrats reintroduced Lieberman's bill, the Public Education Reinvestment, Reinvention, and Responsibility Act, from the previous Congress, hoping to cut a deal quickly. The Bush blueprint borrowed heavily from the New Democrats' proposals: it called for consolidation of the fifty-four elementary and secondary education programs into five categories reflecting federal priorities: (1) educating disadvantaged students; (2) teacher quality; (3) English fluency; (4) school choice; and (5) school safety.

Between January and April, the President's negotiator, Sandy Kress, engaged in a form of alliance politics designed to bring Edward Kennedy, the Health, Education, Labor, and Pension Committee's ranking Democrat, to the negotiating table. The administration feared that HELP chairman Jim Jeffords (at that time, still a Republican), allied with Kennedy and the other liberal Democrats on the Senate HELP Committee, would produce a bill that too closely resembled President Clinton's priorities, with set-asides for class-size reduction and aide for school construction. Yet Kress and the New Democrats knew that on the Senate floor, it would be extremely difficult for them to hold their bloc of thirteen together if Kennedy were not on board. Kennedy's years of leadership on education policy meant that he was a cue provider to his fellow Democrats.

Thus the White House opted to convene negotiating talks outside the committee structure, all the while trying to get Kennedy to want to join. Kress's negotiating group was comprised of approximately seven to nine senators, a mix of Republicans and New Democrats, with whom they believed they would be able to bargain productively. This group consisted of Republicans Judd Gregg (R-NH), Tim Hutchinson (R-AR), Jim Jeffords (R-VT), Susan Collins (R-ME), Bill Frist (R-TN), and New Democrats Evan Bayh (D-IN) and Joseph Lieberman (D-CT), and occasionally, Blanche Lincoln (D-AR) and Mary Landrieu (D-LA). Beginning in January, this group met with the purpose of negotiating a substitute amendment to the committee bill for floor action.

In February, though, Jeffords convened the HELP Committee's official work. Once these meetings had begun, the White House did not support Jeffords's work in committee but Gregg's informal negotiations (adding to the complication was that Gregg, Hutchinson, and Collins were members of both groups). According to Elizabeth Fay, education aide to Senator Evan Bayh (D-IN), "The White House continued to pretend that they were working with the committee when all the time they were negotiating with us."[21] As in the 106th Congress, a member of Majority Leader Trent Lott's staff attended HELP Committee meetings with the purpose of supporting Judd Gregg's positions.

In early March the Republican Party leadership gave Jeffords a final date by which they would need a committee bill for introduction on the floor in April. Jeffords was still grappling with various accountability provisions and told them that he would get it to them when he was ready. Lott gave Jeffords an order to get the bill to the floor within a week, regardless of whether it was ready. "At that time, Jeffords's staff was getting a little upset, saying, well, if the chairman of the committee feels the bill isn't ready, then it isn't ready," explained Bayh's aide Elizabeth Fay. Lott and his staff were dismissive of Jeffords, continuing to defer to Gregg.[22] Jeffords demanded that the committee work during the day. But the Republicans in the negotiating group often met at night from 5 until 10 P.M., which created double duty for some members.

Jeffords used the 2000 version of the 3R's as the base for the committee "mark," or draft on which the committee would vote. It did not contain any provisions for private school vouchers, Straight A's, nor the traditional Clinton priorities of class-size reduction and school repair.

The Senate committee Republicans, unsurprisingly, did not like what was proposed. "Jeffords and Kennedy came out with their bill for markup. And we all sort of said, 'this isn't really what we want,'" recalled Holly Kuzmich, education aide to Republican member Tim Hutchinson.[23] However, Gregg directed the committee Republicans not to get too involved in battles over the substance of the bill, since the sideline negotiations were still actively under way to produce a substitute bill to introduce on the floor. This is a major reason why the committee vote approving the Better Education for Students and Teachers Act on March 8 was a unanimous 20–0. The pressure from the party leadership for Jeffords to report out any bill so they could move to the floor was overwhelming.

Meanwhile, throughout April, the negotiating group was making progress toward its goal of producing a substitute bill. Kennedy had decided that he wanted the Congress to pass an education bill; and when he learned about the outside negotiating group, as Kress had hoped, he decided he did not want to be cut out of the legislative action. Kennedy realized that some version of what Gregg was negotiating with the White House and Kress would have to be passed, since his committee Democrats were not ideologically close to the rest of the Democratic caucus. Kennedy's first action was to let the White House know that they should deal with *him*, not just with Lieberman and Bayh. According to an education aide to a Democratic HELP Committee member, Kennedy reminded Bush that the President would ultimately need to deal with *him*: "Kennedy went to Bush and said: 'You said from the beginning that you wanted to work with me. You're not going to get an education bill out of this Congress without me. Do you want to work with me or not?' And Bush realized that it was much to his advantage to have Kennedy on his side."[24] So Kennedy, along with Senator Christopher Dodd (D-CT), joined the negotiating group. Thus Kennedy was working both on and off the committee, involved with two different versions of the bill at the same time.

By unanimous consent agreement, the negotiating group's alternative package was introduced on the Senate floor in April as a "managers' amendment," a package of numerous individual amendments agreed to by both sides in advance. Chairman Jeffords and Kennedy were the bill's initial managers. Usually a managers' amendment contains only technical adjustments to the committee bill; by contrast, this was essentially a whole new bill. Since the Democratic members of the HELP Committee had not yet seen the new negotiated managers' amendment, Kennedy gave them ample time to read it before it was brought to a vote on the floor. These Democratic members—notably Hillary Clinton, Murray, Reed, and Wellstone—were upset that Kennedy had bypassed them for purposes of political expediency and that the negotiations had involved two Democrats who were not committee members. They continued to offer Kennedy their support, however, because they acknowledged that many of his compromises would hold New Democratic votes on the floor.

CONCLUSION

Both politically and substantively, the New Democrats' "Third Way" was to prove successful once the ideas were freed from the association with the Clinton administration, and the various interests worked to forge No Child Left Behind. Andrew Rotherham's proposal became the basis for Bush's blueprint and Lieberman's floor bill in the 106th. The New Democrats' ideological territory became comfortable for more and more members of Congress as party leaders sought a compromise. While the 3R's proposal to consolidate ESEA programs into five funding streams proved politically impossible, the bill that ultimately passed consolidated programs into performance-based funding streams and targeted the funds more effectively to high-poverty states and districts. Thus, while the parties would wrangle over a range of issues, from testing to vouchers, the New Democrats' plan would prove a successful framework for a compromise.

Though Bayh's and Lieberman's influence over the process was eventually curbed by Kennedy, the workings of the outside bipartisan negotiating group alienated key HELP Committee members like Murray, Wellstone, and Reed. Perhaps it was true, as New Democrats suggested, that the Democratic HELP Committee members were too far to the left and too aligned with traditional interest groups to represent the Democratic caucus's position on education. But these excluded Democratic committee members would later have their opportunity to make demands.

Chapter 7

Bargaining: Choice, Accountability, Testing, and Funding

Well, I have to admit it, I voted for that awful bill. I came here to eliminate the Department of Education, so it was very hard for me to vote for something that expands the Department of Education. But this is one of [the president's] big agenda items, and I did not want to be the person—and I have people who follow me—to keep it from going on. I may vote against it when it comes back out of the conference committee. I'm ashamed to say it was just blatant politics. I can't even remember another time when I've actually voted against my principles. . . . The way it worked in the Congress was, they started at the center and moved left.

—Majority Whip Tom DeLay (R-TX)
to radio talk show host Rush Limbaugh, August 8, 2001[1]

During the period before Jeffords switched parties in May of 2001, the House and Senate passed their respective versions of the bill that after much negotiation between and within parties, would become No Child Left Behind. Choice, testing, funding, and accountability were at the heart of the debate. As Representative DeLay made clear on the airwaves, the politics that produced the two bills were not just intracommittee, but intraparty. President Bush continually distanced himself from his party's conservative caucus during this period leading up to what would be a brief period of Democratic control of the Senate.

VOUCHERS: "DON'T LEAVE THE RESERVATION"

Private school choice and vouchers were central to Bush's articulated philosophy: Parents ought to have a choice in pulling students out of chronically failing schools. In Texas, Bush as governor had advocated vouchers in the 1999 legislative session; they were a top policy priority for the state's

Christian Coalition. He did not fight for them energetically, however, and was unable to persuade one key Republican representative from blocking the movement of the bill to the floor.[2] Thus, when he proposed vouchers as part of the No Child Left Behind, congressional Democrats were cognizant that President Bush might be willing to walk away from that part of the package, and they fought it from the first day he proposed it. Fairly early in the negotiations, Undersecretary of Education Eugene Hickok stated that the President and Kress did not wish "to sacrifice accountability on the altar of school choice."[3]

Vouchers had become an increasingly unpopular legislative proposal in the House during the 1990s: The margins of defeat of proposed bills had grown larger and larger.[4] Representatives Petri and Armey's proposals to introduce vouchers to private schools into Title I had failed in the 106th Congress. Yet Bush, as a presidential candidate, kept the issue alive by proposing that parents ought to have a choice in pulling students out of chronically failing schools. On the campaign trail, he had proposed that parents of students in failing schools be eligible to receive a voucher of $1,500 to enroll their children at other schools, including private and parochial.

In his introduction of the No Child Left Behind plan, Bush advocated for vouchers as part of a set of options for parents when schools failed:

> In order for an accountability system to work, there [have] to be consequences, and I believe one of the most important consequences will be, after a period of time, giving the schools time to adjust and districts time to try different things, if they're failing, that parents ought to be given different options. If children are trapped in schools that will not teach and will not change, there has to be a different consequence.[5]

In his State of the Union address in January of 2001, Bush mentioned vouchers as one of his goals for the bill, but he did not say that he would veto an education bill that did not include them.[6] Sally Lovejoy, senior education aide to the Republicans on the House Committee on Education and the Workforce, said that many House Republicans wanted the president to fight harder for vouchers than he did:

> The party leadership wasn't always on board with the President, particularly on testing. And then particularly when the President dropped vouchers so quickly, that really made a lot of conservative Republicans upset. We didn't have the votes, in the committee or in the House, to pass vouchers. We've been there, done that before. But I think a lot of Republicans felt that the administration dropped that like a hot potato and didn't push harder for it.[7]

The House committee's debate over vouchers in Title I was rancorous. Republicans argued that vouchers were the only way for disadvantaged children to escape failing schools, while Democrats countered that vouchers would squander valuable resources and that the monies available were insufficient to help the students. Chairman Boehner said "We build ships with lifeboats, but we don't give kids a way out of dangerous, poor-performing schools." Lynn Rivers (D-CA) compared vouchers as a way to help ailing schools to medieval doctors' use of blood-sucking leeches to treat illness. Other Republicans, like Bob Schaffer (R-CO), emphasized loyalty to the president: "Don't abandon President Bush. Don't leave the reservation."[8]

But Boehner also knew he needed Democratic votes. As *Congressional Quarterly Weekly* summed up his problem, there was "nothing easy about steering a bill through the House with conservative Republicans unhappy and liberal Democrats looking for a good reason to bolt."[9] The Miller amendment in committee removed language that would have required schools to offer parents vouchers for an amount equal to the district's per-child Title I funding (about $600 nationally on average) that could be used at private schools. It also stripped out the supplemental services option after a year in corrective action status, provisions authorizing grants for local private school voucher programs, and districts' ability to use funds under the Title VI block grants to expand private school choice for disadvantaged students in failing schools.[10] The committee vote on the Miller amendment was 27–20, with five Republicans joining all of the Democrats and one voting "present" to pass it.[11] For committee Democrats, this vote was the key to their continued support.

On the House floor Majority Leader Richard Armey (R-TX) offered two voucher amendments, repeats of the "unsafe or failing schools" and the pilot program he had offered in the 106th. Both failed. It is notable that the margin of defeat for Armey's "Unsafe and Failing Schools" amendment was larger than in the previous Congress: it was defeated 273–155, as compared to 257–166 in the 106th, signaling that even fewer members of the Republican party were supportive despite the White House's voucher proposals. The final vote on No Child Left Behind in the House was 384–45, with Republicans comprising three-quarters of the "no" votes. Thus the key to passage in the House was defeating Armey's amendments to the committee-approved bill, which didn't contain vouchers.

The teachers unions were vociferous in their opposition to the bill's choice requirements. Kara Haas, aide to moderate Republican Representative Michael Castle (DE), described how the National Education Association was quite clear from the outset about its opposition to choice: "We met with [the NEA] early on—as soon as the President's plan was released. Private school choice particularly existed in seven different areas. We went through the list, and we said: 'What about this? Could you do this?' And they just said: 'No, no, no, no, no.'" Joel Packer, a lobbyist for the NEA, confirmed that "vouchers were quite unacceptable to us."[12]

In the Senate the main political difference was the presence of Senator Judd Gregg. Though vouchers were not approved in the committee process, he was determined to add choice provisions to the bill on the floor. There he proposed an amendment that would have authorized $50 million per year to fund private school choice initiatives in ten school districts in three states that applied for the money. Attempting to meet voucher critics' objections, Gregg designed the proposal so that only children in schools that had been designated as low-performing for three years would be eligible, and their family income would have to have been less than $32,000 per year. The dollars allocated to fund the demonstration program would not be diverted from the public school system, as a new program would be created.[13]

When Gregg's amendment failed 41–58 on June 13 and did not fall neatly along party lines, he vocally blamed the Democrats. "What is it they fear?" he asked. "They fear that it may threaten those unions who for years have told us mediocrity works. They fear that this may actually disrupt the public school system."[14] Three Democrats voted in favor while eleven Republicans opposed it. While many conservative Republicans shared Gregg's view that true accountability necessitated parental choice that included the private sector, there were several dissenters among that group. One was HELP Committee member Senator Mike Enzi of Wyoming. According to his education aide Amanda Farris, Senator Enzi was "also very concerned about a federal voucher program changing the focus of education to the federal level. If you institute a federal voucher program, that is the federal government really being the impetus behind educational reform. And that's not something he's comfortable with."[15]

THE COMPROMISE: GREGG'S SUPPLEMENTAL SERVICES

When vouchers for private schools in Title I dropped out of the negotiations, it became apparent that there was room for bipartisan compromise. The removal of private school vouchers from Title I shaped the Democrats' compromise on supplemental services, which allowed federal dollars to be used by parents of students in schools not showing improvement for three years to purchase tutorial services from non-school-based providers, including religious groups and private companies. These could include tutoring and other academic interventions such as after-school enrichment. The requirement applying to all supplemental services was that they had to be provided outside the regular school day. The Republicans needed to have the equivalent of the parent making the choice, as Bush had initially proposed, so offering parents a choice to purchase tutorial services was the compromise, picking up Senator Gregg's Tuition Assistance Grants proposal from the 106th.

Senator Kennedy's position on supplemental services shifted during the process. Initially, in the HELP Committee, when Gregg first introduced his portability amendment allowing children in failing schools to use Title I dollars to transfer to a private school or obtain tutorial services, Kennedy opposed him: "Title I has been targeted on poverty, not on individual students, on the concentration of poverty."[16] After he began to negotiate with Sandy Kress in March, however, Kennedy dropped his opposition and convinced the Democrats that this was a compromise they could live with. An appropriate compromise, he maintained, was that the state would approve the institutions eligible to be service providers. So long as the legislation was clear about what entity provided them and who chose them, this was fair. The providers could be nonprofits, including faith-based groups; for-profit entities; school districts; public or private schools, and colleges and universities. Districts would have to give priority to the lowest-achieving students, and only low-income families in schools identified as low-performing were eligible.

Both parties found something compatible with their ideological stances with supplemental services. Sally Lovejoy, Boehner's chief education staffer on the House committee, reported that she reminded members who were disappointed about losing vouchers; "'You know what you're getting with supplemental services is a huge deal. For the first time we'll have federal dollars paying for private services. Even in Catholic schools, for the summer or for tutoring or whatever.' That's a huge issue, and I just think because they didn't get vouchers, they thought that was nothing."[17] For other Republicans, getting supplemental services in place was a strategy for more privatization measures in future reauthorizations. Mike Kennedy, an education aide to House education committee member Thomas Petri (R-WI), said, "At least this time we were able to get supplemental services. That was a big victory . . . hopefully, that's the camel's nose under the tent, six years from now they can maybe expand it . . . it's at least a start, a precedent maybe six years from now, upping the amount of money . . . that's one of the best things in the bill, really."[18] Likewise, Senator Gregg saw another advantage to supplemental services. As one aide who preferred anonymity recalled about a meeting with Republican Senate committee members right before the committee voted: "Gregg was explaining why they should vote for the bill . . . and he said, 'Well, the supplemental services are a foot under the door for vouchers. They're going to show that these schools aren't working properly, and we'll finally be able to show that the schools aren't doing well. The assessments are going to prove the same thing.'"[19]

While some Democrats were upset about the use of public money in private settings, many found it consistent with their views of accountability. Charles Barone, Representative George Miller's legislative director, noted that Head Start and the America Reads program were both set up for some contracting out of services, so this was not a massive difference from what other programs allowed. Democrats negotiated a 15 percent cap on the amount of Title I dollars that a district could use to pay for supplemental services. (The law mandated that a district spend a minimum 5 percent of its Title I allocation to pay for the services if they were needed.) Barone emphasized that there were numerous checks on the privatization: "It could be the district taking over services. There's nothing that says that you have to have Sylvan and these other people in. I mean, you have to give parents some choice. . . . It's a little fuzzy. It's definitely the intention of the people who pushed it to have Sylvan or Kaplan or these other people come in." He emphasized that the implementation would vary by locale, and that the law gives states the ability to leave private providers off the approved list. Further, districts have veto power over the providers. Barone said, "Miller doesn't have a problem with a school contracting for services with a private entity, as long as the money stays in the public school system, and they oversee the money."[20]

As Senator Kennedy convinced Democrats to make such compromises, he had to give the major education interest groups far less than what they wanted. From the powerful senator that the groups had always gone to, they got almost nothing. As reported in the *Washington Post*, one education lobbyist remembered that at a session with him just before the Senate took up the bill, "Kennedy just read us the riot act. 'You may not have noticed,' [Kennedy] said, 'but we don't control the White House, the Senate or the House. I'm doing my best, but I'm not going to let you stop this.'"[21] In fact, one Republican aide had heard that Kennedy personally called the NEA and demanded that they not oppose the bill; ultimately, the union took no position on it.[22] Having decided that he was going to compromise with the Republicans and the White House, Kennedy would not be able to meet all of the groups' demands.

As in the 106th Congress, all sides knew that private school vouchers in the ESEA were not a passable provision. The expansion of supplemental services, however, meant that parents would be able to use some of their Title I allocation to purchase outside instructional services. The accountability measures mandating public school choice after a school was identified as not making adequate progress had bipartisan support, as they had had in the 106th. Both of these provisions were built into the sanctions of the bill's accountability system and were designed to apply pressure to low-performing schools.

ACCOUNTABILITY: THE TECHNICAL AND POLITICAL DEBATE

The issue of adequate yearly progress in Title I highlights how ideas developed in the 106th entered the agenda stream in the 107th. Lawmakers from both parties in the 107th agreed that sanctions for continuously low-performing schools should be specified in the law. Education aides, however, would have to grapple with setting goals for improvement for schools and determining how many schools identified as failing would be politically unacceptable. Academic researchers would also weigh in with analyses of the provisions, though their effect on the outcome was to be minimal.

As described earlier, in the 106th Congress, Senator Lieberman had incorporated Bingaman's accountability blueprint into his 3R's proposal, while Representative George Miller had successfully guided similar requirements through on the House side. The Education Trust, strong proponents of the benefits of such a model of accountability for poor and minority students, was active in drafting language for both Miller and Bingaman. Thus the accountability language had been vetted on the Hill long before Bush adopted it.

Senator Jeffords was not enthusiastic about the particular model of subgroup accountability with a specified timeline. His committee staff director, Mark Powden, made a presentation showing National Assessment of Educational Progress results from three states—Texas, North Carolina, and Connecticut—and argued that a majority of schools would be labeled "failing" according to the bill.[23] The Congressional Research Service released a study in August that examined the Senate bill and concluded that the vast majority of schools in Texas, North Carolina, and Maryland would have been labeled "failing" under its definition.[24] A corroborating research paper by Thomas Kane of UCLA and Douglas Staiger of Dartmouth concluded that more than 98 percent of the schools in Texas and North Carolina would have failed to meet the proposed federal expectations in at least one year between 1994 and 1999.[25] Since Texas and North Carolina were considered models of how annual testing and accountability ought to work, Congressional aides argued that these findings were cautionary.

HELP Committee senators Jim Jeffords, Judd Gregg, Christopher Dodd, Hillary Clinton, and Tom Harkin became concerned about what the results would be if they stayed with the formula. Powden's analysis had extrapolated that under Texas's system, the achievement goals could have been reached by all students in twelve years. So the Senate changed its version from ten to twelve years. The requirements for racial and economic subgroups were less stringent than those in the House and allowed states more flexibility on how to set targets. The Senate bill would judge states by a complicated formula that would weigh more heavily the performance of subgroups performing "at a level furthest from the proficient level" and that made the greatest improvements. It required that the performance of each subgroup increase at least one percentage point annually; however, data could be averaged over the current school year and the previous two years. Thus schools could not be labeled as failing simply because minority students did not see their test scores rise in a single year.

The House bill, on the other hand, was somewhat more stringent. Schools would have to make steady progress toward proficiency for all students in reading and math in twelve years. It required that increasing percentages of students in the racial and economic subgroups make the same amount of progress as all students in the school. The House's fidelity to this model was mainly the result of George Miller's insistence. As it had in the 106th Congress, the Education Trust continued its vocal push for the tougher accountability provisions.

According to aides, White House negotiator Sandy Kress sent mixed messages about adequate yearly progress. In April, before the Senate bill went to the floor, Kress attempted to back away during negotiations from the subgroup model of accountability. The White House was uncomfortable with a fixed point of achievement, and in the middle of the Senate negotiating group's meetings, it appeared as though Bush were siding with Jeffords. The story that the national media picked up, however, was that Democrats were stalling on the education bill. When a reporter asked Minority Leader Daschle at one of his daily briefings (called the "Dugout") whether the Democrats were obstructing the negotiations, he countered that, in fact, the White House was trying to gut the accountability. "For an entire week the White House got its head kicked in by the national media, that it was trying to strip out the accountability provisions," recalled Senator Bayh's aide Elizabeth Fay.[26] Ultimately, though, Kress adjusted the Senate formula but not the fixed point of achievement for all groups that remained in both bills. It would fall to the conference committee to reconcile the accountability provisions in the House and Senate bills.

"THE CAMEL'S NOSE UNDER THE TENT": NEW FEDERAL TESTING MANDATES

The White House proposed requirements that every state would test all students every year in Grades 3 through 8, one of the most significant departures from current law. Because this policy would mean an expansion of the federal role, it was controversial among Republicans.

Congressional Democrats, with a few exceptions, were generally not opposed to further testing requirements in Title I. The 1994 reauthorization during the Clinton administration had strengthened the requirements for Title I assessment. Clinton, too, had proposed a national test in his State of the Union address in January 1997. Congressional Republicans, led by then House committee chairman Goodling, had spent the rest of Clinton's second term opposing it. Yet there also were Democrats who viewed Bush's proposal as an overly burdensome and expensive regulation of the states, or simply too much testing. For instance, Senator Patty Murray (D-WA) wasn't opposed to testing in general, but she found the proposed three through eight system to be excessive. One of her aides described her opposition: "Her concern was that testing is expensive, and it takes time and energy and focus. . . . You're really focusing on something other than teaching and learning, and it not only becomes a measure, it becomes an end in itself."[27]

Testing in Texas during the 1990s had been a vital part of the reform strategy that Bush had supported as governor. It was also strongly endorsed by the business community. Edward Rust, cochairman of the Business Coalition for Excellence in Education, testified to the House Education Reform Subcommittee in March 2001, saying, "We know it from a business standpoint that you have got to measure progress or you will never know whether or not you are getting close to your goal."[28]

Sally Lovejoy, the chief legislative aide to the majority on the House side, summarized the conundrum for the Republicans in supporting the bill's testing provisions:

> We had a president that wanted to do things that a lot of our members did not support. When we had spent a good part of the time before then objecting to testing . . . this is a different test, but our guys saw this as the camel's nose under the tent for the national test, which we had spent six years fighting. . . . Mr. Goodling led the battle to fight testing. So that would have been a big barrier for [Goodling] if he had been the chairman.[29]

The testing requirements of the proposed Bush law were potentially disruptive to the existing accountability policies in many states and districts. Under the 1994 law, states had latitude to propose their own assessments for reading and mathematics and to design their own accountability systems. As long as all students were included in the same assessment system—no separate, different tests for Title I students—the federal requirements could be met.

Bush's new policy required that states test all students every year in Grades 3 through 8 (the prior law already required that the assessments be administered once in high school). At the time the legislation was proposed, only fifteen states had such a system. The bill also added science to reading and mathematics as a third subject that states would have to assess by the academic year 2005–06 (though only in one grade in each grade span of 3–5, 6–9, and 10–12). The question then became how much money they would have to spend on testing development and administration. The kind of instruction students would receive in such an intensively test-driven system was not seriously debated, but Congressional Democrats like Senator

Paul Wellstone and numerous interest groups raised questions about the uses of the results for instruction.

In the House one single feature of the bill lost more Republican votes than any other: Bush's proposal that states be required to give the National Assessment of Educational Progress as a "check" on the rigor of state tests. It would awaken many conservative Republicans' fears about the evolution of a de facto national test. Representative Mark Souder (R-IN) said, "I have great fear of a national test. I fear the solution is going to be worse than the problem."[30] The Cato Institute, a libertarian think tank, issued a report in April that decried the proposed bill's increased funding and testing requirements, including the use of NAEP.[31]

Moderate Republican Michael Castle (R-DE), however, had formerly been a governor and was of the opinion that governors respond to the competitive pressure of where states place in comparative rankings and he persistently lobbied for the inclusion of NAEP in the bill. Because conservative Republicans such as Tom Tancredo, Mark Souder, and Peter Hoekstra were wary of NAEP, they amended the House bill to provide that states could have alternatives to NAEP, they could use it or another test to verify the state results.

The trouble in the Senate over NAEP had to do with an individual concern of Judd Gregg. The design of the NAEP test is that of a sample—a cross section of students in a state takes it rather than every student. But in New Hampshire, in order for there to be validity, every student would have to take it every year. This infuriated Senator Gregg, who saw NAEP as an enormous burden on his state's schools. He ended up with a compromise position, with a clause in the Senate bill saying that if a state has only 0.25 percent of the Title I students in the country, then they should only be required to take NAEP every other year. Ultimately, Gregg's biennial policy was what ended up in law applying to the whole country because the House could not agree on what was meant by an "alternative" to NAEP.

In a much bigger challenge to the testing requirement, Democratic Senators Murray, Dodd, and Reed joined Senators Ernest Hollings (D-SC) and Paul Wellstone (D-MN) in a move to make the new testing optional to the states, striking the word *shall* and substituting *may*. It was supported by a coalition of very conservative members who did not believe in telling the states what to do and very liberal Senators who had other concerns about testing, such as the quality of assessments and the tests' effects on instruction.

Senator Hollings argued that states were already spending millions on testing every year, and that Congress was setting up a "straw man" by claiming that there was neither testing nor accountability in states under the status quo. Further, he asserted, the mere identification of low-performing schools via testing did nothing to improve their performance: "I could flunk

30 or 40 in South Carolina this afternoon with this so-called quality test, and students do not have another school to go to and you cannot close their school down. So we spend billions, and we are in the same place as we are this minute."[32] The Hollings-Wellstone amendment was defeated on June 13 by a vote of 78 to 22. Washington, Hawaii, and Minnesota were the only three states from which both senators cast votes in favor.

Interest group politics surrounding testing were quite mixed. The National Conference of State Legislatures was furious about the testing mandates and what it saw as an overly intrusive role. Calling both S1 and HR1 "seriously and perhaps irreparably flawed," the group's letter to the Hill read as follows:

> The testing requirement at the heart of both bills is an egregious example of a top-down, one-size-fits-all federal reform. There is no convincing argument that an effective accountability system must include annual testing in multiple subjects . . . the requirement to use a standardized statewide testing instrument ignores successful state accountability systems that use a *combination of state and local testing*.[33]

The National Governors' Association played a lower-key role than it had in the 106th, a major explanation being that its Republican leader, John Engler, was a close Bush associate. The NGA did write to share its concerns about the testing provisions, however. In August 2001, NGA cochairs Engler and Paul Patton (D) of Kentucky sent a letter to Congressional leaders, emphasizing that funding of testing was imperative:

> Recognizing that development and administration of state assessment systems and NAEP create a financial burden on states, local education agencies, and schools, Governors believe the responsibility for funding any additional federal testing requirements in all states should fall on the federal government. Although federal mandates may reflect well-intentioned policy goals, they often impose unfunded cost and regulatory burdens on states.[34]

Democratic governors spoke out separately at the August meeting of the NGA, expressing their displeasure with the testing mandates. They had originally understood that Washington would pay 40 percent of testing costs, but then learned that the authorized amount was closer to 15 percent. At a news conference called by the Democratic governors, Tom Vilsack of Iowa made this statement:

> The federal government has not fulfilled its promise. The election last year was not about making the president a super school superintendent. We know what's best for our students. We understand accountability. But what we really need from Congress and the president is support, the funding we were promised.[35]

Senator Paul Wellstone (D-MN) proposed an amendment, subsequently defeated, that would have delayed Bush's testing plan until Title I was funded at triple its current level, at least $25 billion. Another Wellstone amendment passed, requiring the assessments to be certified as valid for each purpose for which the state used them. His objective was to make sure that states did not use tests designed for state-level accountability to make decisions about individual students. Wellstone was particularly worried about the effects that intensive testing might have on the teaching profession, as he expressed in this floor statement:

> We have parents, children, young people—really starting in the suburbs, interestingly enough—who are rebelling. We are having more and more reports coming out that the really gifted teachers, the very teachers we need in the school districts where children are most underserved, are leaving the profession because they do not want to teach to the standardized test; they do not want to be drill instructors.[36]

The Senate approved a "trigger" about testing activities: States would be permitted to defer the development and administration of new tests if the President's budget did not provide at least $370 million for that purpose in fiscal year 2002, and an increase of that amount in each of six succeeding fiscal years. This was designed as insurance that states would not bear all of the costs of the new mandate. An amendment by Senator Wellstone also authorized bonus money to reward those states whose assessments were deemed by an independent expert review panel to be of particularly high quality. When Judd Gregg alleged that the proposed amendment meant that a "politically correct" external review panel would weaken Bush's testing proposal, Wellstone responded that testing experts had pointed out the importance of high-quality assessments:

> I have drawn from everybody in the testing field. I have drawn from all the people in the States. I have drawn from all the people who are doing this work. And they are all saying: Let's make sure the bonus incentive goes to the States for doing the assessments as well as possible as opposed to doing the assessments as fast as possible.[37]

A handful of Republicans found Wellstone's amendment acceptable; it passed by a vote of 57 to 39.

The alliances against testing in the House were similarly from far-flung segments of the political spectrum. In the House committee markup, Congresswoman Betty McCollum (D-MN) offered an amendment to strike all of the requirements from the final bill. In a press release she criticized the bill for "imposing federal student testing without covering its full cost. This is a terrible bill for Minnesota school children and our state's future." Her press release cited an estimate that Minnesota would incur $4.33 million in unfunded testing costs passed on to the state and its local districts.[38] McCollum later joined fellow Education and Workforce Committee members David Wu, Bobby Scott, Lynn Rivers and Donald Payne in supporting the Frank-Hoekstra amendment restricting all new testing provisions. The pairing of Barney Frank, a liberal Massachusetts Democrat, and Peter Hoekstra, the conservative Republican from Michigan, exemplified the liberal Democrat–conservative Republican axis of opposition to the new requirements. The vote on the Frank-Hoekstra amendment produced some odd geographical alliances against testing. There was support for the amendment in south Texas and along the border in New Mexico, where Latino representatives feared that their constituents' children might be penalized if stakes became attached to the test, and also in Vermont, which administered only limited tests and where local control was a long-held educational priority. South Carolina's districts were fairly evenly split on the motion, while in Georgia, only Representative John Lewis (D) of Atlanta's Fifth District voted in favor.

The White House was concerned about the possible success of the amendment; strategist Karl Rove and Chief of Staff Andrew Card made visits to the Hill to attempt to win over reluctant Republicans. The Business Roundtable circulated an e-mail to its membership, asking them to lobby in support of testing.[39] Secretary of Education Rod Paige rose to the occasion to defend the administration, writing, "Anyone who is against annual testing of children is an apologist for a broken system of education that dismisses certain children and classes of children as unteachable."[40] The amendment's defeat, by a comfortable margin of eighty-two votes, was a major victory for the White House, which by now was confident it could hold the Democrats on the final vote on the bill. The May 16, 2001, *White House Bulletin* quoted a "House GOP source" as saying, "You could not pass the bill (HR1) with Republican votes, but the White House has a much better idea of where they are with the Democrats, and they were very optimistic about the numbers."[41]

Congressman Tim Petri, a generally conservative Wisconsin Republican, was one committee member who felt unhappily pressured to support testing. Wisconsin did not yet have statewide standards, but it did have local standards, and it administered tests in Grades 4, 8, and 10 (as well as a reading test in Grade 3) in response to the 1994 Title I law requirements. Thus Wisconsin had in place a little less than half of what they would need in order to comply with the Bush bill. Petri supported the provision in the bill, but was not enthusiastic. His education aide Michael Kennedy said: "I don't know if Boehner is all that big on it. He seems to be, but it's something we fought against when we were fighting against Clinton. . . . Clinton wanted a national test, and it's not exactly what we're doing. But with the expansion of NAEP, we're getting close to that, anyway."[42] Wisconsin's Superintendent of Public Instruction, Elizabeth Burmaster, had publicly opposed the new testing requirements, saying, "The plan doesn't seem to be leaving no child behind. It seems more like 'leave no child untested.'"[43] According to Michael Kennedy, Petri had met with Burmaster to hear her concerns, and "sort of agrees with her, up to a point. But that battle was basically lost when Bush was elected."[44]

The legislative success of testing contradicted the Republicans' prior position: While the Clinton administration had been attacked by congressional Republicans for proposing a national test, the Bush administration succeeded in winning support for making federal dollars contingent on mandatory testing for every American student. On the Senate floor, it was clear that the politics of the 106th Congress were not completely dead, in that anything resembling a former Clinton administration initiative was defeated along party-line votes. Most of the Democrats' amendments for set-asides for new teachers, principals, school construction, and class-size reduction were voted down. Patty Murray (D-WA), who sponsored the amendment for class-size reduction, said that Republicans had turned their backs on the program simply because Clinton had initiated it. One notable exception to this pattern, to be described later, was bipartisan support for ESEA funding increases. The Senate approved Senate Bill S.1 on June 14 by a vote of 91–8.

DEMOCRATIC LEVERAGE: KILLING THE STRAIGHT A'S BLOCK GRANT

While Senator Jeffords's May 2001 defection from the Republicans did not have great substantive importance to the bill, it did create an opening for the new Senate Majority Leader, Tom Daschle, to make demands of the White House. Besides the defeat of vouchers, two areas in which Democratic leverage was particularly effective were increasing funding and targeting for Title I and watering down the Republicans' Straight A's proposal in the Senate while blocking it entirely in the House.

Once the Republicans realized that vouchers were off the table, securing the block-grant provision called "Straight A's" loomed far more important. Prior to the House committee vote, President Bush called Representative Miller and asked him to support the seven-state demonstration program that had been proposed in the 106th. Miller said no.[45] The House Republicans, in general, did not favor the Straight A's that Senator Gregg had championed in the 106th because of the power it gave to governors; why should they support a measure that would take decision-making power away from local districts? Yet others were passionately in favor. Both Repsentatives

Thomas Tancredo (R-CO) and Peter Hoekstra (R-MI) cited the watering-down of Straight A's as their reason for ultimately voting against the final bill. It had become something that true conservatives demanded. Sally Lovejoy of Representative Boehner's staff on the House Education and Workforce Committee called the block grant a "fall-on-the-sword" issue for Republicans, and added, "Straight A's became like Goals 2000. . . . It became a political fight. It wasn't a substance fight."[46] The fight, in this case, would make it all the way to the President for a final decision.

When Representative Jim DeMint (R-SC) offered Straight A's as an amendment on the House floor, Boehner told Bush that it would end Miller's cooperation. The White House convinced DeMint to pull it in order to save the bill, with Bush offering assurances that he would later push for it in conference. Naturally this angered many Republicans; as Representative Mark Souder (R-IN) said in a floor statement, "A few minutes ago, a group of conservative Republicans had been hauled down to the White House for a combination of persuasion and subtle threats" over the block-grant obstacle.[47] Charlie Barone, legislative director for Miller, a leading opponent of the measure, described what took place:

> They pulled the amendment, but Bush said: "I'll fight for this in conference." That's what he promised DeMint: you pull it, and I'll fight for it in conference. So there was a hope engendered with the conservatives by the president and by other people that this would come back in conference.[48]

But the Democrats, according to Barone, kept saying:

> "No, we're serious. We're not kidding. I mean, we're not agreeing. If this is in the bill, we're walking. This is code for asking our members to rip off poor school districts. And destroying the federal role in education, and we're not doing it." And so that reality took a while to sink in.[49]

Instead, the House narrowly passed a proposal known as "Super Local Flex" allowing 100 districts, two per state, the opportunity to apply for agreements that would allow them to consolidate several categorical program funds and waive requirements; these programs included the Title II teacher recruitment and professional development money. This compromise for Straight A's was developed largely by Representative Timothy Roemer (D-IN) and other New Democrats. Representative David Wu (D-OR) was one liberal Democratic member who firmly opposed even this watered-down provision. He chided the Republicans, "For the folks who just passed a huge, huge mandate on local schools, mandatory national testing, I find this flip-flop of positions absolutely breathtaking," and added, "I think most Americans want some accountability for public dollars spent for public purposes, that is the least that we can do for Federal funds that are spent for identifiable purposes in this bill."[50]

The Senate Republicans, too, found themselves at a disadvantage with Straight A's, because the provisions were at odds with their rhetoric of local control. As it was written, the governor still had control over the federal funds. When Bill Frist (R-TN) introduced his amendment for the Straight A's pilot in the HELP Committee in March, Patty Murray (D-WA) pointed out, "This is actually exactly the opposite of local control."[51] She contended that local districts receiving federal funds for special needs would have to hire a lobbyist to get their share of the block grant. Senator Tim Hutchinson's (R-AR) education aide Holly Kuzmich said: "The thing that we fought about most in Straight A's was that the Democrats on the committee usually felt more comfortable holding the purse strings at the federal level so that they could have more control as to how to direct the funds, whereas the Republicans by and large sided with the states."[52] The Republicans, she conceded, ultimately found it impossible to resolve this contradiction of policy.

Senator Gregg, however, was determined to have some version of Straight A's on the floor, and it turned out to be Senator Kennedy who offered a compromise. While governors would not have control over the funds, which Gregg had sought in the 106th, seven states and twenty-five districts could apply to consolidate programs and waive regulations, excepting several categorical programs like Title I. This compromise was called "Kennedy-Gregg Straight A's," to the consternation of many Senate HELP Committee Democrats. As for Kennedy, an unnamed Democratic aide on the Senate side recalled, "He knew he'd eventually have Miller," meaning he knew Miller would fight Gregg in conference in order to preserve the categorical programs most important to Democrats: Title I, bilingual education, and migrant education.[53] Senator Dodd proposed an amendment that would remove the $846 million of the 21st Century Schools After-School money from the list of programs states could consolidate under the Straight A's block grant. Republicans fiercely opposed the amendment and it was defeated 47–51 with three New Democrats voting no and Jeffords and Olympia Snowe (R-ME) voting in favor. Senator Bill Frist (R-TN) said after the vote, "If that had won today, it would have put the whole bill in jeopardy," noting the compromises on consolidation to which Republicans had already agreed.[54]

The controversy over which state-level actors should administer Title I funds resurfaced when the National Governor's Association advanced an amendment to S1, introduced on the floor by Senators George Voinovich (R-OH) and Evan Bayh (D-IL), requiring that governors approve all Title I and consolidated state plans and that program improvement plans be jointly prepared by the governor and state education agency. "Governors are willing to be held accountable but it is imperative that the federal government give Governors the authority to help determine reform through federal education programs," NGA's cochairmen Parris Glendening (D-MD) and John Engler (R-MI) wrote to Senate Leaders Lott and Daschle.[55] The Council of Chief State School Officers' Executive Director, Gordon Ambach, quickly mobilized around twenty education interest groups, including the National School Boards Association and the NEA, to oppose the amendment. "It is unsound policy to splinter the authority for making decisions about the use of the federal funds by adding governor's decisions on top of SEA decisions," Ambach wrote in a letter to Senators. "The types of decisions to be made in the plans and administration of ESEA Title I and other programs are based on educational practice. SEAs are established precisely to make such decisions."[56] The Chief State School Officers' interest group coalition lobbying strategy was effective: the Bingaman/Hatch/Kennedy second-degree amendment, which provided for consultation with a governor on Title I plans, rather than establishing a federal mandate, prevailed with a final vote of 63–37. Senators were apparently wary of the governors' bid for a major legislative change that would have given them greater leverage over the direction of state-level reforms, likely due to the perceived risk of tampering with their home state's constitutional provisions.

Flexibility was a political issue that had grown in symbolic importance to the GOP from the 106th to the 107th Congress. When Bush heeded Boehner's wishes to concede Straight A's, it showed that the President was willing to challenge both his own party's governors as well as his own conservative base.

DEMOCRATIC LEVERAGE: THE POLITICS OF INCREASED FUNDING AND TARGETING

After thirty-five years of a program in which it had been politically difficult to target to the poorest districts because of the House, the House approved such changes under the leadership of Boehner, a suburban Republican. Suddenly, targeting of Title I funds was politically possible in the 107th, and the new interparty competition was the reason.

The majority of Title I funds are allocated according to two formulas: basic grants and concentration grants. Most of the money goes out under basic grants, but the poverty threshold is so broad that more than 90 percent of districts receive at least some money. The concentration grants are more targeted, but the formula still encompasses 9,000 of the nation's approximately 15,000 districts. When Congress reauthorized the law in 1994, debate about rewriting the formulas had been predictably contentious. A provision for targeted grants, which would give more money to districts with higher percentages or numbers of disadvantaged students, was added to the law in 1994, but the formula was never used despite President Bill Clinton's continued requests to appropriators to do so.

In the 107th Congress, the White House and New Democrats set the tone for the approval of funding targeted grants, and the House responded. There are several explanations for the House's receptivity. First, Republicans found education had become an issue on which they wanted to be seen as leaders, and voting for funding increases fit with their strategy of rivaling the Democrats' priority. Second, Boehner, unlike his predecessor Goodling, became a believer in targeting Title I money. Kara Haas, legislative assistant to Representative Michael Castle (R-DE), explained:

> There was a real kind of back-to-basics approach, and I think Mr. Boehner really led that. When these programs were all created, they were intended to target the most disadvantaged and to help give them a leg up. Yet they were being spread so thin that really poor schools were only getting a portion of what they needed, whereas in other states and other districts, relatively well-off schools were getting Title I funds. And while it was sometimes hurtful to some of our members, the realization is that the federal government does a better job of equalizing than the states do. . . . Members didn't really seem to question it. . . . I think that the increases helped cushion some of the potential criticism over that.[57]

George Miller's legislative director, Charles Barone, concurred about Boehner: "I had an easier time working with him and his staff on targeting money than I ever had with Democrats . . . they didn't even look at the runs [computer-generated lists of which districts would gain money and which would lose]. We would negotiate and we'd say, we think we ought to start in this program by poverty. How do you do it, boom, this is it, okay, we agree to it—the runs came in later."[58] Some Democrats also commended Bush for what they perceived as his leadership on targeting. Representative Major Owens (D-NY) stated on the House floor: "President Bush should be given credit for pushing aside all of the temptations of our majority party in this House certainly to take what education funds were available and try to spread them as much as possible regardless of how much wealth a district already had."[59]

Third, House members were willing to support targeting to poor districts because of the overall increases in funding. The House bill increased authorized funding for ESEA programs by $5.5 billion to $24 billion in FY 2002, a 32 percent increase. In addition, the bill provided for future increases by doubling the authorization for Title I by FY 2006 to $17.2 billion. Further, the funding of the "hold-harmless" provisions was a guarantee to members that their districts would not see decreases the following year. Initially, in

May, Democratic Senators Landrieu, Jack Reed, and Wellstone voted against bringing the bill to the Senate floor until Bush made a commitment to fully fund Title I. Bush had proposed an increase of about 3.7 percent in ESEA funding, which the three Senators said was inadequate. Kennedy, however, made the case to Democrats to proceed with approving the bill, resolving that he would increase pressure on the administration.[60]

CONCLUSION

President Bush was tacking decisively toward the center, willing to take on the most conservative members of his party, while he had made the New Democrats' plan the core of the reauthorization bill. The most difficult and unpredictable period, however, was to follow, as the Democrats were to suddenly gain control of the HELP Committee, with Ted Kennedy as its new chair. With the House and Senate versions of the bill still varying widely in their accountability provisions and Democrats able to make demands for greater funding and targeting, quite a lot remained on the conference committee's bargaining table.

Chapter 8

The Politics of Passage: No Child Left Behind Becomes a Law

Senator Jim Jeffords left the Republican Party and became an Independent in May 2001, giving control of the Senate to the Democrats. His departure was precipitated by his irritation with the Republican White House for their refusal to fund the Individuals with Disabilities Education Act (IDEA). The IDEA was not scheduled for reauthorization until the following year, but Jeffords had long sought assurances from the Bush administration that they would endorse ample IDEA funding as part of the negotiations over No Child Left Behind.

SENATOR JEFFORDS LINKS SPECIAL EDUCATION FUNDING AND ESEA REAUTHORIZATION

In both houses, the debate on special education was about whether IDEA should be fully funded. Federal law requires a 40 percent federal contribution to the total cost to states of compliance with program regulations, but federal appropriations were still just 15 percent. On the Senate floor in May, there had been bipartisan support: an amendment introduced in the Senate by Tom Harkin (D-IA) and Chuck Hagel (R-NE) and vocally supported by Jeffords ultimately passed. The amendment provided for an increase in the federal share by $2.5 billion a year until the 40 percent level was reached in 2007. Further, the amendment would directly fund the program, not just authorize the funds. The program would no longer be on the discretionary side of the federal budget, but the mandatory side. The connection between the ESEA and the IDEA was clear, argued Jeffords: until the states had the necessary resources to provide for the education of students with disabilities, federal compensatory dollars would be diverted for that purpose. The Bush administration, pressing for its tax cut, was adamantly opposed to Harkin-Hagel, maintaining that any major funding increases ought to be debated concurrent with the upcoming IDEA reauthorization in 2002. Since the House passed no comparable provision, it would fall to the conference committee to resolve the discrepancy with the Senate bill.

With regard to full funding of the IDEA, the National Governors' Association now walked a fine line between their own interests and those of Bush, a former member. In the past the NGA had consistently supported full funding for the IDEA. However, during the legislative process the NGA did not visit the Hill in favor of full funding. According to Jordan Cross, the education aide to Senator Susan Collins (R-ME), there was internal conflict because Governor Tom Ridge (R-PA) had told the membership that they should not demand provisions that the Bush administration vehemently opposed. Cross explained how Ridge's pressure for loyalty to Bush meant that the association took a position inconsistent with their prior one: "From the governors' perspective, there's no reason to oppose mandatory full funding of special education. It's guaranteed to go over with the governors. And so it was clearly a situation in which they were fronting for the administration."[1]

During strained negotiations with the White House about whether he would vote with the GOP on the tax cut, Jeffords said that full funding of the measure was his condition. When Bush refused, the senator announced his decision to switch his party affiliation to become an Independent on May 23, rendering the balance 51–49 in the Democrats' favor.

Jeffords described himself as being out of step with the Republican Party leadership:

> Increasingly, I find myself in disagreement with my party. I understand that many people are more conservative than I am, and they form the Republican Party. Given the changing nature of the national party, it has become a struggle for our leaders to deal with me and for me to deal with them.[2]

The decision by White House leaders and the Senate to drop $305 billion in spending for special education from the final budget was what finally made up his mind: "When they took all that out, that was it."

Jeffords' switch did not change the substance of the House bill in May. But by giving the balance of power to the Democrats and the chairmanship of the committee to Kennedy, his switch ensured that Democrats would now have more leverage for setting the agenda and the legislative timetable.

BARGAINING CHIPS

Funding became the Democratic majority's bargaining chip. The new Senate Majority Leader, Tom Daschle (D-SD) caused controversy by suggesting to reporters that once the conference was over he might delay its final passage until the White House agreed to commit to more resources. "It certainly wasn't my intention to throw down any gauntlets," he said when criticized. "I just suggested that before we can complete our work, we have to know what kind of resources are going to be there."[3] Representative George Miller was more direct: "Reform without adequate funding is cruelty."[4]

Democrats had already secured bipartisan support in the Senate bill to authorize an added $132 billion for Title I funding over ten years. They also voted to quadruple money for bilingual education programs and to add $120 billion for children with physical and learning disabilities. The previous majority leader, Trent Lott, had predicted that most of the increases would be stripped out during the appropriations process. The president's budget resolution, after all, capped increases in domestic spending to 4 percent, so the votes hardly seemed realistic.[5] Kennedy, however, said it would be hard for the Republicans to later back away from those increases, since they were on the record now in support: "This president and the administration [had] better get used to the fact that we will hammer this issue again and again and again. We are going to make that case at every single opportunity."[6] Senator Olympia Snowe (R-ME), who voted for many of the increases, hinted that the mood of the electorate was different: "I think the votes carry some weight this year. It's different than in the past."[7]

LANDRIEU AND THE TARGETED GRANTS

Once the Senate Republicans had begun to bargain with the New Democrats, they found they had relentless members to contend with, notably Mary Landrieu (D-LA). She was the New Democrat who in the 106th Congress had unsuccessfully pressed for altering the formula by which Title I money was distributed to the poorest states and districts. In the 107th, her ESEA amendment stating that any appropriation above current levels for Title I should go toward the targeted grants was approved 57–36 in June. In New Orleans the district was frequently in the position of having to tell schools with 84 percent of students eligible for free or reduced lunch that no Title I money was left for them.[8] On the Senate floor she spoke passionately about the need for reforms to be funded:

> I intend to be heard on these matters. I don't want to see a bill come up which will turn into a mess out here that allows these ideas to go down the drain and the President claiming a bipartisan achievement because a few Democrats go along with something that isn't adequately funded, doesn't provide for the true reforms that are needed; and we end up doing some real damage to kids.[9]

Landrieu's education aide Kathleen Strottman engaged the media, local administrators, and grassroots organizations to draw public attention to the issue. She explained her boss's success in making funding equity among the states a credible issue: "It was the one place where we could reach out to Republicans and say: If there is any such thing as an appropriate role for the federal government to play, this is it."[10] When Senator Landrieu was offered the chance to give the Democratic response to the January State of the Union, she used much of the time to talk about funding for poor schools.

The vote on her June 2001 amendment did not fall along party lines. The thirty-six senators who opposed it presumably were from states that would not fare well under the new provision. For instance, the pairs of senators from Kansas, Missouri, Oklahoma, Idaho, Maine, Kentucky, Mississippi, Iowa, and Virginia voted against it.

Part of Landrieu's strategy after June was to coordinate the ESEA reauthorization with the approval of education spending legislation in November. She offered an amendment, approved 89–10, funding both "targeted grants" and the "state education finance incentive" formulas in Title I for the first time. The latter formula was designed to reward states that spend more on education relative to their per capita income, as well as states having less disparity in per pupil spending between the poorest and wealthiest districts.[11] States such as New Mexico, Alabama, and her home state of Louisiana with low per capita incomes should be rewarded for focusing money on education, she said.

After Jeffords's switch, Senator Tom Harkin (D-IA) became chairman of the Labor, Health and Human Services, and Education Subcommittee of the Appropriations Committee. Long an advocate of changing Title I to reward states that did better at finance equalization between poor and wealthy districts, Harkin could powerfully affect how the formulas were written. Landrieu's staff engaged Harkin in a compromise process, convincing him that the state finance incentive Title I formula should be fixed to solve two problems at once: states that put a greater share of their own resources into education should get more federal assistance (Landrieu's goal), and so should those that better equalized spending between poor and wealthy local districts (Harkin's long-time goal). Harkin was persuaded, and the formulas were changed. Title I would be better targeted, and states would be rewarded for equalization. Once the targeted grants were funded, it was calculated that the fifty school districts nationwide with the highest percentage of students in poverty would get an immediate boost. Of course, the success of all of the new reengineering of the formulas would ultimately depend on the Bush budget.

SECOND THOUGHTS ON ACCOUNTABILITY

As the bill entered the conference phase, the White House began to recognize the political danger of the accountability provisions' labeling too many schools as failures, which might alienate suburban voters and squander limited federal resources. At the same time, many education observers, both practitioners in the field and members of beltway associations, reacted to the proposed provisions.

In an August 2001 speech to the National Urban League, President Bush said, "Some of my allies in reform want to require dramatically improved performance—immediately, everywhere. I appreciate aiming high, but setting impossible expectations means setting no expectations."[12] The administration faced a balancing act. It had a political reason to want to see nonimproving schools identified so that NCLB's options to exit such schools for better ones or receive private supplemental instruction would produce visible results of Bush's educational innovations in the first term. There was political interest in identifying lots of failing schools.

That rewards and sanctions would be so heavily dependent on continuous annual gains was troubling to researchers Thomas Kane and Douglas Staiger. Writing about the implications of their research findings in the *New York Times* in August 2001, they made the following argument:

> The central flaw is that both versions of this bill place far too much emphasis on year-to-year changes in test scores. Under either, every school in America would have to generate an increase in test scores each and every year or face penalties like having to allow its students to transfer to another public school, being converted into a charter school or being taken over by a private contractor. . . .
>
> However, the path to improved performance is rarely a straight line.[13]

Further, the authors wrote, racially diverse schools would face the harshest penalties, since each and every group would be required to make the progress required by the formula. Kane and Staiger recommended that every state be able to devise its own rating systems for schools, and that states should withhold sanctions "until there is real evidence that disadvantaged minority students are being allowed to lag behind. The Secretary of Education should develop a way to determine this with statistically justifiable methods."[14]

As they learned over the summer of 2001 about the accountability provisions in the passed bills, state and local education leaders also began to vocalize what they saw as the problematic aspects for practice. On a July panel at the National Press Club, Roy Romer, superintendent of the Los Angeles Unified School District, said that the provisions' effect would be to encourage local authorities to lower the levels of proficiency in order to avoid sanctions. "You'll have people out there gaming the system," he warned.[15] David Hornbeck, the former superintendent of Philadelphia schools, however, approved of the House bill's stricter provisions and opined, "We've got to quit masking the disaggregated failure" of groups within schools.[16]

The goal of moving all students to proficiency over ten or twelve years also drew fire from state leaders. In interviews with the *New York Times*, Missouri's assistant commissioner of education Stephen Barr called it "an impossible dream," while Charles Zogby, the chief state school officer in Pennsylvania, said, "It's unrealistic to think that in some places where 90 percent of the children are below basic that we're going to turn this around in ten years. And then everybody is going to throw up their hands and say none of this is possible."[17] One consequence of the committees' having moved the legislation without lengthy hearings in the winter (the Senate HELP Committee had had a single hearing with Secretary Paige as the sole witness) was that practitioners could only raise these concerns in the summer, that is, when it was too late.

The information and analyses that academic researchers brought to bear on the debate in August caused some midcourse modifications on the part of negotiators, but the information was used selectively. By that time both sides had decided that some sort of sanctions had to be attached to the requirement that schools narrow the racial achievement gap along a multiyear timeline. Therefore, the effect of the research was to cause Senate and House conferees to tinker with their formulas, not to abandon the model altogether.

THE CONFERENCE

The conference committee is sometimes referred to as the "third house," as it is a newly formed group comprised of selected members from both houses whose job it is to resolve discrepancies in the separate House and Senate bills. The conference phase lasted from July through early December, and involved one of the largest conference committees ever appointed. On July 10, the Senate named its conferees; there were twenty-five, fully a quarter of the chamber. All HELP Committee members were conferees, joined by Jeffords. The Democrats then added Lieberman and Bayh, while the Republicans added Wayne Allard (R-CO), Michael DeWine (R-OH), and John Ensign (R-NV).

The House delegation was comprised of eight Republicans and six Democrats. The White House had almost no involvement in the conference itself. White House negotiator Kress was not invited in by the leadership; by this time, according to one aide, he had "burnt bridges" with aides on both sides through his deal-making.[18]

The terrorist attacks on September 11, however, heightened President Bush's pressure on the "Big Four" leaders (Boehner, Kennedy, Gregg, and Miller) to complete the bill. It was quickly apparent in the aftermath of the attacks that the education bill was Bush's last opportunity for a major domestic piece of legislation before having to address homeland security and defense. Secretary Paige even linked education to national security: "The events of September 11th didn't make an education bill less important, it made it more important. Education is a national security issue. This is not something we can put on the shelf and come back to later."[19] In the several months after September, there was a tone of bipartisanship and unity behind the President in Congress, and this added to the leaders' willingness to reach an agreement.

The conference began with 3,000 "notes," or discrepancies in passed measures between the two laws, requiring resolution before the final version of the bill could be sent back for approval by both chambers. Some of these were as minor as wording (e.g., whether to write about "school completion" versus "dropouts"); others were as large as resolving mandatory full funding for the IDEA (the Senate) versus no money for special education (the House).

The debate over full funding of the IDEA had reached a boiling point. Senators Kennedy, Harkin, and Jeffords gave the issue a high public profile, arranging for busloads of parents of disabled children to show up unannounced the day of the conferees' vote. The Bush administration was equally adamant in seeking the defeat of the provisions of the Harkin-Hagel amendment because it coincided with the debate around the tax cut, their top domestic priority. In an August 13 letter addressed to conferee Representative Rob Andrews (D-NJ), Secretary Paige wrote that it was imperative that the IDEA not be removed from the annual appropriations process and called attention to the fact that the Bush administration's proposed funding increase for the program was a historic $1 billion.[20] The Senate conference delegation began the vote and passed it, with several Republicans joining the 17–8 majority in favor. But when it was the House delegation's turn, not a single Republican conferee would break ranks to support it; the measure was defeated 8–6. One Senate-side Democratic aide recalled: "[The President] kept them in line, we were amazed; we really thought that we might pull a Republican or two from the House because of that, but he kept them."[21]

This defeat was reason enough for Senator Jeffords eventually to vote against final approval of the bill. He wrote in the *New York Times*:

> I fear we may pass legislation that will do far more harm than good.
>
> Earlier this year the Senate agreed without objection to a bipartisan amendment introduced by Senators Tom Harkin and Chuck Hagel that would require Congress to fund the 40 percent of special education costs in full. This was a great victory for all our children. I am outraged, however, that a majority of my colleagues on the conference committee voted not to include this amendment. . . .
>
> I have been in Congress for more than 25 years and have never voted against an education bill. But to pass this bill as it stands would be counterproductive. It is better to approve no bill than to approve a bad one.[22]

The authorization levels were also finally resolved. The conference agreement authorized $26.5 billion for the next fiscal year for K–12 education. While this was $6 billion less than what Senate Democrats had sought, it was $4 billion more than what Bush had wanted. Title I in particular would get a $5 billion increase in fiscal year 2003, which with the targeting meant that the fifty districts with the largest concentrations of poor children would receive an immediate boost.

The number of programs consolidated was far less than what either Bush or the New Democrats' 3 R's had called for. The Improving America's Schools Act had had fifty-five programs; NCLB ended up with forty-five. Safe and Drug Free Schools and Ready to Learn Television were examples of programs that had been slated for consolidation but were separated in conference. Still, the New Democrats' model of consolidation and higher funding worked in many areas. For instance, the conference agreement included the first-ever funded formula grant program for bilingual education in the ESEA. Bilingual programs were consolidated into a single program. Federal funds would be targeted with the goal of assisting English language learners to become proficient in English after three years of attending school in the United States.

As had been the case with the 1994 reauthorization, social issues provided the final stumbling blocks in the negotiations.[23] Conservatives wanted to require schools to show that they were not banning constitutionally protected prayer, to withhold funds from districts discriminating against the Boy Scouts or groups that barred homosexuals, and to assure nondiscrimination in hiring by religious providers of supplemental services. In response, Representative Miller and Senator Kennedy insisted that there be provisions preventing supplemental service providers affiliated with religious groups or churches from discriminating against both children and employees before they would ratify the conference agreements.[24] It became a serious disagreement on November 29, right before the bill was set to go to the floor. According to an unnamed aide to the House Republicans on the Conference Committee, the civil rights provisions could have killed the whole process:

> This was sort of [the Democrats'] last gasp, trying to defeat supplemental services . . . they wanted to say that if you were a religious organization, you could not hire based on religion. So you could not, for example, if you were a Catholic program, hire people who were Catholic, because they were Catholic and were going to be serving kids. It was so far-reaching. . . . I mean it was a complete no-go. We rejected it out of hand. . . . Senator Kennedy's staff got just absolutely, insanely livid that we would not even approach the subject.[25]

After a fifteen-hour negotiating session that went until 1:30 in the morning, the four leaders agreed that a compromise would have to be reached for the final negotiations to continue. Kennedy's staff prevailed, getting language barring religious discrimination against recipients of the services and employees alike, while requiring a neutral, nonideological curriculum. The Republicans prevailed in allowing federal funds to be stripped from any school district that discriminated against Boy Scouts or similar groups barring homosexuals, as well as in requiring that schools had to certify that they were not preventing "constitutionally protected" prayer.

Though conferees' education aides convened to agree on core principles of adequate yearly progress, the final definition was ultimately resolved by the leadership, mainly Representatives Boehner and Miller, closely assisted by Senator Bingaman. The terms of the agreement were that states would have to design a plan to raise students in all racial and ethnic subgroups to get all students to a "proficient" level in reading and math within twelve years. Miller remained adamant about the subgroup accountability until the deal was reached. States would set cut scores corresponding to three performance levels—basic, proficient, and advanced—as well as the initial goals for target percentages of students to be proficient on state reading and math tests. The final bill allows states to set relatively low "starting points," equal to either the percentage of "proficient" performers in the state's lowest scoring subgroup or the percentage of "proficient" students in a school that ranks at the 20th percentile in the state, whichever is higher. A critical addition was that states would be required to raise the bar for those goals (i.e., percentages of students in each group with proficient scores). For their determinations of proficiency, states would have to use data from their previous years' assessment results until the new testing system was phased in. There was also a "safe harbor" provision added: If a school had one subgroup not making AYP but reduced by 10 percent the number of students not proficient, the school could avoid penalties. Schools not meeting either goal would be placed in "school improvement" status, followed by "corrective action." After a fourth year of a school's not making requisite progress, states had to take one of a list of corrective actions consistent with state and local laws. Missing from the list of sanctions was financial penalties for Title I schools not making progress, a Bush campaign proposal. Thus the compromise resembled the House bill and was almost identical to the Texas accountability blueprint.

Further, the law specified the responsibilities of states for intervention in low-performing districts. States would now be required to undertake one of the following actions in districts in "corrective action" status: deferment of programmatic funds; implementation of a new "research-based" curriculum; replacement of district administrators; or appointment of a trustee or receiver to replace the superintendent or school board. Another of the crucial "notes" the committee had to resolve was what to do about the National Assessment of Educational Progress. The House bill allowed an alternative to NAEP, while the Senate did not. With the House Democrats vehemently in support of NAEP but many Senate Republicans opposed to it, Senator Gregg's proposal to require that states administer NAEP every other year ended up as the compromise. The conference report also said that NAEP would be given in fourth and eighth grade provided that it was funded. No federal rewards or penalties could be based on NAEP results, but states could reward either schools or teachers for progress.

The core of the testing provisions for Grades 3 through 8 remained intact, though they were still making members nervous at this final stage. A letter was circulating in the House about testing, expressing support for the idea that state and local assessments should be used instead of annual tests to satisfy the requirements. Over twenty-one members from both parties signed.[26] During the conference phase numerous national education groups, including both major teachers unions, voiced their objections to testing. In part, the late reaction was due to the fact that education groups were only slowly realizing how far-reaching the legislative provisions were going to be.[27] By August of 2001, however, many were alarmed. National Education Association President Bob Chase said in his keynote address at the union's annual summer meeting that "the soul of education is being jettisoned in the name of testing."[28] But this opposition was ineffective. The bill's proponents were not listening to the education professionals and interest groups.

The final version of NCLB contained flexibility provisions that were dramatically different from the Straight A's pilot that both houses had approved in the 106th. The new version did not exempt states and districts from meeting adequate yearly progress requirements; the states and districts could apply to gain more control over federal education funds by negotiating "performance agreements" with the Education Department. While programs such as Technology and Safe and Drug Free Schools could be included in these agreements, Title I, bilingual education, and migrant education could not. The Senate Democrats fought and lost battles over the inclusion of some programs.

There were also "local flexibility demonstration projects," in which a district could pool its funds under the major ESEA programs (excepting Title I) and sign an "accountability contract" with the federal department. Finally, all districts could shift up to 50 percent of their non-Title I funds between programs, referred to as "transferability." The final agreements were far from the "charter states" model Bush had proposed in the blueprint when he took office in January. Nevertheless, Senator Gregg's tenacity in fighting for block grants won him favor with the White House. According to an unnamed aide to a Senate Committee Democrat, "Gregg got to be the person the White House needed because he carried their water when nobody else would," and by the time the bill was signed, "if anybody could go back to the White House and say, 'I want something from you,' it would be Gregg.[29]

Besides the extensive testing requirements, there were several provisions in the law that expanded the federal role in defining instructional inputs and practices. The first was the language requiring that there be a "highly qualified teacher" in every classroom by 2005–06, and that effective in fall 2002, no new hires in Title I schools could be unqualified. Paraprofessionals, or instructional aides, whose work Title I had long been funded by compensatory education dollars, would now be required to either have completed two years of college or pass a rigorous state assessment certifying their competence. Representative George Miller disagreed strongly with the NEA when it fought mandatory state competency testing for teachers in Title I schools. To Miller, the situation in his home state of California, where some 42,000 teachers had emergency certification credentials, was nothing short of a disaster for poor children. Since he had introduced his teacher quality bill in 1999, Miller had insisted that the federal government ensure that all teachers be "highly qualified" in the subject areas in which they taught. The unions were largely supportive of that provision, but opposed measures to require teachers to take further tests after having already proven themselves in the classroom. After all, the implication was that if current teachers could not pass a test, they risked removal from their jobs. Both unions prevailed in getting an alternative to competency testing included in the bill: Teachers could instead prove their competence by another kind of professional assessment.

Yet as they encountered such efforts by Congressman Miller and others to force states to regulate teacher quality, the unions found themselves in a different political environment than they ever had before. Miller's legislative director Charles Barone contended that the NEA in particular found itself on the losing side of the trend toward accountability in the profession: "They were at risk of marginalizing themselves in this bill, I think they actually did." Referring to the new requirements that all teachers in Title I schools be highly qualified by 2005, Barone added: "I'm not under any illusion about what it takes to do that in four years, Miller's not under any illusions. You're going to have to pay people more, you're going to have to improve the working conditions. But don't say you can't do it. The profession ought to be for it."[30]

The second instructional issue was language specifying that grants would be awarded to those districts that drew on "scientifically based reading research" and that included "the essential components of reading instruction." The bill lists those essential components as "phonemic awareness, phonics, vocabulary development, reading fluency, including oral reading skills, and reading comprehension strategies."[31] The education community, including both teachers and state and district administrators, were concerned right away about the federal government's explicit endorsement of phonics-based reading, and interpreted the statute to mean that only projects with this instructional approach would be funded.

The third instructional provision, one that was quite controversial, was that programs and interventions in low-performing schools be based on "scientifically based research" or "promising effective practices," terms that the law did not define. These stipulations raised far more questions than they answered, particularly since the U.S. Department of Education had no guidance about what level of evidence constituted "scientifically based research." The conference report does reveal that several times conferees chose language specifying that programs should be "scientifically based" rather than founded on "rigorous field experiments in multiple sites."[32] The term was used approximately 120 times in the bill, signifying that Congress wanted to require states and districts to adopt programs that worked, but left to the Department of Education the job of offering guidance about what exactly the term meant.

INTEREST GROUPS: A LATE MOBILIZATION

While the leadership resolved the accountability formula dilemma in September, it was not announced until the final conference bill had been completed in order to avoid opening the issue up to interest groups.[33] Once the conference began, most education advocates were deliberately kept in the dark about the content of the provisions. "They've managed to keep a pretty good lid on this," said Richard Long, head of the National Association of State Title I Directors, in October.[34] Jordan Cross, an aide to Senator Susan Collins (R-ME) who had also been involved earlier in the process as a lobbyist for the American Association for School Administrators, concurred: "I've never seen people so tight-lipped about what was going on in a conference. I was, you know, on the outside of that at first as a lobbyist. . . . Everybody would meet at the Committee for Education Funding. There'd be some thirty lobbyists in the room, and everybody would say, "What's going on? We don't know."[35]

The freezing out of interest groups at this stage was a decision supported by both parties. An unidentified aide on the House side recalled, "I had very little interaction with outside groups because they told us as conferee staff early on, 'Don't talk to groups. Don't tell them what's going on,'" adding that the directive came from Democrats and Republicans alike.[36] One group that was particularly concerned by the leadership's blackout of information about key agreements on testing and accountability was the bipartisan National Governors Association. In a letter sent to conferees in late September they said, "as those who bear the greatest responsibility for implementing any changes enacted by Congress, we would hope there would be full consultation with the nation's governors prior to any agreements on key issues."[37] The strategic agreement made during the conference to prevent interest groups from learning about the substance of the negotiations was effective. NEA lobbyist Joel Packer recalled that not only interest groups were kept in the dark, but often conferees also were:

> They didn't share stuff with other members. At one meeting I had with Senator Jack Reed, who's a Democratic member and a conferee, I was asking him if he could help convince Kennedy to at least have a briefing for the groups in between when they finalized it and when it went to the floor, so at least we could take some time and see it. And he said, "That's a great idea, because then maybe I could go to the briefing and find out what's in the bill."[38]

About much of the education community's response to the bill after its enactment, Packer noted, "I think some of the questions that are now coming up might have been able to have been slightly better clarified in legislative language if people had been able to see [it]."[39]

Not all interest groups were excluded, however. One whose visibility continued to rise during the process was the Education Leaders' Council. Now that one of ELC's founders, Eugene Hickok, the former chief state school officer from Pennsylvania, had been appointed Undersecretary of the Education Department, the group enjoyed enhanced access to both White House officials and congressional leaders. Their top issues had been state and local control, with less federal involvement in schools, and increased school choice. Their executive director, Lisa Graham-Keegan, the former chief state school officer of Arizona, had long been an advocate for increased flexibility for states in the administration of federal categorical programs. Secretary Paige appealed to the organization when he told them at an October conference: "You are the right people at the right time to do something about this. Your voice in the national dialogue must be loud, and we need your help in a big way."[40] One example of the council's influence came during the conference process, when they and the Heritage Foundation advised conferees on the House side to accept the provision requiring states to use NAEP because of its value as a "sunshine" instrument.[41] A mutual interdependence was growing among the ELC, the administration, and some Republican Hill staff: As Secretary Paige's remark suggests, the department needed a group that would champion a controversial new law to state administrators. Following the bill's passage, Boehner commended the group, saying, "It wouldn't have been possible without the work of Lisa Keegan and the Education Leaders' Council, who were instrumental in the successful effort to turn the President's vision for education reform into legislative action." He added, "ELC has played a vital role in bringing new purpose to a federal law that has lost its focus and never met its promise."[42]

The majority of interest groups who spoke out during the conference, however, were dismayed about the legislation. In November, very late in the conference, the National Caucus of Black State Legislators issued a report calling on the federal government and the states to provide funding for class-size reduction, better teacher training, and more parental involvement in schools. Resources for minority students ought to accompany the bill's provisions for identification of failing schools, the group's leadership contended.[43] Similarly, the legislative director of the Council of Great City Schools, Jeff Simering, criticized the bill for demanding too much accountability with insufficient guarantees of resources. The American Association of School Administrators (AASA), the National School Boards Association, and the National Conference of State Legislatures were all major education interest groups officially opposing the final bill. In a letter to congressional leaders, the AASA argued that the act federalized the establishment of teacher qualification requirements and thereby violated the act that had created the federal Department of Education. "From a more practical perspective," wrote lobbyist Bruce Hunter on behalf of the organization, "we do not believe that the 7% federal contribution justifies such prescriptive intrusion in the operations and staffing of local public schools."[44] One factor that led to some of these interest groups' opposition to the final bill was that they had backed themselves into a corner politically with their stance on IDEA full funding. Representative Michael Castle's education aide Kara Haas said, "I think I understand how they boxed themselves in. . . . They got all the grassroots all fired up, and then when [full funding] didn't happen, what could they do?"[45] On the other hand, NCLB was also a disappointment to the conservative think tanks and coalitions that had been among the most influential in the 106th, such as Fordham, Heritage, and EXPECT. Despite their advantaged position with Bush in office and a majority-Republican House and Senate, they were not able to dictate the agenda to the extent that theories of "unified party government"[46] would have predicted.

The conference committee finished its work on December 11. The conference report was adopted by the House on December 13 by a vote of

381–41, with conservative Republicans comprising thirty-three of those voting against passage. Majority Whip Tom DeLay, who had expressed his unease about the bill back in the spring, was one of those. The Senate followed suit on December 18 with a vote of 87–10; three Republicans, Robert Bennett (UT), Chuck Hagel (NE), and George Voinovich (OH) opposed the bill.

President Bush signed the No Child Left Behind Act into law on January 8, 2002. House Education and Workforce Committee chairman John Boehner got credit in a very visible way: Bush signed the bill in Hamilton, Ohio, located in his suburban district. In his remarks, Bush commended what he described as the spirit of bipartisanship that had produced the bill: "We made it because proud Members of the House and the Senate, loyal to their parties, decided to set partisan politics aside and focus on what was right for America."[47] In fact, it was the partisanship of the House Republicans—their loyalty to President Bush and willingness to vote for his bill—that made NCLB possible.

CONCLUSION

The events of the 107th Congress demonstrate the pressures on both parties to break through gridlock on the issue of education. The impending election had been largely responsible for the gridlock in the previous Congress, but in 2001 the pressure of public opinion for Congress to work in a bipartisan fashion following a national crisis marked the temporary end to the impasse. While those Republicans adhering to Newt Gingrich's 1994 message of "no federal role" had dwindled to a handful, with Boehner himself emblematic of the change, most conservative Republicans had not altered their views about a limited federal role. The Republican Party moved because Bush moved. I consider the broader change of the GOP's defection from its prior ideology in the final chapter.

It is instructive to compare Republican votes for the 1994 reauthorization bill and their votes on NCLB in 2001. Only 19 percent of House Republicans voted in favor of the Improving America's Schools Act in 1994, a lower percentage than had voted for the original act in 1965 (27 percent) when the concept of federal aid was quite controversial.[48] Eighty-five percent of House Republicans voted for No Child Left Behind, returning their level of support to that of the range on education bill votes during the 1970s and 1980s. The contrast between the 1994 and 2001 Republican Senate votes is also notable: in 1994, 53 percent of Republican Senators voted yea, while 94 percent did so in 2001 (there were only three Republican nays). This was a level of Republican support not seen in the Senate since the 1988 reauthorization. Bush's particular style of leadership on education, enhanced by the national mood following September 11, made it possible for his party to give overwhelming support to an education bill that was far more pervasive and coercive than the one it had opposed in 1994.

That Bush was able to pass the reauthorization bill while Clinton could not is partly explainable by theories of unified party government. That is, Clinton battled the GOP-controlled Congress, while Bush could readily find the support he needed (with the exception of the last six months of 2001 when Democrats held control of the Senate). But just as critical a political factor was Bush's staking a claim on a movement over which administration did not have a great deal of power: the legacy of the Clinton administration in promoting state-based standards reform as a condition of receipt of federal education funds. Bush capitalized on this momentum, taking the New Democrats' proposal that called for program consolidation and tightened school-level accountability and challenging Congress to pass it as his administration's bill.

Both parties altered their ideological positions in order to pass the bill. As the next chapter describes, this created fissures within the GOP during the first several years of the law's implementation.

Part IV

IMPLICATIONS FOR EDUCATION POLICY: 2002 AND BEYOND

How the new law presented implementation challenges, garnered opposition, and was enforced by the Bush administration; what the 2004 congressional and presidential elections signify for the future of the federal role.

Chapter 9

A Rocky Start to Implementation, 2002–2004

The political environment from which the bill emerged was an unusual and powerful amalgam. Moderate Republicans, the White House, centrist Democrats, and many liberals had managed to find common ground. The leadership was under enormous pressure from President Bush to pass something. Between the increased targeting and funding and the racial subgroup accountability provisions, NCLB was in some ways progressive. With the exception of mandatory full funding for the IDEA, Democrats were successful in securing Republican support for higher funding levels. Yet conservatives prevailed in provisions that would allow Title I dollars to pay for private tutoring services, a measure that Democrats had fought since the 1980s.

No Child Left Behind signified a considerable expansion of the federal role, and suddenly a presidential administration that in most other ways was conservative began a reach into the operations of local schools and districts. The federal government in most places provides only about 8 percent of local districts' education expenditures, but the law changes the regulatory environment for states considerably. Neither Democrats nor Republicans really confronted the fact that the bill might have been demanding a degree of leverage over state policy that was not commensurate with the still low proportion of federal funding.

This chapter considers some of the major policy implications for Title I and gives an overview of some of the initial controversies once implementation began in states and districts. Further, it describes how the Bush administration softened its initially rigid enforcement stance over a two-year period in order to render the law more palatable to state officials.

POLICY IMPLICATIONS FOR TITLE I

The "policy talk"[1] from both parties during the debate over Title I across the two Congresses revealed how much the discourse about compensatory education had changed. "Closing the achievement gap" was now the articulated goal of both parties for Title I. The legislation completed Title I's evolution from a program based on inputs to one based on outcomes, and the rhetoric of both parties was about results and accountability.[2] But there was a notable absence of discussion on Capitol Hill, whether in hearings or in the committee, about what the new bill would actually mean *inside* high-poverty schools. For instance, a major focus of the 1994 reauthorization was encouraging adoption of "schoolwide projects," whereby concentrated-poverty schools would enrich instruction throughout the whole school instead of pulling students out of the regular classroom for remedial instruction. None of the major players in the 107th, from the Bush administration to the Progressive Policy Institute, discussed what had been learned from this particular policy initiative, how widespread its adoption had been, or how a new testing regime would affect it. Further, policymakers paid scant attention to the consequences of annual testing in the elementary grades for secondary school completion rates. President Bush spoke about testing as necessary for measuring schools' performance. Yet no one in Congress suggested that the policies might have the effect of increasing high school dropout rates if large numbers of students were held back because districts adopted tougher promotion policies. (Senator Wellstone, however, sought guarantees that tests would only be used for the purposes for which they had been designed.)

One exception to the trend of not examining the research base was the attention of George Miller and other members given to the problem of qualifications for teachers and paraprofessionals in Title I, which they saw as a major obstacle to improving instructional opportunity in high-poverty districts. Reports from the Department of Education had documented a problem of lack of teacher qualifications, as had groups like the Education Trust and the Civil Rights Project at Harvard. Miller managed to keep the issue alive throughout deliberations in both the 106th and 107th, weathering criticism from the unions and ultimately enacting very tough provisions. With the exception of the blanket observation of politicians of both parties alleging that Title I had failed to meet its original goals, the policy discourse was not focused on the condition of instruction in high-poverty schools so much as on accountability and getting kids out of schools that "failed." The embedded assumption in the bill is that turning up the heat on teachers and administrators in high-poverty schools will close the achievement gap. But as Richard Rothstein writes in his book *Class and Schools*, the gap cannot be closed if the purpose of the tests is "to assess whether schools are reaching an impossible goal—equalizing achievement between children of different social classes while we fail to reform the economic and social institutions that ensure unequal achievement, on average, for children of different social classes."[3]

The tightened requirements for interventions in failing schools and districts under Title I also assumed a level of state and local capacity for response. Richard Elmore refers to this problem in Title I implementation as "the capacity gap"[4]—the gulf between what the law mandates that states, districts, and schools do and the resources and expertise they possess. Along with a critique, it is important to state that the designation of schools in improvement status is, in itself, a desirable Title I policy, because a measure of extra resources and funding are directed to high-poverty schools once they are so designated. The unintended consequence of NCLB accountability, however, is that it may trigger a list of schools so long that states will not be able to effectively target their interventions. Lawmakers' assumptions about the capacity of local school districts to effectively intervene in low-performing schools, even to administer the sanction of fundamental overhauls of school organization through "reconstitution," are not based on empirical research. School reconstitution in Chicago, Baltimore, San Francisco, and New York during the 1990s had very mixed success in raising student achievement in high-poverty schools. NCLB further mandates eventual state intervention in high-poverty, low-performing districts. The aftermath of the 1989 mandate for interventions in several of New Jersey's districts (Newark and Patterson) revealed no dramatic changes in student performance.[5] States are not eager to wield this sort of administrative power over local school districts. For instance, since 1989, Maryland has identified about one hundred schools as "reconstitution eligible," but has only sanctioned three schools through private takeovers.[6] When states have intervened, they often lack the capacity and knowledge to run programs effectively. Even where there have been some improvements following a state intervention, usually gains in the early grades, there has not been an instance of a state intervention that has resulted in the achievement gains on the scale that NCLB envisions.

The clearest manifestation of the capacity gap at the state level is the severe staffing limitations for interventions in low-performing schools. A few states, like Maryland and New York, already had systems in place for identifying continuously low-performing schools and mandating interventions, but the majority of states' technical assistance units have very small staffs, and state budgets are not allowing for additional hiring. In NCLB, the federal funding for technical assistance units was "zeroed out" and rolled over into Title I. There is a resulting problem of balance in accountability. The law places numerous added responsibilities on states, from testing to intervention in schools to overseeing choice programs while 95 percent of Title I funds are required to go to the local level via formula. So the statute splits responsibility for administering accountability between districts and states, but the additional money is not accessible to states for technical assistance.

Many in the civil rights community noted that the bill's mandates for eliminating racial achievement disparities might not be realistic in the short or medium term, but hailed the codification of this commitment into federal statute. Christopher Edley, Jr., of the Civil Rights Project at Harvard University, compared the legislation's commitments to outcome equity for minority students to the seemingly unreachable environmental targets in the Clean Air Act in the 1970s. Just as industries had complained then that the goals were unfair because they did not possess the technology and knowledge for full compliance, but the statute drove their compliance to the higher standards over time, so it would be with the education community under No Child Left Behind. By this view, lawyers needed a commitment in federal statute as their foothold for fighting for equity.[7] What the statute required might be impracticable, but it was still the right kind of gain. The bill was a testament to the federal government's commitment to the achievement of minority and economically disadvantaged students, as well as those with disabilities and limited English proficiency.

The version of federalism embodied in the new law is a directive one. States had to adopt a particular framework for their accountability systems, one that mandated that schools make annual progress along a twelve-year timeline. At the time of the law's enactment, only sixteen states had a testing system that was in compliance with the new requirement to test students in every grade. Further, only twenty-two states had the required single accountability system in place to measure the performance of all schools according to the same definition of adequate yearly progress.[8] While the 1994 law had mandated that states develop content and performance standards to which local districts could align their instructional programs, the 2001 law mandated that states adopt a uniform test. Thus the further along a state had been in developing its standards and assessments, such as Maryland, the more sweeping changes in its assessment program it might have to make to comply. Further, with many more curricular and testing decisions accruing to state-level officials, it was unclear how much discretion local administrators, school board members, and teachers would retain over instructional issues. The statute dictates that local schools operate under the enormous external pressures of test-driven accountability with strong sanctions.

NCLB in one sense continued the federal strategy of fostering standards-based reform at the state level, as it required states to measure student performance via testing.[9] The law also kept in place the 1994 IASA requirement that a state have a single set of standards, assessments, and accountability for all students. Yet the law's implications for preexisting systems of state standards were unclear. If the multiyear testing requirements proved expensive, for instance, it might be an incentive for states to drop their performance-based assessments in favor of cheaper and easier-to-administer norm-referenced tests. Further, one of the possible consequences of the mandate that all students be "proficient" in math and science might be that states would adopt tests at a lower level of difficulty. As Jack Jennings has written, one of the many factors that led to the standards movement in the first place was that educators and policymakers recognized that a proliferation of low-skills tests in the 1970s and 1980s had led to poor skills and low levels of instruction.[10] NCLB builds on the standards-based reforms in the states that had gained so much momentum over the past decade, but it is uncertain what kind of standards states will put in place in order to comply with the new testing requirements.

As state assessment policies changed, so would the incentives for schools, particularly those with racial minorities. Most states had set proficiency levels before NCLB's enactment because of the 1994 requirements. Because of the new law's goal of narrowing the racial achievement gap by getting all students to the "proficiency" performance level, those schools with substantial minority populations would have to make the most rapid gains. Given this context of states needing to map growth trajectories for schools toward proficiency, it is clear that the National Assessment of Educational Progress must play an important role in the determination of how the key goals of the law are being met. First, NAEP will provide a basis of comparison for where states set their proficiency levels. Second, it will be important in terms of verifying and validating achievement score gains. There will be pressure on schools with substantial minority populations to raise their test scores, but one measure is not a particularly accurate barometer of whether students' achievement is improving over time.[11]

POLITICS AFTER THE PASSAGE OF NCLB

The implementation of the new law began slowly and in many states and districts, with confusion and resistance. The first two years of the law's implementation, from the administration's education budget to states' experience with defining baseline standards and implementing school transfer policies in the fall, revealed many of the political and practical problems that NCLB posed. The aftershocks of the GOP's ideological defection reverberated as state legislatures, notably ones with Republican majorities, passed resolutions against the law because of its alleged unfunded mandates. In 2004, as the election neared, the administration made a few adjustments to the accountability provisions.

The first major clash was between constituency groups and the administration over the negotiated rule-making process by which the Department of Education receives input prior to writing the regulations for standards and assessments. Several groups alleged that the department had not fulfilled what the law required in assuring representation of several constituencies, notably, parents. A lawsuit filed by four groups led by the Center for Law and Education (CLE) charged that the department had ignored a mandate to give parents and students an "equitable" voice in the rule-making process.[12] The CLE and other groups' complaint was twofold: First, in the negotiated rule-making for the regulations on standards and assessments, the department had appointed education officials who possessed a high level of technical expertise about test validity and alignment, but then "appointed lay parents without such expertise."[13] According to the CLE, this left the parents "with little ability, even when they raised concerns, to critically and expertly evaluate the responses of the education officials." Second, the sessions devolved into negotiations between the department and state and local officials.[14] One observer, Paul Houston of the American Association of School Administrators, agreed: "They only wanted people who agreed with them. If you weren't a cheerleader, they didn't want you there."[15] The suit did not gain standing in the courts, however; in 2002, the District Court granted the Education Department's motion to dismiss the case based on lack of standing, and the federal Court of Appeals affirmed the lower court's decision in January 2005.

Congressional Oversight

In May 2001 the Senate HELP Committee began its official efforts to monitor the department's guidance to states about the statute. Senators, including Kennedy, sent a letter to Secretary Paige, saying they were troubled that accountability provisions were being watered down into a "patchwork" of state assessments. Senator Hillary Clinton, for instance, sent Paige a letter that read: "It was our intention, those of us who went along with the increase in testing, to ensure that every state had a coherent testing system that allowed for comparisons between school districts."[16]

Representative George Miller suggested that the department's guidance for meeting the "highly qualified" teacher provisions did not match with the law. The department's draft regulations would have categorized a trainee enrolled in an alternative program "highly qualified," while a certified teacher assigned a class outside his or her area of expertise would not be qualified. Miller said, "It's up to the department to scrutinize the states to find out whether states are living up to the law, not to grant a blanket exemption to alternative certification systems." He added that he did not believe that the regulations complied with either the law or the intent of Congress.[17]

Struggles in the States

Governors, state legislatures, chief state school officers, and state boards of education were the first level of implementers to struggle with the law's mandates. Many of NCLB's new provisions would require approval by the legislature or the state board of education. At issue was whether the boards would give the authority to the state department to impose sanctions, particularly reconstitution or taking away a school's accreditation. Funding the improvement activities, too, was enormously difficult, both fiscally and politically.

In February 2001 the month after the new law was signed, the National Governors Association asked the Bush administration to ease the new requirements substantially. The new testing requirements, for instance, were estimated by the National Conference of State Legislatures to cost the states $1 billion a year. The states would also have to assume the costs of data processing and developing systems for the longitudinal tracking and disaggregation of test score data; this was estimated to cost between $20 million and $100 million per state, depending on the state's existing system. Implementation of the sanctions in Title I—busing and supplemental services—also meant further new costs for states. The law mandated that states set aside 5 percent for busing, 5 percent for supplemental services, and an additional 10 percent for either or both. Since Title I funding increases went up less than 20 percent, that amount is usurped by just the administration of the law's rewards and sanctions.

Democratic governor Howard Dean of Vermont was one of most vocal initial critics of the new requirements. He said the cost of an overhaul of the state testing system ought to be investigated and suggested it might not be worth it to Vermont to comply. One estimate found that the Vermont would receive $56 million but spend $151 on compliance. Governor Dean stated in March 2001:

> It's going to be incredibly expensive and require us to do our work all over again. I don't think the people who wrote this bill had much consideration for the taxpayers, because this is going to cost people all across this nation.[18]

New Hampshire legislators and state school board members were also wary of the new mandates. Dean Michener of the New Hampshire School Boards Association said: "I am amazed that this Republican administration would be promoting such legislation that is really invasive into the local control process—much more than any other federal program I've seen come down the pike."[19] Louisiana governor Mike Foster (R-LA), who complained to President Bush about what he saw as federal intrusion, promised a fight:

"States still have some rights," Foster said. "I have a lot of friends in Washington. If they don't give us some flexibility in the law, I'll tell you this: We won't go quietly."[20]

By spring of 2003, some state legislatures, facing desperately meager budgets, were showing signs of resistance to the law. Hawaii was one of three states (along with Washington and Minnesota) from which both senators had voted in favor of the Hollings-Wellstone amendment to strike the bill's testing requirements. In April 2003, the Hawaii House of Representatives passed a resolution encouraging school officials not to comply with No Child Left Behind and advocating that the state send its federal Title I funds back to Washington. The resolution's sponsor, Representative K. Mark Takai, stated that it was unreasonable "to make the 'adequate yearly progress' required by the act given the high level of student needs and the low level of federal funding."[21] The state Department of Education, however, said that refusing Hawaii's $35 million of Title I funds was not practical.

Beyond the cost, there were numerous concerns about the effects of the testing mandates on states' instructional programs. The April 2002 General Accounting Office report found that most states' assessment systems were unprepared for the new changes and reiterated the problems of compliance with the 1994 statute.[22] Researchers pointed to the difficulty of the set goals for limited-English-proficient and special education students, score inflation, and validity of the new assessments. Especially worrisome was the fact that the performance of small numbers of students could affect the whole school's designation. Regardless of where states set the mark for proficiency on their assessments, states in the South and West were projected to have the highest number of failing schools because they were more racially diverse.[23]

The Administration's Initial Tough Enforcement Stance

As discussed earlier, the implementation of the 1994 Improving America' Schools Act was uneven and the Clinton administration's enforcement of it relatively weak. A major reason was the fight for survival that the Department of Education's leaders faced after the 1994 elections, when Gingrich's Contract with America had called for its abolition. The question of what level of enforcement would be politically acceptable for the Bush Education Department was one of the first questions posed by both policymakers and practitioners. Undersecretary Eugene Hickok was adamant that in contrast to the Clinton administration, he would not give waivers to states for No Child Left Behind.

Particularly because states would define proficiency and mandate progress for schools differently, it was difficult to see how enforcement would be both fair and consistent. The year 2000 had been designated the year for full compliance with IASA; by January of 2001, only eleven states were in compliance with Title I assessment requirements, and over thirty states had received waivers from the department allowing them one to three additional years to comply fully with the law's mandates.[24] Many states were not in compliance with the requirements to have a single set of standards and assessments for all students, such as those who were limited English proficient, had disabilities, or were migrants, while others had not implemented the disaggregation of data by racial and ethnic subgroups.[25] While most states had adopted standards of some variety in the six years since the 1994 reauthorization, the quality of the assessments and technical knowledge about their use was low in many state departments of education. The report by the General Accounting Office (GAO) in April 2002 found that states were struggling to ensure that student Title I performance data was complete and accurate. The GAO reported that most states hired contractors to score Title I assessments and that about two-thirds monitored the contractors' scoring; several states had found errors with the results, from miscalculating scores to wrongly identifying schools in need of improvement. Many state officials reported that inadequate funding had been an obstacle to compliance.[26] As Richard Elmore writes, "This situation should have signaled to the Bush administration and Congress that there were complex issues of institutional capacity at the state and local level that could not be brushed aside by simply tightening the law's requirements."[27]

As states developed their Title I plans, several, including California, said that they would have to reduce the bar for "proficiency." Secretary Rod Paige, in a letter to the chief state school officers in October 2002, decried those state leaders he said were manipulating the law:

> Unfortunately, some states have lowered the bar of expectations to hide the low performance of their schools. And a few others are discussing how they can ratchet down their standards in order to remove schools from their lists of low performers. Sadly, a small number of persons have suggested reducing standards for defining "proficiency" in order to artificially present the facts. This is not worthy of a great country. . . . Those who play semantic games or try to tinker with state numbers to lock out parents and the public, stand in the way of progress and reform. They are the enemies of equal justice and equal opportunity. They are apologists for failure. And they will not succeed.[28]

Despite Paige's portrayal of them as duplicitous, most state education officials said they lacked clear and consistent guidelines about what kind of plans the Department of Education would find acceptable.[29] The department's final regulations for the accountability component of state Title I plans, for instance, were not issued until the end of November 2001, two months before the plans were due.

In particular, states with the toughest standards or toughest accountability systems appeared to be the ones that would be penalized the most. For instance, in summer of 2002, Michigan had 1,513 "failing" schools, the highest tally in the nation. A spokesman for the Michigan Education Department, T. J. Bucholz, said that state officials would request a meeting with the department to assure that they were not penalized for having high standards.[30] By spring of 2003, however, Michigan cut that number of schools to 216 by adjusting downward the number of students in a school scoring at the proficiency level.[31]

The states' plans for acceptable growth trajectories for all their students reaching proficiency levels by 2014 was also an area of great guesswork. Dr. Joseph Johnson, the federal compensatory education director, told the National Association of Federal Education Program Administrators in April 2001: "People are looking at the data and saying, 'This is going to be catastrophic because there are going to be so many low-performing schools and this isn't going to work.'"[32] Though Johnson himself urged a more positive response, by June he had submitted his resignation.

As states began to devise their growth trajectories for schools, for instance, some analysts noted that they were betting that Congress would make midcourse corrections around 2007 to the law's seemingly unreachable goals. The state of Ohio, for instance, submitted a plan that envisioned the steepest achievement gains between 2007 and 2014. While state officials defended the goals as valid, it was counterintuitive to what one would actually expect to see occur: short-term gains in teaching to the test in the early years, with the most ambitious gains toward the end.

"Research-Based" Methods

Many teachers and administrators were convinced that the administration was going to base its funding of the new Reading First grants on programs endorsed by the National Reading Panel (NRP), a panel charged by Congress with reviewing the evidence on effective reading programs. The NRP had screened approximately thirty-eight studies of reading and concluded that phonics-based instruction programs had been shown to be the most effective. Educators' and legislators' apprehension was based on a section of the statute requiring that funded programs be grounded in "scientifically-based research" and that they address five components of reading instruction identified in the NRP report. These were phonemic awareness, phonics, fluency, comprehension, and vocabulary. By spring 2002, the perception that the department would only endorse phonics-based programs was widespread among educators, publishing associations such as the Association of American Publishers, and groups like the International Reading

Association. Many district administrators who attended the department's Reading Leadership Academies came away with the impression that based on the examples offered by federal officials, only phonics-based programs were acceptable. For instance, at one of the winter Reading Leadership Academies, department officials listed three examples of acceptable reading programs: McGraw-Hill's *Open Court Reading*, Harcourt's *Trophies*, and *Houghton-Mifflin Reading*.[33] Federal officials at the workshops did not explicitly state that a district could put together its own overall strategy with multiple components that met the law's requirements as a whole. Nor did officials discuss the option of a district's using a "home-grown" program if it is designed with a basis in research findings.

That the Department of Education did not clearly dispel these perceptions in the education community about a narrow range of approveable programs only added to the early confusion. When the Senate Health, Education, Labor, and Pensions Committee held a hearing in April, however, Assistant Secretary for Elementary and Secondary Education Susan Neuman, who was also a University of Michigan professor, and Undersecretary Hickok stated that there was no "approved list" of programs eligible for Reading First.[34] Still, given the administration's endorsement of NRP's findings, many district administrators were convinced that only phonics-based literacy programs would win approval in the Reading First grant competitions.

Assistant Secretary Neuman did little to counter the fears of many members of the education community that the Bush administration wanted to foster specific teaching methods. The Stockton, California, *Record* reported her comments on a visit to a local university:

> Susan Neuman said the new federal No Child Left Behind Act, if implemented the right way, will put an end to creative and experimental teaching methods in the nation's classrooms. "It will stifle, and hopefully it will kill (them)," said Neuman. "Our children are not laboratory rats."[35]

Neuman resigned in January 2003 to return to her university teaching job, creating not so much surprise as uncertainty about how her successor in that office would administer the law.

Implementation of School Transfer Policies

In large measure, much of the confusion in states and districts was due to the fact that the Department of Education's final regulations were not issued until November 2002. Thus, during much of the year, state and local officials were reacting to the new requirements in the absence of clear information. For instance, the school transfer provisions caused great confusion.

In some states, the question was how many had been identified as being in "needs improvement" status. Then there were questions about timing. In Rhode Island, for instance, no schools were named as in corrective action because a new assessment system had been put in place less than three years prior to the law taking effect.

As the beginning of the 2002–03 school year approached, school districts experienced confusion about how to implement the policy that children be able to transfer out of schools "needing improvement." Districts made the determination of receiving schools variously, depending on performance, capacity and location. The *New York Times* reported in August 2002 that due mainly to the lack of slots in better schools, the number of transfers in large urban districts would be relatively few:

> In Baltimore, of 30,000 children eligible to transfer to better schools, 347 have applied to fill 194 slots, school officials said. In Chicago, 145,000 students can theoretically leave struggling schools, but only 2,425 applied to transfer and fewer still, 1,170 students, will get to. In Los Angeles, an overcrowded system with 223,000 children in 120 failing schools, officials say there is no room in better schools for any to transfer to.[36]

The U.S. Department of Education clarified that districts needed to offer parents more than one choice for where to send children if their school had been identified as "needing improvement." Space constraints specified in safety codes were the only reason for schools to not accept transfers. Undersecretary Hickok said that the department was willing to be tolerant of districts' difficulties during the initial phase of implementation. Yet he added that federal officials would not be tolerant of locals "thumbing their nose" at the law.[37]

As 2002 drew to a close, the Department of Education began to emphasize interdistrict transfer in the law's implementation. In December the Department issued guidance stating that school districts that lacked space for children wishing to transfer out of failing public schools "must, to the extent practicable," forge cooperative agreements with other districts to accept those students.[38] Underscoring its philosophical commitment to giving parents alternatives, an Office for Educational Choice and Innovation was established under the auspices of the Office of the Undersecretary to make grants to local groups and to disseminate information about charters and choice.[39]

Another complication arose when several southern school districts became confused about how to implement the new transfer law when it appeared to conflict with long-standing desegregation orders. In 2002 in Richmond County, Georgia, still operating under a 1971 court order, the school board attorney successfully argued to a federal judge that transfers might upset the racial balances in the schools if the county did not take the time to plan for adequate transportation. The court required that within each attendance zone in the Richmond County schools, there be 60 percent white and 40 percent African American students, which would shift if students from low-performing schools transferred to higher-performing ones.[40] Undersecretary Hickok told county officials that they should tell the court that they needed to make changes to comply with the federal law, and Secretary Paige referred to county officials as "foot-draggers."[41] But Judge Dudley Bowen gave the school system a year's delay to study how to implement the law without upsetting the court-mandated balances. In the summer of 2004, a federal district judge in Pinellas County, Florida, handed down similar rulings exempting the county from implementing NCLB choice based on a similar rationale: that through the Supremacy Clause of the Constitution, federal court rulings trumped statutes on constitutional matters.[42]

The Zelman Voucher Decision: Philosophical Tensions

As school districts wrestled with the implementation of public school choice, the Supreme Court ruled on June 27, 2001, on the *Zelman v. Simmons-Harris* voucher case. In a 5–4 decision, the Court upheld the constitutionality of the Cleveland voucher plan through which parents could spend state tax dollars for their children to attend religious schools. As President Bush traveled and promoted the bill in the summer of 2001, his focus shifted somewhat toward private school choice once the Supreme Court had ruled. At that point, Bush revived his voucher proposal from the campaign, even saying "the voucher system is a part of the strategy" of improving public education with No Child Left Behind.[43] Some pointed out, however, that the goals of a voucher system appear inconsistent with a focus on improving public schools. The conservative wing of the Republican Party wanted the President to actively endorse vouchers, and he obliged them with several speeches, one in which he called the *Zelman* decision the most historic one in terms of educational equity since the 1954 *Brown v. Board of Education*.[44] The Department of Education in fall 2002 formed a new office on school choice initiatives, headed up by Nina Rees, a former Heritage staff member and aide to Vice President Cheney.

At a July 2001 congressional hearing, Undersecretary Hickock stated that the *Zelman* ruling "does not have a significant impact in terms of where we are" with No Child Left Behind. He added: "Somewhere down the road, I think it might as school choice and supplemental services become a bigger part of the puzzle."[45] Education interest groups on the conservative side of the spectrum were energized by the decision. As Krista Kafer, an education policy analyst for the Heritage Foundation, said, she "wouldn't be surprised" to see some kind of vouchers in Title I given consideration in the next reauthorization.[46] A few state legislatures approved voucher measures, as the Colorado legislature did in April 2003.[47] Following a lengthy congressional battle, the 108th Congress passed a pilot voucher program to serve the District of Columbia by appending it to a January 2004 appropriations measure; shortly thereafter, Secretary Paige called on states and districts to adopt private school choice strategies.[48] Moreover, he used the Fund for Innovation in Education, the main pot of discretionary federal education dollars, to award $77 million to a handful of proeducational privatization advocacy groups, including the Black Alliance for Educational Options, Hispanic CREO, and the Education Leaders Council.[49] This is a significant sum of money aimed at strengthening and amplifying the voices of voucher advocates whose activities likely will include congressional lobbying with the goal of changing the votes of Republicans and Democrats alike.

Funding Adequacy

Adequate funding of the education law has been the major point of contention between congressional Democrats and the President since the law's passage. During the congressional debate over the reauthorization in 2001, Representative George Miller, (D-CA) charged, "Reform without adequate funding is cruelty."[50] On the first anniversary of the signing of the No Child Left Behind Act in January 2002, Senate Democrats, including Edward Kennedy and Joseph Lieberman, sent President Bush a letter which read in part, "America's public schools cannot overcome the enormous obstacles they face on the cheap."[51] Their letter demanded a $7.7 billion increase in the federal education budget for the next fiscal year (2004). Bush, by contrast, proposed a $1.1 billion increase, saying that the country could not afford more in time of war. The administration also proposed cutting 40 education programs at $1 billion. The *American Prospect* reported in June 2002 that "after-school programs and bilingual education are slated to receive the same funding next year as they did this year—which amounts to a cut, due to the projected increase in enrollment. As a result, 33,000 children will go without after-school programs in 2003, and 25,000 will be deprived of bilingual education."[52]

Meanwhile, states were already cutting education budgets across the board. When moderate Republicans complained that the Bush administration was not keeping its funding commitments for NCLB, Budget Director Mitchell Daniels defended the underspending, referring to the law as the "explosively larger education bill."[53] The 1.1 percent net increase in K–12 federal education funding, to many state policymakers' thinking, was not commensurate with the changes being demanded. Wisconsin Attorney General Peggy Lautenschlager, after a review of the law, wrote in June of 2004 that the statute might be successfully challenged in court on the grounds that it is inadequately funded relative to its demands on states to comply with testing and accountability provisions.[54]

CONCLUSION

There were at least four perceptible changes in the federal education policy landscape during the law's first two years of implementation. The first was the strong rhetoric of federal education officials and how it evolved. As states struggled to adjust their accountability systems based on very little guidance about the law, Secretary Paige sought to publicly shame those officials who, he claimed, were cheating parents and students. When Undersecretary Hickok was pressed for operational details—about the transfer policy, for instance—he replied that of greatest importance was that the law was about trying to change the culture of public education.[55]

However, the 2004 election provided an incentive for federal officials to soften their stance by making adjustments to the law. Two Republican-dominated legislatures, Utah and Virginia, passed resolutions against the law, criticizing it as an unfunded mandate, and Senate HELP Committee Democrats sent a lengthy letter to Secretary Paige asking for modifications.[56] Secretary Paige in March 2004 told a group of state legislators, "In the last few months, there have been audible cries from some states and districts. Believe me, we've heard you."[57] Soon after, the Department of Education loosened some of the tougher demands on states, such as testing special education and limited-English-proficiency students, the proportion of students required to take the tests, and the requirement that teachers must have a degree in every subject they teach.

Second, the initial implementation phase coincided with the decline of governor-led education reform that had peaked in the 1990s. If that era's beginning is marked by the 1989 Charlottesville, Virginia, Education Summit, its end might well be marked by the 2002 fiscal retrenchment, which ensured that governors would not have the resources to be the activist reformers they had been in the recent past. This is not to say that governors would not promote K–12 reforms or that states would abandon their standards-based systems. But the January 2003 one-year anniversary of the signing of NCLB witnessed most states facing enormous budget deficits and scaling back their expenditures from the fiscally flush 1990s.[58] As described earlier, many governors and state legislators had begun to challenge the law's goals, especially in light of the lack of accompanying resources. At the same time, many governors have used the law as a lever for justification and continuation of their agendas.[59]

Third, the Supreme Court's 2001 *Zelman v. Simmons-Harris* ruling gave the advocates of private school voucher plans the "green light" of constitutional legitimacy, and this meant that the *politics* of the education policy landscape at state and federal levels would inevitably shift some too. President Bush reacted to the ruling by claiming that NCLB and enhanced private school choice were part of a single strategy of educational improvement. Yet there is a measure of philosophical incompatibility between standards-based reforms to improve public education and the simultaneous endorsement of publicly funded vouchers for private schools; the GOP will continue to wrangle with it in the coming years.

Finally, because the Bush administration's rhetoric about compliance with NCLB was so strong, the Democrats had great difficulty in crafting any kind of new education message. In the November 2002 midterm elections, the Republicans regained control of the Senate and retained a majority in the House for the 108th Congress. With the Democratic Party having failed to effectively convey a message on domestic policy to the electorate, education was but one of the issues over which its leaders would need to wrangle internally before it could point again to an "edge" in education. Furthermore, many education interest groups representing practitioners, particularly the American Federation of Teachers and the National Education Association, had a difficult time crafting new political messages in the midst of the "pro-accountability" rhetoric in which Paige, Hickok, and many education organizations had insulated the new law.

A major fact about federal authorizing legislation is that Congress always plans to revisit it. When elements of the law prove unworkable or unpopular, Congress often alters them. As Eugen Eidenberg and Roy Morey wrote in their study of the ESEA, "Most often the conflict continues, inside and outside Congress, and new laws are proposed which reshape the issues and ground rules of previously fought battles."[60] In the case of the NCLB, the law expires five years before the twelve-year timeline for students' "proficiency" is complete. While the law's passage portended a powerful realignment of federal, state, and local responsibilities in elementary and secondary education, it is also not Congress's last word on the subject. It was the framing document for a work in progress.

Chapter 10

Epilogue: The Future of Federal Education Policy in the Twenty-First Century

This epilogue, written after the 2004 election, considers the major implications of these two Congresses for the future. What does this past ESEA reauthorization portend for the future of federal education policy for elementary and secondary education, particularly in light of a second presidential term for George Bush and a strengthened GOP majority in Congress? A starting place for thinking about this question is placement of NCLB into several comparative contexts. For instance, to understand the statute's implications for intergovernmental relations, one must consider whether the trend of increased regulation might match trends in other federal social policies. In order to think about the future role of interest groups and think tanks in fashioning federal education policies, it is necessary to review why the groups representing educators were displaced the way they were during the five-year period covered in this book. And in order to predict whether the next Congress will be more "partisan" over education, we need to review what the term really meant during the 106th and 107th Congresses.

THE REPUBLICANS' IDEOLOGICAL DEFECTION

This book has considered how partisanship and ideology worked in very different ways across these two Congresses. "Partisanship" in the 106th meant that the GOP declined to pass Clinton's education bill on the eve of an election. The two parties' ideological stances were far apart, with the GOP continuing to invoke "local control" while the Democrats fought privatization measures. By contrast, partisanship in the 107th was manifested by loyalty to President Bush: conservative Republicans followed his exhortation to pass a centrist bill and parted with their long-held ideological tenets. Democrats made fewer ideological concessions, though many of the liberal Democrats opposed the mandatory testing requirements that were accompanied by what they saw as inadequate resources for poor schools.

No Child Left Behind was consistent with Bush's demonstrated ability to discipline the far right of his own party in the House. As with the overhaul of Medicare in 2004, in which Bush tamed his most vociferous ideological opponents in the House, he demonstrated that he could inspire ideological defection. President Bush and the GOP gained political capital from the bill's passage; the 107th Congress definitively proved that education would no longer be the sole terrain of the Democratic Party. Along with that new capital came public accountability: Having committed itself so visibly to an enlarged and active federal role, the Republican Party may find it difficult in the decades ahead to retreat to the policies of the Reagan era. The legislation embodies a federal commitment to eradicating achievement disparities among students of different racial groups and socioeconomic groups, not at all resembling the federal retreat from setting educational priorities that characterized the Reagan years.[1]

ESEA was first passed in the context of the formation of Lyndon Johnson's Great Society antipoverty programs. As Frederick Hess and Patrick McGuinn write, "The rise of the new conservatism that first emerged in 1964 provided Republicans with an opportunity-oriented alternative to the Great Society–style liberalism that they charged with undermining the nation's sense of responsibility, unraveling its cultural fabric, and threatening its economic well-being."[2] Clinton and the New Democrats, by embracing standards and accountability, while simultaneously calling attention to the educational needs of the poor, were able to escape the negative labeling of this Great Society liberalism. What Bush has done, on the other hand, with "compassionate conservatism" and education, is an uncertain legacy:

> Bush's stance strengthened the Republican hand on education and a broad array of policy debates, but it proved to be an unhappy bargain for traditional Republicans and for the radical critics of federal interventionism. The expanded federal role marked a historic departure from Republican doctrine and created the likelihood of future conflicts between the proponents of the opportunity society and the traditional defenders of state and local prerogatives.[3]

Despite the awkwardness posed by Republican governors crying foul of the law's increased regulations, NCLB has enabled the GOP to be on the side of the "opportunity society" without having to commit significant additional fiscal resources.

RETHINKING THE ROLE OF THE PRESIDENT IN AGENDA SETTING

The events in the 107th Congress also reinforce the centrality of the president in determining the course of a major readjustment in the federal role in education. Bush's placing elementary and secondary education as his top domestic priority affected the leadership's actions: Boehner and Gregg were not going to halt his initiative, and Kennedy and Miller very much wanted the bill. Very little about the substantive content of the bill was new; the difference in the 107th was Bush's relationship to the four committee leaders.

In his article, "Short-Circuiting the Bureaucracy in the Great Society Policy Origins in Education," Hugh Davis Graham contrasts President Lyndon Johnson's "task forcing" approach to building the architecture of the ESEA in 1964 with the education "iron triangles," spawned by the legislation itself, that formulated policies during the 1970s.[4] Clinton was a "hands-on" education governor and president, ensuring that standards-based reform drove the 1994 IASA. President Bush's style of legislative leadership differed from that of all of these predecessors. Aside from his support for testing, accountability, reading, and, initially, vouchers, he was not particularly interested in the crafting of policies. Neither the White House nor the Education Department proposed legislative language, and Secretary of Education Paige was not involved in the fine details of policy formulation. Instead, Bush's strategy was to embrace the core principles in the New Democrats' bill and then allow Congress to work out the specifics. Once the bills had passed both houses, however, the White House actively tamed the right flank of the House leadership, blocking the two most conservative proposals, vouchers and block grants.

My interpretation of Bush's role with No Child Left Behind is that it is apt to be viewed by historians as rather anomalous in terms of an executive fashioning education policy. When one considers Secretary Paige's post–9/11 invocation of education as a national bulwark against terrorism and Bush's insistence that Congress pass the bill to demonstrate that it had not been immobilized, it is evident that NCLB's passage was an unusually symbolic political event. It was the prerogative of the President to have the legislation, and he exercised it aggressively.

One of the guiding questions for this study was agenda setting: Which groups in the "primordial policy soup" (as Kingdon terms the atmosphere on Capitol Hill) were most determinative of the agenda? Answering that President Bush was seems an obvious answer, particularly since he played an active role in reigning in conservative House Republicans. However, if the problem that NCLB was intended to solve was too-lax accountability, that problem was actually defined by Democrats as early as the 1999 passage of Ed-Flex. Issue entrepreneurs like PPI and Fordham (portability), as well as the Education Trust, got the most mileage for their ideas. Clearly, the Clinton administration helped develop the policy alternatives, though many never made it any further because of partisanship and the climate of politics (class-size reduction, school construction). Senator Bingaman and Representative Miller, along with organizations like the Education Trust, kept the subgroup accountability model alive. The political opening was electing Bush, who claimed credit for a school accountability system in Texas that neatly matched what many beltway groups, including civil rights organizations, had already been advocating. A second window for passage opened after September 11, as the President demanded compromise. But perhaps the most important finding in this case about Kingdon's agenda setting is the one relating to what he calls the "national mood."[5] Policy alternatives were constrained by intense political divisions in both Congress and in the electorate, but right now, there is no evidence that the electorate en masse is eager to see changes to the law.

INSTITUTIONAL IMPLICATIONS: CONGRESS, THE EXECUTIVE BRANCH, AND INTEREST GROUPS

I have argued that many of the political conditions and institutional relationships that produced No Child Left Behind developed during the 106th Congress, when Republican staff turned away from the Clinton Education Department's proposal and the traditional education interest groups and looked for alternative policy ideas. In the 106th and 107th Congresses, it was apparent that the former model of drafting education legislation via stable relationships, reliance on acknowledged "specialists," organizations' access to committee staff, and close coordination with administrators, was no longer operative. My argument is not that the groups in the education establishment stood in opposition to the substantive reforms of No Child Left Behind such as testing, public school choice, and accountability, as these groups had been in the coalition that had solidly supported standards-based reform in the 1990s. Rather, I found two slightly different reasons for their exclusion across the two Congresses. While in the 106th, these groups were excluded because of the GOP's association of them with the "status quo," in the 107th, both Democratic and Republican leaders shut them out during the conference for expediency, that is, not having to be responsive to a set of disparate voices that would slow down the producing of a bill.

It is important, however, to distinguish between the *access* groups had to the legislative process and the *impact* that they actually have on the final legislation. That is, even though the liberal interest group coalition enjoyed far more limited access to the Congress, their impact is nonetheless apparent in the passage of No Child Left Behind, which in many ways builds on the ideas and structures of the bipartisan standards movement of the 1990s.

Throughout much of the 1970s and 1980s, it was committees' negotiation with pluralistic interests, with a relatively ideologically disunited Democratic majority in power, which kept the liberal-leaning education policy network functioning. Another change is that the membership base of groups representing education professionals and their clients declined steadily throughout the 1990s. As states became the key actors in the political arena in the late 1980s and 1990s, these groups' dominance was challenged by state education policymakers and the groups that represent them.[6] The Republican Party gained control of the Congress in 1995, and thus was in control of the entire legislative agenda when the ESEA came up for reauthorization in 1998. Many of the Republican committee staff did not perceive the interest groups as a pluralistic network, but as monolithic—the status quo or "big learning organization bureaucracy," meaning the former players in the more liberal interest group coalition. The pattern shifted, however, between 1998 and 2001: the traditional education interest groups found they had to work harder to gain access to the legislative process, while members of Congress and their staff were responsive to a host of new actors and interests. Groups representing state leaders, namely the Education Leaders Council and the National Governors Association, gained new visibility and access to the legislative process. Moreover, past patterns of partisan loyalties did not consistently hold: Senator Kennedy and Representative Miller, for instance, challenged the NEA's oppositional stance to greater teacher accountability measures.

NCLB presented both the AFT and the NEA with a challenge. The NEA has openly opposed the law and attempted to find a plaintiff state to sue the federal government claiming that it is an unfunded mandate, while the AFT has expressed far more support of the law's goals of testing and subgroup accountability.[7] AFT president Sandra Feldman warned delegates in 2003: "If all we do is focus on the potential harm that can be done by the law, then we'll be doing a disservice to our students, our profession, our union, and to each and every individual teacher. When anxiety gets whipped up into a generalized, simplistic 'down with the law' mantra, it jeopardizes Title I."[8]

It is unclear exactly how the unions will reposition themselves during the second Bush term, though the administration has more friendly ties with the AFT, which has not wanted to risk damaging its image by objecting to the law. Secretary of Education Rod Paige was openly contemptuous of the National Education Association, referring to the group as a "terrorist organization" at a January 2004 meeting of the National Governors Association. (Both unions issued statements of objection to the remark, and Paige did apologize.)

Many practitioner interest groups and civil rights groups have sought to defend the law. The newly formed Achievement Alliance, a group whose goal is to deepen understanding of the law, is composed of the Citizens' Commission on Civil Rights, the National Alliance of Black School Educators, Just for the Kids/National Center for Educational Accountability, the Education Trust, and the Business Roundtable. Such diverse coalitions that include business and civil rights interests (but not the teacher unions) are a harbinger of a likely new advocacy model in the DC education policy subsystem.

There was also a vacuum in terms of Congress's consideration of educational research. The hearings in the 106th Congress were dominated by governors and chief state school officers. When academics like Kane and Staiger did weigh in about the likely effects of NCLB accountability—namely, the overidentification of racially diverse schools as "failing"—the political process pushed right past them. The kind of information provided by think tanks is very different from the scholarly expertise provided by researchers. This is part of a larger trend of the displacement of expertise and the reliance on the public-relations kind of strategy of think tanks.[9] As Andrew Rich has written, a long-defended idea in political science was that "the social science expert was most effective as a detached analyst, producing research that would serve a common and neutral view of the public interest."[10] However, Rich writes, the growth in recent decades of think tanks' involvement during all phases of formation of legislation has challenged the ideal of scholars' neutrality:

> Out of the developments among think tanks—and largely due to their efforts—research is often produced from many sources that represent many sides of every issue. What these experts produce is often far from a neutral or objective analysis of what serves the public interest. And experts are quite politically active. Few policy makers believe that experts are neutral or detached. The evidence suggests that political scientists should not hold that belief either.[11]

Particularly with a Republican House and Senate and second term for President Bush, practitioner-based and urban interests groups are apt to retain their "outsider" status,[12] but strategize about how to regain their influence in education policymaking, either through direct access to congressional staff or through grassroots-style tactics of mobilizing their constituent bases. NCLB has already spawned new coalitions of interest groups, such as the Achievement Alliance, whose mission has been to respond to the state-level backlash against the law by building support for its basic tenets of accountability and equity. Meanwhile, it is likely that think tanks with education policy programs will continue to coordinate and build alliances with similarly ideologically aligned ones, both on the right and the left. (One new entrant is the Center for American Progress, a center-left think tank founded by Clinton's former Chief of Staff, John Podesta.)

From a political perspective, the exclusion of Democratic Senate HELP Committee members from the core of deal making has powerful implications for the future of federal education policy. Especially with the new 55–44–1 Republican majority in the Senate in the 109th Congress, the GOP's bypassing of Senate committee Democrats in favor of the New Democrats is likely to continue, and not just on the education committee. This pattern has been evident in legislation for several areas of domestic policy in recent years, for instance, with both the 1995 welfare reform bill and the conferencing of the Medicare/prescription drug bill passed in 2004.

Over the past thirty-five years, education subgovernments functioned from a base at the committee level, where staff negotiated with a pluralistic constituency, including the numerous education interest groups.[13] Moreover, until 1994, the Democrats were the majority party, but not an ideologically coherent majority. Federal agencies were a critical component of this subgovernment. Now, however, there is not only a highly disciplined Republican majority, but it is the party leadership, not the committee, that has become powerful in agenda setting. Education interest groups that had been accustomed to providing input into program decisions and wielding influence with Democratic committee staff, have been largely excluded from the process. Republican staff considered these groups a self-interested monolithic entity—the "blob"—and showed a tendency to consult center-right think tanks and groups of state education administrators, such as the Education Leaders Council and the National Governors' Association. Congress is thus less effective from the perspective of researchers' and educational practitioners' access to the process.

IMPLICATIONS FOR FEDERALISM

As political scientists Kathryn McDermott and Laura Jensen have written, the federal government has recently used its conditional spending power—its ability to require states and localities to satisfy certain conditions in order to receive funds—to leverage compliance with national directives in many areas of social policy, such as social welfare, transportation, and criminal justice. NCLB "attaches newly stringent conditions to elementary and secondary school subsidies, ratcheting up the level of Federal control over policies and programs that previously fell within the purview of state and local educational authorities."[14] Further, as state and local governments have become increasingly invested in education, it is very difficult for any state to walk away from aid and thus avoid accepting the conditional aid "strings" of teacher quality; requirements for student, school, and district performance; and clear responsibility for interventions. McDermott and Jensen find that "the major problem with conditional federal spending is that it limits the states' policy choices, thickening the intergovernmental regulatory web and increasing intergovernmental tensions while tipping the federal balance that was meant to protect liberty and ensure governmental accountability."[15] This narrowing of states' policy choices, along with the increased fiscal demands of the law on states, is a large part of why governors are now in a peculiar position with respect to NCLB. Governors of both parties have put intense pressure on the Department of Education to change the accountability requirements. Not all governors have pushed back on Washington, however; indeed some have used the law's ambitious goals as a platform for pushing their own reforms and priorities.[16]

Even if state policymakers' options have been narrowed through increased regulation, one important consequence for Title I is that there is now a more clearly defined measure of its program effectiveness than in the past.[17] It is clear to all that there should not be separate assessments used to measure the academic progress of Title I students and everyone else: they are one and the same instrument. While the 1994 reauthorization made this programmatic correction, NCLB's specified goals ensure that states will implement it.

Thus conclusions about federalism and NCLB are best examined against recent trends of how the federal government has used conditional aid in other areas of social policy. Governors will no doubt continue to push back against the regulations, but states' compliance seems assured by their need for the money. The quality of state policy instruments, such as instructional programs and tests, and the capacity of states to intervene in low-performing schools is, however, an entirely separate question from that of compliance. As the first phase of implementation revealed, state resources for reaching the law's goals were highly uneven.

An important but still largely undiscussed implication of NCLB for federalism is its relationship to school finance equity and adequacy lawsuits. Some legal scholars, such as Professors Goodwin Liu and Stephen Sugarman of Berkeley, have suggested that in the long run NCLB might provide momentum for reconsidering an issue left open by the Supreme Court in its 1973 decision, *San Antonio v. Rodriguez*—namely, whether the United States Constitution guarantees some level of adequacy in educational opportunity.[18] In *Rodriguez*, the Court held 5–4 that large spending inequalities resulting from a locally driven school finance scheme do not violate the Equal Protection Clause. However, the Court did not decide whether a minimum floor of opportunity is required. By requiring states to define "adequate yearly progress" outcomes for all students and to eliminate an achievement gap in

Title I, NCLB adds support to state lawsuits alleging a duty to provide students with an "adequate" education and has motivated educational cost studies seeking to define educational adequacy in greater detail. The gradual evolution and strengthening of conceptual and empirical notions of adequacy may provide a basis for reexamining whether there is indeed a federal constitutional right to a certain standard of educational "adequacy" for all students regardless of where they attend school. While it seems implausible that a conservative-leaning Supreme Court would actually overturn *Rodriguez*, the broader point is that NCLB does provide a new framework for school finance advocates' consideration of what the federal constitutional obligation to equity and adequacy might plausibly be.

THE 109TH CONGRESS: WIDER MARGINS, LIMITED ALTERNATIVES

The 2004 elections portend a period of relative stability in K–12 education policy over the next four years. Four new southern Republican senators replaced retiring Democrats Zell Miller (GA), Ernest Hollings (SC), John Breaux (LA), Bob Graham (FL). The loss of "Blue Dog Democrats" who could work across the aisle means that the Senate's polarization will become even more pronounced.[19] The GOP increased its margins in both houses: the Senate at 55 Republicans, 44 Democrats, and 1 Independent, and the House at 231 Republicans, 200 Democrats, and 1 Independent. Senator Mike Enzi (R-WY) replaced Judd Gregg as HELP chair. One possible implication of this change is that the special challenges of rural states in complying with provisions like choice and teacher quality will get higher priority.

The two presidential candidates did not propose radically different policies, though Senator Kerry, who had voted for NCLB, charged that the Bush administration had underfunded the law by $27 billion. Unless governors succeed in lobbying for further relief from selected testing and accountability regulations, opportunities to change NCLB are more constrained for the simple reason that Democrats now have diminished political leverage in Congress. Vouchers and choice, extending mandatory testing to the secondary grades, amendment of some of the accountability provisions in NCLB are likely proposals for the 109th Congress, along with the reauthorization of Head Start and the Higher Education Act. The competition between parties over message on education will continue, but without control of the committees, the Democrats' ability to use the media to gain advantage on the issue with the electorate has diminished significantly. As with all other areas of the federal domestic budget in 2005, education is apt to have very few increases over the next five years because of the deficit.

Politically, education as a national issue has become the shared domain of the Republican and Democratic parties. The law has made unprecedented performance demands on poor schools and tightened the federal requirements of states for intervention, but it has done so in a context of diminishing resources and unclear rules about the terms of federal enforcement. President Bush's expansive education policies are the mirror image of Reagan's, but the fiscal context of domestic policy during 2003 and 2004 resembles that of the 1980s: tax cuts, rising deficits and military spending, and impending cuts in social programs. As discretionary dollars vanish, the margin for interparty competition on message narrows. As there is less room for expansion of existing K–12 education programs, let alone ambitious new initiatives, the range of policy instruments available to the federal government is growing ever more constricted. Congress can fine-tune accountability mechanisms and most likely place further regulations on states. An example is the Bush campaign proposal to expand NCLB testing into the high school grades. Perhaps most ominous of all for compensatory education is that the nation's poverty rate rose by almost a half point in 2003, the third yearly rise in a row, to 12.5 percent, or one of every eight Americans, according to the U.S. Census Bureau.[20] In 2004, one in six of every American children lived in poverty, while one in eight had no health insurance.[21] Federal compensatory dollars are going to have to be spread thinner, serving fewer numbers of eligible children, and the reform of high-poverty schools will become all the more difficult. Further, given the international and fiscal crises facing the Bush administration, addressing the underlying causes of child poverty will remain a low priority in the second term.

ACCESS, INFLUENCE, AND SUBSTANCE

Given the lack of impetus for major changes and the hold of the Bush administration, the substance of the law is unlikely to be overhauled. The centrist compromise will certainly hold, if for no other reason than that the Democrats will be unable to set the agenda or thwart that of the GOP. The vital political question from a democratic perspective is *which* groups and interests will now be admitted to the process of policymaking. While it is unsurprising that teacher unions and urban interest groups had their dominance challenged during the period chronicled here, there is a serious danger in the continued systematic exclusion of researchers and practitioners from the legislative process. The future effectiveness of Title I depends on what many scholars have called for since the early 1970s: not just more funds, but "more funds plus an ambitious plan of systematic experimentation. Different programs [have] to be carefully compared and the same programs tested under different conditions so that promising approaches could be isolated."[22] The federal Institute of Education Sciences' aspiration is to conduct a program of systematic, "scientifically based" research. Yet the conduct of well-planned experimentation and research is a significant investment, and the nation's increasing deficits mean that the money to conduct such work has been severely curtailed.

Because of the present lack of a federal commitment to programs designed to ameliorate family and child poverty, and the accompanying lack of funds in the domestic budget to support them, the outlook for the improvement of compensatory education does not appear bright. Its best hope is that the formation of future educational policy will rely to the greatest degree possible on the knowledge base about both high-poverty schools as organizations and also students in poverty. The danger is that this kind of foundation for Title I will continue to erode because of "message politics." Perhaps the most sobering lesson of the events of these two Congresses is that the more heated the parties' competition over education becomes, the harder it is for empirical knowledge to enter the policy stream.

Appendix A

Methods

From the beginning of this study, which was my doctoral dissertation, I conceptualized it as both a case study of legislative action and also a history of what had taken place. That is, I wanted to both document the facts of what occurred and analyze their political and institutional significance. With the stalemate of the 106th Congress, however, I recognized that the interesting story was not just about the substance of Title I, but about ideological divisions between and within parties and the implications of changes in Congress for changes in the substance of federal policy.

DATA COLLECTION

My data collection was based on the principle that, as Yin has written, "any finding or conclusion in a case study is likely to be much more convincing and accurate if it is based on several different sources of information, following a corroboratory mode."[1] The multiple sources of information I relied on included not only interviews, but governmental reports, selected internal staff memoranda, and numerous congressional members' policy briefs or official public statements on education issues, legislation and committee reports, transcripts of hearings as well as media accounts and one major Title I trade publication. In addition, I utilized the Congressional Record and videotapes of floor debate. Feasibility is one reason that I decided against requesting interviews with members of Congress themselves, as I was writing and researching a doctoral dissertation. There is, however, a strong rationale for interviewing aides, namely, that past work in political science has shown that aides play an important substantive role in the formation of legislation.[2]

During the 106th Congress, I conducted four major rounds of interviews and document-gathering in Washington, DC. The first three were interviews with aides, audiotaped, and approximately forty minutes in length. The final round of interviews was with representatives of various interest groups, as well as three selected members of the Department of Education and former Undersecretary of Education Marshall Smith. The interest group interviewees were mostly either legislative or K–12 education policy directors within their organizations. My decisions about when to conduct a round of interviews mirrored the progress of the bill: I went to Washington whenever either a major legislative step had been taken or was anticipated.

During the 107th Congress, I conducted two major rounds of interviews in January and February 2002 following No Child Left Behind's passage and signing into law. This delay was dictated largely by aides' unavailability during the conferencing of the bill, which was somewhat chaotic due to post–9/11 anthrax attacks on the Hart Senate Office Building.

In the course of data collection during the 106th Congress, the outcome of the passage of a final bill was in doubt. Therefore, many questions I asked of staff were about the substance of proposed changes to Title I, but also about their perceptions of the political climate and how it affected the formation of the agenda. In the earliest phase of interviewing, in the House of Representatives, I tried to learn what members of both parties saw as their top priorities, and the issues on which they believed they could compromise and those where they were unwilling to do so. These interviews did not follow formal protocols, though there were common questions asked of aides in the different rounds of interviews. Examples of the kinds of questions were both about procedures (what legislative developments had recently occurred, what kinds of internal meetings had taken place, what measures would they be sponsoring as an amendment), and their perceptions (what was happening to the program, what was driving the formation of the agenda, what were their constituents telling them, what was the source of a particular idea or proposal, with which external groups or other members of Congress did they collaborate).

By the time of my last round of interviews during the 106th Congress, and during the two rounds during the 107th, I was able to offer my own perceptions, asking for the interviewee to confirm or disconfirm them. Throughout the study, I treated the issues of choice, testing, and accountability in particular depth. Particularly in the 107th Congress, these surfaced as the issues over which there was the most inter- and intraparty division, and hence, bargaining and negotiation.

While I had not conducted research in the Congress before, I brought to the interviews a certain level of insider knowledge about the U.S. Department of Education. I worked there as a policy analyst from 1992 to 1996 in the research office. It was during those years that the Elementary and Secondary Education Act was reauthorized and the Goals 2000 legislation enacted. I was thus familiar with how the Clinton administration and Congress had changed the law.

SELECTION OF INTERVIEWEES

My data collection deliberately reflected a balance of the two parties, and the composition of the subcommittee and committee levels (see Appendix B, interviews conducted). The data are institutionally representative. That is, I did not try to interview aides of every member of each committee. Instead, I sought interviews with staff of the chairs and ranking members of each committee and subcommittee. (Five aides were interviewed twice). Beyond this initial selection of interviewees, I relied on "snowball sampling." Aides would tell me whose staff I should talk to about particular issues, assuming the role of informant as well as respondent. For instance, I learned in this way about the important role of New Democratic senators who were not Health, Education, Labor, and Pensions Committee members.

In the selection of interest groups, I also sought a balance among institutional missions and political ideologies. These interviews focused on the group's or institution's strategies for gaining access to the political process and their positions on Title I policy. I conducted the set of interest group interviews corresponding to the 106th Congress in October of 2000, shortly before the presidential election. While five months had elapsed by then since the bill had died on the Senate floor, the advantage was that the various actors had had time to reflect on what had happened and make meaning of it.

The key limitation of the data is that the interviews offer only aides' and interest group members' perceptions of the political process. However, it was still possible to attain a reliable picture of how institutional relationships functioned because the interviews were conducted across the governmental and nongovernmental sectors during a three-year-period and included the vantage points of the key actors involved in the policymaking process.

ANALYSIS

As many institutional researchers find, the unfolding of political events over three years necessitated my revision and expansion of the study's theoretical frame. When I initiated the study in 1999, my goal was to write a legislative history that would, as past ones had, document how the legislative agenda for Title I was formed and by which coalitions, and analyze what this meant for high-poverty schools. Thus, the basic theoretical proposition guiding the initial analysis of data from the 106th Congress was derived from Kingdon's themes of "problem definition" and agenda-setting, as well as the education policy community's specification of "alternatives," or policy options.[3] While these concepts remained relevant throughout the study, as political events progressed, my analytic lens on the data broadened. The case of the 106th Congress revealed as much about policymaking in education due to polarization between parties and changes in Congress as they did about the substance of Title I. After May 2000, when the Senate dropped consideration of its ESEA bill, I realized that I had a case about legislative "failure," and the study's more robust framework was the political and institutional factors that led to that failure. Though I persisted with my original goal of writing a thorough legislative history that progressed in chronological fashion, my questions of "what passed when" were deemphasized as I came to view the data as a story about partisanship and institutional relationships. While many of the same theoretical propositions about agenda formation and specifications of policy alternatives carried over to the 107th Congress, this shift in perspective meant that when I collected data in winter of 2002 following the passage of No Child Left Behind, my interviews emphasized inter- and intraparty differences on policy. However, my methods for selecting aides were the same and I kept the substantive focus on testing, choice, and accountability in Title I.

Throughout the construction of the narrative, I used the documents and media accounts as a means of corroborating and augmenting the information from the interviews with aides.[4] I see the study's "chain of evidence"[5] as a consistent one originating with my research questions grounded in Kingdon's framework on agenda formation, utilizing a case methodology designed to gather multiple sources of data about the legislative process and substance of policy proposals, and over time, incorporating questions about partisanship and its limitations.

Appendix B

Interviews

October 1999

Alex Nock, professional staff member (minority), House Committee on Education and the Workforce, 10/26/99.

Kara Haas, legislative assistant, Representative Mike Castle (R-DE), 10/29/99.

Kent Talbert, professional staff member (majority), House Committee on Economic and Educational Opportunities, 10/26/99.

Charles Barone, legislative director, Representative George Miller (D-CA), 10/29/99.

Christine Wolfe, professional staff member (majority), House Committee on Education and the Workforce, 10/28/99.

November 1999

Carmel Martin, chief education counsel, Senator Jeff Bingaman (D-NM), 11/22/99.

Susan Hattan, deputy Republican staff director, Senate Committee on Health, Education, Labor, and Pensions, 11/22/99.

Beverly Schroeder, legislative assistant, Senator Tom Harkin (D-IA), 11/23/99.

Jill Morningstar, legislative assistant, Senator Paul Wellstone (D-MN), 11/19/99.

Denzel McGuire, professional staff member, U.S. Senate Subcommittee on Children and Families, and Senator Judd Gregg (R-NH), 11/19/99.

Laura Chow, legislative fellow, Senator Edward Kennedy (D-MA), 11/18/99.

March 2000

Glen Chambers, legislative assistant, Senator Sam Brownback, (R-KS) 3/30/00.

Laura Chow, education advisors to Edward Kennedy (D-MA), Health, Education, Labor, and Pensions Committee, 3/31/00.

Jill Morningstar, legislative assistant, Senator Paul Wellstone (D-MN), 3/29/00.

Shannon Ashpole, legislative assistant, Senator Patty Murray (D-WA), 3/31/00.

Michele Stockwell, legislative assistant, Senator Joseph Lieberman, (D-CT) 3/31/00.

Elyse Wasch, legislative assistant, Senator Jack Reed (D-RI), 3/28/00.

Kathy Hogenbruen, legislative assistant, Senator Christopher Dodd (D-CT), 3/28/00.

Meredith Medley, legislative assistant, Senator Bill Frist (R-TN), 3/30/00.

Julian Haynes, legislative assistant, Senator Susan Collins,(R-ME) 3/28/00.

April 2000

Marshall Smith, Undersecretary, U.S. Department of Education, 4/20/00.

October 2000

Susan Wilhelm, program analyst, U.S. Department of Education, 10/16/00.

Ann O'Leary, special assistant to the president for the Domestic Policy Council (formerly of the U.S. Department of Education), 10/16/00.

Mary Cassell, Office of Management and Budget, 10/18/00.

David Shreve, National Conference of State Legislatures, 10/18/00.

Jack Jennings, director, Center for Education Policy, 10/18/00.

Bruce Hunter, senior associate, American Association of School Administrators, 10/18/00.

Kelly Amis, education program director, Thomas B. Fordham Foundation, 10/19/00.

Andrew Rotherham, director, 21st Century Schools Project, Progressive Policy Institute, 10/19/00.

Amy Wilkins, principal partner, Education Trust, 10/19/00.

Nina Shokraii Rees, senior education policy analyst, Domestic Policy Studies, The Heritage Foundation, 10/20/00.

Patricia Sullivan, former director, Education Legislation, Human Resources Group, National Governors Association, 10/26/00.

February 2001

Charlene K. Haar, Education Policy Institute, 2/9/01.

January 2002

Alex Nock, professional staff member (minority), House Committee on Education and the Workforce, 1/28/02.

Sally Lovejoy, education aide (majority), House Committee on Education and the Workforce, 1/28/02.

Democratic legislative assistant (name withheld), House side, 1/28/02.

Holly Kuzmich, legislative assistant, Senator Tim Hutchinson (R-AR), 1/28/02.

Kathleen Strottman, legislative assistant, Senator Mary Landrieu (D-LA), 1/28/02.

Amanda Farris, legislative assistant, Senator Mike Enzi (R-WY), 1/30/02.

Professional staff member to the Majority (name withheld), House Committee on Education and the Workforce, 1/30/02.

Jordan Cross, legislative assistant, Senator Susan Collins (R-ME), 1/30/02.

February 2002

Kara Haas, legislative assistant, Representative Michael Castle (R-DE), 2/1/02.

Democratic legislative assistant (name withheld), Senate side, 2/1/02.

Michael Kennedy, legislative assistant, Representative Thomas Petri (R-WI), 2/25/02.

Charles Barone, legislative director, Representative George Miller (D-CA), 2/26/02.

Democratic legislative aide (name withheld), Senate side, 2/27/02.

March 2002

Sarah Youssef, professional staff member, Domestic Policy Council, 3/18/02.

Joel Packer, director of intergovernmental relations, National Education Association, 3/1/02.

September 2002

Elizabeth Fay, legislative aide, Senator Evan Bayh (D-IN), 9/23/02.

Appendix C

House and Senate Education Committee Membership, 106th and 107th Congresses

Members of the House Education and Workforce Committee 106th Congress

Majority: 27 / Minority: 22

Republicans

William Goodling, Pennsylvania, Chair
Thomas Petri, Wisconsin, Vice-Chairman*
Marge Roukema, New Jersey*
Cass Ballenger, North Carolina
Bill Barrett, Nebraska
John Boehner, Ohio*
Peter Hoekstra, Michigan
Howard McKeon, California
Michael Castle, Delaware*
Sam Johnson, Texas
Nathan Deal, Georgia
James Talent, Missouri
James Greenwood, Pennsylvania*
Lindsey Graham, South Carolina*
Mark Souder, Indiana*
David McIntosh, Indiana*
Charlie Norwood, Georgia
Ron Paul, Texas*

Democrats

William (Bill) Clay, Missouri
George Miller, California*
Dale Kildee, Michigan*
Harold Ford, Jr., Tennessee*
Major Owens, New York
Robert Andrews, New Jersey
Tim Roemer, Indiana
Donald Payne, New Jersey*
Patsy Mink, Hawaii*
Robert Scott, Virginia*
Loretta Sanchez, California*
John Tierney, Massachusetts
Carlos Romero-Barcelo, Puerto Rico*
Chaka Fattah, Pennsylvania*
Ron Kind, Wisconsin
Lynn Woolsey, California*
Ruben Hinojosa, Texas*
Rush Holt, New Jersey
Dennis Kuchinich, Ohio*

Van Hilleary, Tennessee*
Bob Schaffer, Colorado*
Thomas Tancredo, Colorado
Ernie Fletcher, Kentucky
Jim DeMint, South Carolina*
Johnny Isakson, Georgia
Matt Salmon, Arizona*
Fred Upton, Michigan
Vernon Ehlers, Michigan

David Wu, Oregon*
Carolyn McCarthy, New York*
Vacancy

*Denotes membership on Subcommittee on Early Childhood, Youth, and Families

Members of the Senate Health, Education, Labor, and Pensions Committee, 106th Congress

Majority = 10 / Minority = 8

Republicans

James Jeffords, Vermont, Chair*
Judd Gregg, New Hampshire*
William Frist, Tennessee
Mike DeWine, Ohio*
Mike Enzi, Wyoming
Tim Hutchinson, Arkansas
Susan Collins, Maine*
Sam Brownback, Kansas*
Charles Hagel, Nebraska*
Jeff Sessions, Alabama

Democrats

Edward Kennedy, Massachusetts*
Christopher Dodd, Connecticut*
Tom Harkin, Iowa
Barbara Mikulski, Maryland
Jeff Bingaman, New Mexico*
Paul Wellstone, Minnesota*
Patty Murray, Washington*
Jack Reed, Rhode Island*

*Denotes member of the Subcommittee on Children and Families

Members of the House Committee on Education and the Workforce, 107th Congress

Majority: 27 / Minority: 22

Republicans

John Boehner, Ohio, Chair
Thomas Petri, Wisconsin, Vice-Chairman

Democrats

George Miller, California (Ranking Minority Member)
Dale Kildee, Michigan

Marge Roukema, New Jersey
Cass Ballenger, North Carolina
Peter Hoekstra, Michigan
Howard McKeon, California
Michael Castle, Delaware
Sam Johnson, Texas
James Greenwood, Pennsylvania
Lindsey Graham, South Carolina
Mark Souder, Indiana
Charlie Norwood, Georgia
Van Hilleary, Tennessee
Bob Schaffer, Colorado
Thomas Tancredo, Colorado
Ernie Fletcher, Kentucky
Jim DeMint, South Carolina
Johnny Isakson, Georgia
Patrick Tiberi, Ohio
Bob Goodlatte, Virginia
Judy Biggert, Illinois
Todd Platts, Pennsylvania
Fred Upton, Michigan
Vernon Ehlers, Michigan
Ric Keller, Florida
Tom Osborne, Nebraska
John Culberson, Texas

Harold Ford, Jr., Tennessee
Major Owens, New York
Robert Andrews, New Jersey
Tim Roemer, Indiana
Donald Payne, New Jersey
Patsy Mink, Hawaii
Robert Scott, Virginia
Loretta Sanchez, California
John Tierney, Massachusetts
Ron Kind, Wisconsin
Lynn Woolsey, California
Lynn Rivers, Michigan
Ruben Hinojosa, Texas
Rush Holt, New Jersey
Dennis Kuchinich, Ohio
David Wu, Oregon
Carolyn McCarthy, New York
Betty McCollum, Minnesota
Susan Davis, California
Hilda Solis, California

Members of the Senate Health, Education, Labor, and Pensions Committee, 107th Congress

Majority: 11 / Minority: 10

Republicans

Judd Gregg, New Hampshire
William Frist, Tennessee
Mike Enzi, Wyoming
Tim Hutchinson, Arkansas
Christopher Bond, Missouri
Susan Collins, Maine
Jeff Sessions, Alabama

Democrats

Edward Kennedy, Massachusetts, Chair
James Jeffords, Vermont**
Christopher Dodd, Connecticut
Tom Harkin, Iowa
Barbara Mikulski, Maryland
Jeff Bingaman, New Mexico

John Warner, Virginia
Pat Roberts, Kansas
Mike DeWine, Ohio*

Paul Wellstone, Minnesota
Patty Murray, Washington
Jack Reed, Rhode Island
Hillary Clinton, New York
John Edwards, North Carolina

---

*Served 2nd session only (as of July 2001)
**Became Independent in May 2001 and yielded Chairmanship to Kennedy

Notes

Chapter 1

1. John "Jack" Jennings, *Why National Standards and Tests? Politics and the Quest for Better Schools* (Thousand Oaks, CA: Sage, 1998), 156.

2. Jennings, *Why National Standards and Tests?*, 172.

3. Legislative histories of the enactment of the ESEA in the context of the War on Poverty include: Robert Bendiner, *Obstacle Course on Capitol Hill* (New York: McGraw-Hill, 1964); Sidney Tiedt, *The Role of the Federal Government in Education* (New York: Oxford University Press, 1966); Eugene Eidenberg and Roy Morey, *An Act of Congress: The Legislative Process and the Making of Education Policy* (New York: W. W. Norton, 1969); John Bibby and Roger Davidson, *On Capitol Hill: Studies in the Legislative Process*, 2nd ed. (Hinsdale, IL: Dryden Press, 1972); Julie Roy Jeffrey, *Education for Children of the Poor: A Study of the Origins and Implementation of the Elementary and Secondary Education Act of 1965* (Columbus: Ohio State University Press, 1978); Stephen Bailey and Howard Samuel, *Congress at Work* (Hamden, CT: Archon Books, 1965); Hugh Davis Graham, *The Uncertain Triumph: Federal Education Policy in the Kennedy and Johnson Years* (Chapel Hill: University of North Carolina Press, 1984).

4. See Jennings, *Why National Standards and Tests?*

5. For a discussion of agendas and alternatives in policy formation, see John Kingdon, *Agendas, Alternatives, and Public Policies*, 2nd ed. (New York: HarperCollins College Publishers, 1995).

6. Elizabeth Fay, interview by author, Washington, DC, September 23, 2002.

7. Erik Roebelen, "Democrats in House Offer Their Own Agenda on Education," Education Week, June 22, 2005, p. 32.

8. Charles Lindblom, "The Science of Muddling Through," *Public Administration Review* 14 (1959): 79–88; Aaron Wildavsky, *The Politics of the Budgetary Process* (Boston: Little, Brown, 1979).

9. Bibby and Davidson, *On Capitol Hill*, 227.

10. Ibid.

11. Ibid.

12. Ibid., 237.

13. For a list of legislative histories of the enactment of the ESEA, see note 3.

14. Eidenberg and Morey, *Act of Congress*, 23–24.

15. J. L. Sundquist, *Politics and Policy* (Washington, DC: Brookings Institution, 1968), 206.

16. Eidenberg and Morey, *Act of Congress*, 35.

17. Randall Ripley and Grace Franklin, *Congress, the Bureaucracy, and Public Policy*, 5th ed. (Pacific Grove, CA: Brooks/Cole, 1991), 145.

18. Ibid., 147.

19. Hugh Davis Graham, "Short-Circuiting the Bureaucracy in the Great Society Policy Origins in Education," *Presidential Studies Quarterly* 12 (3), Summer 1982, 412.

20. Eidenberg and Morey, *Act of Congress*, 93.

21. Bibby and Davidson, *On Capitol Hill*, 246.

22. John Brademas, *The Politics of Education: Conflict and Consensus on Capitol Hill* (Norman: University of Oklahoma Press, 1987), 77.

23. Stephen Bailey and Edith Mosher, *ESEA: The Office of Education Administers a Law* (Syracuse, New York: Syracuse University Press, 1968), 2.

24. Ibid.

25. John "Jack" Jennings, "Title I: Its Legislative History and Its Promise," *Phi Delta Kappan*, March 2000, 516–522.

26. Bailey and Mosher, *ESEA*.

27. Jerome Murphy, "The Education Bureaucracies Implement a Novel Policy: The Politics of Title I of ESEA, 1965–72," in *Policy and Politics in America: Six Case Studies*, ed. Alan P. Sindler (Boston: Little, Brown, 1973), 169.

28. Phyllis McClure and Ruby Martin, *Title I of ESEA: Is It Helping Poor Children?* (Washington, DC: Washington Research Project and NAACP Legal Defense and Education Fund, 1969).

29. Allen Matusow, *Unraveling America: A History of Liberalism in the 1960s* (New York: Harper & Row, 1984), 223.

30. Murphy, "Education Bureaucracies," 168.

31. Theodore Sky, "Concentration under Title I of the Elementary and Secondary Act," *Journal of Law and Education* 1, no. 2 (1972), 171–211.

32. Jennings, "Title I," 519–20.

33. Thomas Timar, cited in Gary Natriello and Edward McDill, "Title I: From Funding Mechanism to Educational Program," in *Hard Work for Good Schools: Facts Not Fads in Title I Reform*, ed. Gary Orfield and Elizabeth DeBray (Cambridge, MA: Civil Rights Project, Harvard University, 1999), 34.

34. Harvey Kantor, "Sustaining the Liberal Educational State: Title I of ESEA and the Politics of Federal Education Policy, 1965–1994" (unpublished paper, 2002), 17.

35. Carl Kaestle and Marshall Smith, "The Historical Context of the Federal Role in Education," *Harvard Educational Review* 52, no. 4 (1982).

36. Richard Elmore and Milbrey McLaughlin, *Steady Work: Policy, Practice, and the Reform of American Education* (Santa Monica, CA: Rand Corporation, 1988).

37. John "Jack" Jennings, "Chapter I: A View From Congress," *Educational Evaluation and Policy Analysis* 13, no. 4 (Winter 1991), 336.

38. Geoffrey Borman and Jerome D'Agostino, "Title I and Student Achievement: A Meta-Analysis of Federal Evaluation Results," *Educational Evaluation and Policy Analysis* 18, no. 4 (1996), 320.

39. Puma, Karweit, et al., *Prospects: Student Outcomes* (Cambridge, MA: Abt Associates, 1997).

40. While the U.S. Department of Education's Planning and Evaluation Service released a report suggesting positive achievement trends following the 1994 reauthorization, there was very little evidence that this was the case; see its *Promising Results, Continuing Challenges: Final Report of the National Assessment of Title I* (Washington, DC: GPO, 1999).

41. Ripley and Franklin, *Congress, the Bureaucracy.*

42. Two of the first to use the phrase "iron triangle" were J. Leiper Freeman, *The Political Process* (New York: Random House, 1965); and Douglass Cater, *Power in Washington* (New York: Vintage, 1964).

43. Hugh Heclo, "Issue Networks and the Executive Establishment," in *The New American Political System*, ed. Anthony King (Washington, DC: American Enterprise Institute, 1978), 95.

44. National Commission on Excellence in Education, *A Nation at Risk* (Washington, DC: U.S. Department of Education), 1983.

45. George Kaplan and Michael Usdan, "Education's Policy Networks," *Phi Delta Kappan* 73, no. 9 (May 1992): 664–72; Carl Kaestle, "Mobilizing School Reform from Above: Five Decades of Federal and National Strategies" (American Educational Research Association Distinguished Lecture, Chicago, IL, April 21, 2003); Jennings, *Why National Standards and Tests?*

Chapter 2

1. Kantor, "Sustaining the Liberal Educational State," 20.

2. Sarah Binder, "Congress, the Executive, and the Production of Public Policy: United We Govern?" in *Congress Reconsidered*, 7th ed., ed. Lawrence Dodd and Bruce Oppenheimer (Washington, DC: Congressional Quarterly Press, 2001), 298.

3. Ibid.

4. C. Lawrence Evans, "Committees, Leaders, and Message Politics," in *Congress Reconsidered*, 7th ed., ed. Lawrence Dodd and Bruce Oppenheimer (Washington, DC: Congressional Quarterly Press, 2001), 227.

5. Ibid., 231.

6. Gary Jacobson, "Party Polarization in National Politics: The Electoral Connection," in *Polarized Politics: Congress and the President in a Partisan Era*, ed. Jon Bond and Richard Fleisher (Washington, DC: Congressional Quarterly Press, 2000), 15.

7. Roger Davidson and Walter Oleszek, *Congress and Its Members*, 7th ed. (Washington, DC: Congressional Quarterly Press, 2000), 190–91.

8. Lawrence Dodd and Bruce Oppenheimer, "Congress and the Emerging Order: Conditional Party Government or Constructive Partisanship," in *Congress Reconsidered*, 6th ed., ed. Lawrence Dodd and Bruce Oppenheimer (Washington, DC: Congressional Quarterly Press, 1997), 396.

9. Barbara Sinclair, "Individualism, Partisanship, and Cooperation in the Senate," in *Esteemed Colleagues: Civility and Deliberation in the U.S. Senate*, ed. Burdett Loomis (Washington, DC: Brookings Institution, 2000), 63.

10. Dodd and Oppenheimer, "Congress and the Emerging Order," 396–97.

11. Jacobson, "Party Polarization in National Politics," 18.

12. David Von Drehle, "Political Split Is Pervasive," *Washington Post*, April 24, 2004, http://www.washingtonpost.com/.

13. Davidson and Oleszek, *Congress and Its Members*, 191.

14. Douglas Koopman, *Hostile Takeover: The House Republican Party, 1980–1995* (Lanham, MD: Rowman & Littlefield, 1996), 139.

15. David Rohde, "Agenda Change and Partisan Resurgence in the House of Representatives," in *The Atomistic Congress: An Interpretation of Congressional Change*, ed. Allen Hertzke and Ronald Peters (London: M. E. Sharpe, 1992), 235.

16. Ibid.

17. Nicol Rae, *The Decline and Fall of the Liberal Republicans* (New York: Oxford University Press, 1989), 197.

18. Bruce Oppenheimer, "Abdicating Congressional Power: The Paradox of Republican Control," in *Congress Reconsidered*, 6th ed., ed. Lawrence Dodd and Bruce Oppenheimer (Washington, DC: Congressional Quarterly Press, 1997), 375.

19. Ibid.

20. Burdett Loomis and Wendy Schiller, *The Contemporary Congress*, 4th ed. (Belmont, CA: Thomson-Wadsworth, 2004), 92.

21. Davidson and Oleszek, *Congress and Its Members*, 191.

22. Carroll Doherty and Jeffrey Katz, "Firebrand GOP Class of '94 Warms to Life on the Inside," *Congressional Quarterly*, January 24, 1998, 155.

23. Ibid.

24. Loomis and Schilller, *Contemporary Congress*, 100.

25. Loomis and Schiller, *Contemporary Congress*, 100–101.

26. Davidson and Oleszek, *Congress and Its Members*, 181.

27. For a consideration of the historical development and contemporary usage of the unanimous consent agreement, see Lawrence Evans and Walter Oleszek, "The Procedural Context of Senate Deliberation," in *Esteemed Colleagues: Civility and Deliberation in the U.S. Senate*, ed. Burdett Loomis (Washington, DC: Brookings Institution, 2000), 78–104.

28. Sinclair, "Individualism, Partisanship, and Cooperation," 59–60.

29. Helen Dewar, "Recasting the Senate as Great Guerrilla Theater," *Washington Post*, May 30, 2000, A8.

30. Ibid.

31. Ibid.

32. Burdett Loomis, *The Contemporary Congress* (New York: St. Martin's Press, 1996), 84.

33. Ibid., 91.

34. Steven Smith and Eric Lawrence, "Party Control of Committees," in *Congress Reconsidered*, 6th ed., ed. Lawrence Dodd and Bruce Oppenheimer (Washington, DC: Congressional Quarterly Press, 1997), 182.

35. Oppenheimer, "Abdicating Congressional Power," 379.

36. Loomis, *Contemporary Congress*, 81.

37. Richard Fenno, *Congressmen in Committees* (Boston: Little, Brown, 1973), 32.

38. Davidson and Oleszek, *Congress and Its Members*, 219.

39. These rankings of the American Conservative Union were obtained from http://www.conservative.org/ratings2000.htm (accessed March 20, 2001). The information may now be found at http://www.acuratings.org/default.asp?ratingyear-2000.

40. Dan Carter, *From George Wallace to Newt Gingrich: Race in the Conservative Counterrevolution, 1963–1994* (Baton Rouge: Louisiana State University Press, 1996), 110.

41. Ibid., 119.

42. Elizabeth Drew, *Showdown: The Struggle between the Gingrich Congress and the Clinton White House* (New York: Simon & Schuster, 1996), 82.

43. John Engler, quoted in Drew, *Showdown*, 83.

44. Drew, *Showdown*, 84.

45. Gingrich, quoted in Drew, *Showdown*, 85.

46. Richard Jung and Michael Kirst, "Beyond Mutual Adaptation, into the Bully Pulpit: Recent Research on the Federal Role in Education," *Educational Administration Quarterly 22*, no. 3 (1986): 80–109.

47. National Committee for Responsive Philanthropy, *One Billion Dollars for Ideas: Conservative Think Tanks in the 1990s* (Washington, DC: author, 1999), 5.

48. Ibid.

49. Andrew Rich, "War of Ideas: Why Mainstream and Liberal Foundations and the Think Tanks They Support Are Losing in the War of Ideas in American Politics," *Stanford Social Innovation Review*, Spring 2005, 18.

50. National Committee for Responsive Philanthropy, *One Billion Dollars for Ideas*, 17.

51. Ibid.

52. Marci Kanstoroom and Chester Finn, eds., *New Directions: Federal Education Policy in the Twenty-First Century* (Washington, DC: Thomas B. Fordham Foundation, 1999).

Chapter 3

1. For an interpretation of the standards movement, see Diane Ravitch, *National Standards in American Education: A Citizen's Guide* (Washington, DC: Brookings Institution, 1995); of systemic reform, see Maris Vinovskis, *History and Educational Policymaking* (New Haven, CT: Yale University Press, 1999); of the justification for and elements of standards-based reform, see Marshall Smith and Jennifer O'Day, "Systemic school reform," *Politics of Education Association Yearbook*, 1990, 233–67.

2. See Smith and O'Day, "Systemic school reform"; Milbrey McLaughlin and Lorrie Shepard, with Jennifer O'Day, *Improving Education through Standards-Based Reform* (Stanford, CA: National Academy of Education, 1995).

3. Jennings, *Why National Standards and Tests?*, 8.

4. U.S. Department of Education, *Improving America's Schools Act of 1993: Reauthorization of the Elementary and Secondary Education Act* (Washington, DC: GPO, 1993), 9.

5. "Scorned School Bill Dies in Senate," *Congressional Quarterly Almanac* 48 (1992), 455–460.

6. Jennings, *Why National Standards and Tests?*, 115.

7. Ibid.

8. Marshall Smith, telephone interview by author, April 20, 2000.

9. Ibid.

10. Ibid.

11. Kati Haycock and David Hornbeck, "Making Schools Work for Children in Poverty," in *National Issues in Education: Elementary and Secondary Education Act*, ed. John Jennings (Bloomington, IN: Phi Delta Kappa International, 1995), 85.

12. Ibid.

13. Marshall Smith, Jessica Levin, and Joanne Cianci, "Beyond a Legislative Agenda: Education Policy Approaches of the Clinton Administration," *Educational Policy* 11, no. 2 (1997), 211.

14. Smith, interview (see n. 8).

15. U.S. Congress, House, Committee on Education and the Workforce, *Statement of the Honorable Richard W. Riley, Secretary, U.S. Department of Education* (106th Cong., 2nd sess., October 2000). The two-thirds reduction comes from comparing the ESEA regulations just prior to the 1994 reauthorization (the Improving America's Schools Act) with the full set of regulations that ended up covering IASA. This latter set of regulations was completed in 1996.

16. Erik Robelen, "Secondary Schools Search for Role in ESEA," *Education Week*, June 9, 1999, 18.

17. U.S. Department of Education, *Targeting Schools: Study of Title I Allocations within School Districts* (Washington, DC: GPO, 1999), 9.

18. U.S. Department of Education, *Challenging the Status Quo: The Education Record, 1993–2000* (Washington, DC: GPO, 2000), 10.

19. Jennings, *Why National Standards and Tests?*

20. Jack Jennings, interview by author, Washington, DC, October 18, 2000.

21. Jennings, *Why National Standards and Tests?*, 174.

22. Ibid., 152–53.

23. Smith, interview (see n. 8).

24. Ibid.

25. Jennings, *Why National Standards and Tests*, 159–60.

26. Ibid., 175.

27. Christopher Cross, *Political Education: National Policy Comes of Age* (New York: Teachers College Press, 2004), 117.

28. David Hoff, "Political Shift Emboldens Clinton to Urge Tests," *Education Week*, February 19, 1997, http://www.edweek.org/.

29. Ibid.

30. Rene Sanchez, "House Votes Down Clinton Plan for National Reading, Math Achievement Tests," *Washington Post*, September 17, 1997, A20.

31. Peter Baker, "Clinton Takes Governors to Task over Education," *Washington Post*, July 26, 1997, A9.

32. "Clinton's National Testing Plan Defeated," *Education Reporter*, Decem-

ber 1997, http://www.eagleforum.org/educate/1997/dec97/test.html (accessed July 31, 2004).

33. Associated Press, "Assessment Board Delays National Student Testing," *Washington Post*, January 23, 1998, A4.

34. U.S. Congress, House, *P.L. 106-25: The Education Flexibility Partnerships Act* (106th Congress, 1st sess., 1999).

35. Kenneth Cooper, "As School Aid Is Relaxed, So Is Response of Many States," *Washington Post*, March 27, 2000, A6.

36. "For the Record: Ed-Flex," *Congressional Quarterly Weekly*, November 27, 1999, 2867–68.

37. Meredith Medley, interview by author, Washington, DC, March 30, 2000.

38. Charles Barone, interview by author, Washington, DC, October 29, 1999.

Chapter 4

1. Paul Peterson, Barry Rabe, and Kenneth Wong, *When Federalism Works* (Washington, DC: Brookings Institution, 1986), 21.

2. Ibid.

3. Jeffrey, *Education for Children of the Poor*, 111.

4. Thanks to Professor Richard Elmore for some of these ideas.

5. Medley, interview (see chap. 3, n. 37).

6. Ibid.

7. Sally Lovejoy, remarks to the American Youth Policy Forum, Washington, DC, November 19, 1999.

8. Floor statement of Rep. Thomas Petri, October 18, 1999, quoted in *On the Air with* Thomas Petri," Radio Show # 638, (Office of Hon. Representative Thomas Petri, Washington, DC, 1999).

9. Glen Chambers, interview by author, Washington, DC, March 30, 2000.

10. Jill Morningstar, interview by author, Washington, DC, March 29, 2000.

11. Cooper, "As School Aid Is Relaxed," A6.

12. Ibid.

13. Ibid.

14. Elyse Wasch, aide to Senator Jack Reed, interview by author, Washington, DC, March 28, 2000.

15. Tammi Chun and Margaret Goertz, "Title I and State Education Policy: High Standards for All Students?" in *Hard Work for Good Schools: Facts Not Fads in Title I Reform*, ed. Gary Orfield and Elizabeth DeBray (Cambridge, MA: Civil Rights Project, Harvard University), 120–29.

16. Barone, interview (see chap. 3, n. 38).

17. Christine Wolfe, interview by author, Washington, DC, October 31, 1999.

18. U.S. Department of Education, Planning, *Promising Results, Continuing Challenges* (Washington, DC: Office of the Under Secretary, Planning and Evaluation Service, U.S. Department of Education; 1999).

19. Ibid., 15.

20. Marshall Smith, interview (see chap. 3, n. 8).

21. "Forum: The Educational Excellence for All Children Act of 1999," *Education Week*, June 9, 1999, 31.

22. U.S. Department of Education, *Measured Progress: The Report of the Independent Review Panel on the Evaluation of Federal Education Legislation* (Washington, DC: GPO, 1999), 12.

23. Catherine Snow, M. Susan Burns, and Peg Griffin, eds., *Preventing Reading Difficulties in Young Children* (Washington, DC: National Academy Press, 1998).

24. Susan Wilhelm, interview by author, Washington, DC, October 16, 2000.

25. Ann O'Leary, interview by author, Washington, DC, October 16, 2000.

26. Ibid.

27. Ibid.

28. Kelly Amis, interview by author, Washington, DC, October 19, 2000.

29. Jim Carl, "Parental Choice as National Policy in England and the United States," *Comparative Education Review* 38, no. 3: 316.

30. Joetta Sack, "Heritage Makes Its Mark in Education Debate," *Education Week*, November 10, 1999, 30.

31. Chester Finn, "First Do No Harm: The Federal Role in Education Reform," *Congressional Digest* 78 (August-September 1999), 217.

32. Ibid.

33. U.S. Congress, House Committee on Education and the Workforce, *Report No. 106-386* (*Academic Achievement for All Act*), (106th Cong., 1st sess., 1999), 24.

34. Charles Barone, interview (see chap. 3, n. 38).

35. Diane Ravitch, "Student Performance: The National Agenda in Education," in *New Directions: Federal Education Policy in the Twenty-First Century*, ed. Marci Kanstoroom and Chester Finn (Washington, DC: Thomas B. Fordham Foundation, 1999), 142.

36. Charlene K. Haar, telephone interview by author, February 9, 2001.

37. Nina Rees, interview by author, Washington, DC, October 20, 2000.

38. Haar, interview (see n. 36).

39. Rees, interview (see n. 37).

40. U.S. Congress, Senate Committee on Health, Education, Labor, and Pensions, *S. Hearing 106-4: Education Reform: Governors' Views* (106th Cong., 1st sess., 1999), 27.

41. Ibid.

42. R. Kent Weaver, *Ending Welfare as We Know It* (Washington, DC: Brookings Institution, 2000), 206–7.

43. See, for instance, Jon Hale, cited in Weaver, *Ending Welfare*, 206–7.

44. See Kingdon, *Agendas*, 122–24.

45. Andrew Rotherham, interview by author, Washington, DC, October 19, 2000.

46. Tim Weiner and Abby Goodnough, "Education Deal a Victory in Politics, If Not Yet Schools," *New York Times*, November 12, 1999, A20.

47. Ibid.

48. The Senate Committee on Health, Education, Labor, and Pensions in the 106th never approved this measure, nor was it included in No Child Left Behind.

49. Office of Hon. Representative Patsy Mink, *Statement of Congresswoman Patsy Mink of Hawaii on H.R. 2300, The Academic Achievement for All Act, Committee on Education and the Workforce, October 13, 1999* (Washington, DC, 1999).

50. Sue Kirchoff, "House Panel Gives and Takes, Setting Tighter Federal Regulations, Giving States Title I Flexibility," *Congressional Quarterly Weekly*, October 16, 1999, 2463.

51. Ibid.

52. Ibid.

53. Sue Kirchoff and Andrew Beadle, "House Bill to Revamp Title I Still Faces Pile of Amendments," *Congressional Quarterly Weekly*, October 9, 1999, 2377.

54. Office of Hon. Representative Thomas Petri, *On the Air*, October 27, 1999.

55. Office of Hon. Representative Thomas Petri, *Support the Petri Amendment to Title I: Let the Money Follow the Child* (Washington, DC, October 18, 1999).

56. Kirchoff and Beadle, "House Bill," 2377.

57. Ibid.

58. Kara Haas, interview by author, Washington, DC, October 29, 1999.

59. Kenneth Cooper, "Senate GOP Draws Lines on Education," *Washington Post*, March 10, 2000.

60. "House Passes Title I Overhaul Bill Minus Vouchers and Broad Block Grants," *Congressional Quarterly Weekly*, October 23, 1999, 2522.

61. Ibid.

62. Mark Hornbeck and Charlie Cain, "Backers Keep Up the Fight, Despite Polls," *Detroit News*, November 3, 2000.

63. Martha Groves, "Voters Ready to Give Vouchers a Drubbing," *Los Angeles Times*, October 26, 2000, A3.

64. Ibid.

65. Jodi Wilgoren, "Vouchers' Fate May Hinge on Name Alone," *New York Times*, December 20, 2000, http://www.nytimes.com/.

66. Lowell Rose and Alec Gallup, "The 32nd Annual Phi Delta Kappa/Gallup Poll of the Public's Attitudes toward the Public Schools," *Phi Delta Kappan* 82, no. 1 (2000), 41–57.

67. Terry Moe, *Schools, Vouchers, and the American Public* (Washington, DC: Brookings Institution, 2001), 380–81.

Chapter 5

1. Laura Meckler, "Gore Offers Education Plan," *Associated Press*, April 28, 2000, http://www.ap.org/.

2. Jay Mathews, "Group Pushes for Vouchers," *Washington Post*, December 19, 2000.

3. Michael Cooper, "Cheney Finds That Bush Plan for Public Schools Hits Nerves," *New York Times*, September 19, 2000.

4. Terry Neal, "Bush Unveils a Reading Skills Plan," *Washington Post*, March 29, 2000, A1.

5. Meckler, "Gore Offers Education Plan."

6. Ibid.

7. Chambers, interview (see chap. 4, n. 9).

8. Jill Morningstar, interview by author, Washington, DC, November 19, 1999.

9. Senator Susan Collins, cited in "Excerpts From the Republican Party's Response to the President's Address," *New York Times*, January 28, 2000.

10. Laura Chow, interview by author, Washington, DC, March 31, 2000.

11. Office of Hon. Senator Judd Gregg, *The Child-Centered Education Act* (Washington, DC, 1999).

12. Ibid.

13. U.S. Congress, Senate, *Educational Opportunities Act: Report of the Committee on Health, Education, Labor, and Pensions, to Accompany* S. 2 (106th Cong., 2nd sess., 2000), 209.

14. Rees, interview (see chap. 4, n. 37).

15. U.S. Congress, Senate Committee on Health, Education, Labor, and Pensions, *S. Hearing 106-4*, 27.

16. Susan Fuhrman and Richard Elmore, "Governors and Education Policy in the 1990s," in *The Governance of Curriculum: 1994 Yearbook for the Association for Supervision and Curriculum Development*, ed. Richard Elmore and Susan Fuhrman (Alexandria, VA: Association for Supervision and Curriculum Development, 1994), 56–74.

17. Weaver, *Ending Welfare*, 209.

18. Fuhrman and Elmore, "Governors," 67.

19. Weaver, *Ending Welfare*, 209.

20. Patricia Sullivan, telephone interview by author, October 26, 2000.

21. Ibid.

22. Ibid.

23. Ibid.

24. Ibid.

25. Rees, interview (see chap. 4, n. 37).

26. Nina Rees, *The NGA's Phony Education Reform Plan* (Washington, DC: Heritage Foundation, 2000).

27. Sullivan, interview (see n. 20).

28. Erik Robelen, "Lawmakers At Odds as Debate Begins in Senate on ESEA Bill," *Education Week*, May 10, 2000.

29. Sullivan, interview (see n. 20).

30. Ibid.

31. The Hon. William Frist, *Congressional Record*, 106th Congress, 2nd sess., May 3, 2000.

32. The Hon. Paul Wellstone, *Congressional Record*, 106th Congress, 2nd sess., May 3, 2000.

33. The Hon. Byron Dorgan, *Congressional Record*, 106th Congress, 2nd sess., May 9, 2000.

34. Ibid.

35. The Hon. Judd Gregg, *Congressional Record*, 106th Congress, 2nd sess., May 3, 2000.

36. Andrew Rotherham, *Toward Performance-Based Federal Education Funding: Reauthorization of the Elementary and Secondary Education Act* (Washington, DC: Progressive Policy Institute, 1999).

37. "Democrats Unveil Education Plan," *Associated Press*, November 16, 1999.

38. Ibid. http://www.ap.org/.

39. Office of Hon. Senator Joseph Lieberman, *The Three R's Bill: A Detailed Summary* (Washington, DC, 2000).

40. Rotherham, interview (see chap. 4, n. 45).

41. Michele Stockwell, interview by author, Washington, DC, March 31, 2000.

42. Joining Lieberman in sponsoring the "Three R's" bill were Democratic senators Bayh (IN) , Landrieu (LA), Lincoln (AR), Kohl (WI), Graham (FL), Robb (VA), and Breaux (LA).

43. David Mayhew, *Congress: The Electoral Connection* (New Haven, CT: Yale University Press, 1974), 76.

44. Chambers, interview (see chap. 4, n. 9).

45. Ibid.

46. Morningstar, interview (see chap. 4, n. 10).

47. Rotherham, interview (see chap. 4, n. 45).

Chapter 6

1. Evans, "Committees, Leaders, and Message Politics," 226–227.

2. Michael Kennedy, interview by author, Washington, DC, February 25, 2002.

3. Erik Robelen, "Bush Has a Loyal Lieutenant in New Education Panel Chairman," *Education Week*, January 21, 2001, 21.

4. Sally Lovejoy, interview by author, Washington, DC, January 28, 2002.

5. Ibid.

6. Alex Nock, interview by author, Washington, DC, January 28, 2002.

7. David Nather, "Finding Education's Center," *Congressional Quarterly Weekly*, January 13, 2001, 112.

8. David Stout, "Bush to Launch Federal Education Plan," *New York Times*, January 23, 2001, http://www.nytimes.com (accessed January 23, 2001).

9. Unidentified legislative aide, U.S. House of Representatives, interview by author, January 28, 2002.

10. Erik Robelen, "Miller Brings Independent Approach to School Concerns," *Education Week*, October 25, 2000, 33.

11. John Boehner, quoted in David Broder, "Long Road to Reform: Negotiators Forge Education Legislation," *Washington Post*, Monday, December 17, 2001, A1.

12. Paul Manna, "Leaving No Child Behind," in *Political Education: National Policy Comes of Age*, ed. Christopher Cross (New York: Teachers College Press, 2004), 127.

13. Sarah Youssef, interview by author, Washington, DC, March 18, 2002.

14. Sandy Kress, quoted in Andrew Rudalevige, "Accountability and Avoidance in the Bush Education Plan: The No Child Left Behind Act of 2001," paper

presented at the Taking Account of Accountability Conference, Kennedy School of Government, Harvard University, Cambridge, MA, June 10–11, 2002, 23.

15. Ibid.

16. Unidentified aide to the majority on the House Education and the Workforce Committee, Washington, DC, January 30, 2002.

17. Nock, interview (see n. 6).

18. Youssef, interview (see n. 13).

19. Youssef, interview (see n. 13).

20. Kathleen Strottman, interview by author, Washington, DC, January 28, 2002.

21. Fay, interview (see chap. 1, n. 6).

22. Fay, interview (see chap. 1, n. 6).

23. Holly Kuzmich, interview by author, Washington, DC, January 28, 2002.

24. Unidentified aide to a Democratic HELP committee member, Washington, DC, February 1, 2002.

Chapter 7

1. "Federal File: Without DeLay?" *Education Week*, August 8, 2001, 36.

2. Molly Ivins and Lou Dubose, *Shrub: The Short But Happy Political Life of George W. Bush* (New York: Random House, 2000), 78–79.

3. Eugene Hickok, quoted in Rudalevige, "Accountability and Avoidance," 30.

4. Thad Hall, "Congress and School Vouchers," *Public School Choice versus Private School Vouchers*, ed. Richard Kahlenberg (New York: Century Foundation Press, 2003), 115–22.

5. David Sanger, "Bush Pushes Ambitious Education Plan," *New York Times*, January 24, 2001, A1.

6. Rudalevige, "Accountability and Avoidance," 22.

7. Lovejoy, interview (see chap. 6, n. 4).

8. Julie Miller, Michael Levin-Epstein, and Lynn Cutler, "Congress Moves toward Bipartisan ESEA Bill," *Title I Report*, May 2001, 10.

9. Nather, "Education Bill Passes," 1256.

10. Miller, Levin-Epstein, and Cutler, "Congress Moves," 10.

11. The five Republicans on the House committee who joined with the Democrats were Judy Biggert (IL), Fred Upton (MI), Todd Platts (PA), Tom Osborne (NE), and Marge Roukema (NJ). Michael Castle (DE) voted "present."

12. Kara Haas, interview with author, Washington, DC, February 1, 2002.

13. Julie Miller, "Senate Passes ESEA Bill," *Title I Report*, June 2001.

14. Lizette Alvarez, "Senate Rejects Tuition Aid, a Key to Bush Education Plan," *New York Times*, June 13, 2001, http://www.nytimes.com/.

15. Amanda Farris, interview by author, Washington, DC, January 30, 2002.

16. Diana Schemo, "Senators Start Work on Bill to Require State Tests for Students," *New York Times*, March 8, 2001, http://www.nytimes.com (accessed March 8, 2001).

17. Lovejoy, interview (see chap. 6, n. 4).

18. Kennedy, interview (see chap. 6, n. 2).

19. Unidentified Senate aide, interview by author, Washington, D.C.

20. Charles Barone, interview by author, Washington, DC, February 26, 2002.

21. Broder, "Long Road to Reform," A1.

22. Kara Haas, interview by author, Washington, DC, February 1, 2002.

23. Paul Manna, "Leaving No Child Behind," 135.

24. Michael Fletcher and Dana Milbank, "Bush Urges Realistic Education Standards," *Washington Post*, Thursday, August 2, 2001, A02.

25. Thomas Kane and Douglas Staiger, "Unintended Consequences of Racial Subgroup Rules," in *No Child Left Behind? The Politics and Practice of School Accountability*, ed. Paul Peterson and Martin West (Washington, DC: Brookings Institution, 2003), 152–76.

26. Fay, interview (see chap. 1, n. 6).

27. Unidentified education aide, interview (see chap. 6, n. 24).

28. U.S. Congress, House, *Report of the Committee on Education and the Workforce on HR1 Together with Additional and Dissenting Views, Report 107–63 Part I* (107th Cong., 1st sess., 2001), 271.

29. Sally Lovejoy, interview (see chap. 6, n. 4).

30. Rep. Mark Souder, quoted in Miller, Levin-Epstein, and Cutler, "Congress Moves."

31. Erik Robelen, "Federal File: Testy about Testing," *Education Week*, May 2, 2001, 26.

32. The Hon. Ernest Hollings, *Congressional Record*, 107th Cong., 1st sess., June 13, 2001, 147 *Cong. Rec.* S 6147.

33. Letter from National Conference of State Legislatures to Congress of September 26, 2001, excerpted from "State Group: ESCA Polls Seriously Flawed," *Education Week*, October 10, 2001, 31.

34. National Governors Association, *Letter from Cochairs of National Governors' Association to Boehner, Miller, Kennedy, and Gregg*, August 17, 2001.

35. B. Drummond Ayres, Jr., "Despite Split on Bush, Governors Find Common Ground," *New York Times*, August 6, 2001, http://www.nytimes.com/.

36. Senator Paul Wellstone, quoted in Miller, Levin-Epstein, and Cutler, "Congress Moves," 8.

37. The Hon. Paul Wellstone, *Congressional Record*, 107th Cong., 1st sess., June 6, 2001, 147 *Cong. Rec.* S 5846.

38. Office of Hon. Representative Betty McCollum, "Press Release, 12/13/01," http://www.house.gov/mccollum/pr_121301edubill_nochild behind.html.

39. Rudalevige, "Accountability and Avoidance," 33.

40. Secretary of Education Roderick Paige, cited in "Federal File: The Word on Tests," *Education Week*, May 23, 2001, 25.

41. "Intra-GOP Sparring On Education Continues," *White House Bulletin*, May 16, 2001.

42. Kennedy, interview (see chap. 6, n. 2).

43. Jodi Wilgoren, "State School Chiefs Fret Over U.S. Plan to Require Testing," *New York Times*, July 17, 2001, http://wwwnytimes.com (accessed July 19, 2001).

44. Kennedy, interview (see chap. 6, n. 2).

45. Broder, "Long Road to Reform," A1.

46. Lovejoy, interview by author, Washington, DC, January 28, 2002.

47. Rep. Mark Souder, quoted in Miller, Levin-Epstein, and Cutler, "Congress Moves."

48. Charles Barone, interview (see n. 20).

49. Charles Barone, interview (see n. 20).

50. The Hon. David Wu, *Congressional Record*, 107th Cong., 1st sess., May 22, 2001, 147 *Cong. Rec.* H 2396.

51. Julie Miller, "Senate Committee Approves Bipartisan ESEA Bill," *Title I Report*, March 2001.

52. Kuzmich, interview (see chap. 6, n. 23).

53. Unidentified aide, interview by author, Washington, DC, February 27, 2002.

54. Erik Robelen, "Education Bill Ready to Face Final Hurdles," *Education Week*, June 20, 2001, 34.

55. National Governor's Association, Letter from Vice-Chairman Parris Glendening and John Engler to Majority Leader Trent Lott and Democratic Leader Thomas Daschle (Washington, DC: author, May 9, 2001.

56. Council of Chief State School Officers, "Oppose National Governor's Assocciation Amendment for Governors to Administer ESEA" (Washington, DC: author), May 9, 2001.

57. Haas, interview (see n. 22).

58. Barone, interview (see n. 20).

59. The Hon. Major Owens, *Congressional Record*, 107th Cong., 1st sess., December 12, 2001, 147 *Cong. Rec.* H 9767.

60. Helen Dewar, "Senate Moves Toward Action on Education," *Washington Post*, Wednesday, May 2, 2001, A4.

Chapter 8

1. Jordan Cross, interview by author, Washington, DC, January 30, 2002.

2. Katherine Seelye and Adam Clymer, "Senate Republicans Step Out and Democrats Jump In," *New York Times*, Friday, May 25, 2001, A18.

3. Robelen, "Education Bill Ready," 34.

4. Frank Bruni, "Bush Pushes His Education Plan, and in a Calculated Forum," *New York Times*, August 2, 2001, http://www.nytimes.com (accessed August 2, 2001).

5. Rudalevige, "Accountability and Avoidance," 34.

6. Lizette Alvarez, "In a Vote on Teacher Hiring, Winning Streak Ends for Senate Democrats," *New York Times*, May 16, 2001, A20.

7. Ibid.

8. Erik Robelen, "Off Target? Political Considerations Cause Title I to Bypass Many Needy Schools," *Education Week*, September 5, 2001, 46.

9. The Hon. Mary Landrieu, *Congressional Record*, 107th Cong., 1st sess., April 24, 2001, 147 *Cong. Rec.* S 3813.

10. Strottman, interview (see chap. 6, n. 20).

11. Julie Miller, "Senate Votes to Fund Targeted Grants," *Title I Report*, November 2001.

12. Fletcher and Milbank, "Bush Urges Realistic Education Standards," A2.

13. Thomas Kane and Douglas Staiger, "Rigid Rules Will Damage Schools," *New York Times*, August 13, 2001, http://www.nytimes.com (accessed August 16, 2001).

14. Ibid.

15. Diana Schemo, "School Leaders Contend Laws May Cause Lower Standards," *New York Times*, July 13, 2001, http://www.nytimes.com (accessed July 18, 2001).

16. Ibid.

17. Wilgoren, "State School Chiefs Fret."

18. Elizabeth Fay, interview (see chap. 1, n. 6).

19. Education Secretary Rod Paige quoted in Christopher Lee, "Paige Predicts Education Accord," *Dallas Morning News*, November 1, 2001, http://dallasnews.com/.

20. U.S. Department of Education, *Letter from Secretary of Education Roderick Paige to Rep. Rob Andrews*, August 13, 2001, http://www.ed.gov/News/Letters/010813a.html (accessed November 22, 2002).

21. Interview (see chap. 6, n. 24).

22. James Jeffords, "Back to School," *New York Times*, December 13, 2001, http://www.nytimes.com (accessed December 13, 2001).

23. See Jennings, *Why National Standards and Tests?*, 136.

24. Unnamed aide, interview (see chap. 7, n. 53).

25. Unnamed aide to majority, House Committee on Education, interview (see chap. 6, n. 16).

26. Diana Schemo, "Congress May Ease Plans for School Accountability," *New York Times*, August 10, 2001, http://www.nytimes.com (accessed August 10, 2001).

27. Jack Jennings, quoted in Julie Blair, "Testing Opponents Speak Out in ESEA Home Stretch," *Education Week*, August 8, 2001.

28. Julie Blair, "Testing Opponents Speak Out in ESEA Home Stretch," *Education Week*, August 8, 2001, http://www.edweek.org (accessed November 1, 2001).

29. Interview (see chap. 6, n. 24).

30. Barone, interview (see chap. 7, n. 20).

31. Stephen Metcalf, "Reading between the Lines," *New Republic*, January 28, 2002, http://www.thenewrepublic.com/.

32. See for instance, U.S. Government Printing Office, *No Child Left Behind Act of 2001: Conference Report to Accompany H.R. 1* (Washington, DC: author, 2001), 802, n. 37.

33. Siobhan Gorman, "Bipartisan Schoolmates," *Education Next*, Summer 2002, 39.

34. Julie Miller, "Key Lawmakers Close to ESEA Deal . . . But Will It Stick?" *Title I Report* 3, no. 9 (October 2001).

35. Cross, interview (see n. 1).

36. Unidentified Democratic House Committee aide, interview by author, Washington, DC, January 28, 2002.

37. David Broder and Michael Fletcher, "State Officials, School Groups Worried about Education Bill," *Washington Post*, October 10, 2001, A2.

38. Packer, interview (see chap. 7, n. 12).

39. Ibid.

40. Secretary Rod Paige quoted in Joetta Sack, "No Longer a 'Splinter,' ELC Flexes New Political Muscle," *Education Week*, October 10, 2001, 26.

41. Joetta Sack, "ESEA Negotiators Near Accords, But Snags Remain," *Education Week*, December 5, 2001.

42. Education Leaders Council, Press Release, January 10, 2002, http://www.educationleaders.org/elc/pressreleases/020110nclbceremony/.html (accessed August 9, 2004).

43. Michael Fletcher, "More Funds Sought for Ailing Schools: Black State Lawmakers Criticize Bush Plan," *Washington Post*, November 28, 2001, A33.

44. American Association of School Administrators, *Letter to Representative John Boehner*, November 8, 2001, http://www.aasa.org/government_relations/esea/11-08-01_ESEA_Boehner_letter.htm (accessed November 20, 2001).

45. Kara Haas, interview (see chap. 7, n. 22).

46. See Loomis and Schiller, *Contemporary Congress*, 122–24.

47. "Remarks of the President on the Signing of the No Child Left Behind Act," *Public Papers of the Presidents of the United States*, January 14, 2002.

48. Jennings, *Why National Standards and Tests?*, 126.

Chapter 9

1. See David Tyack and Larry Cuban, *Tinkering toward Utopia: A Century of Public School Reform* (Cambridge, MA: Harvard University Press, 1995), 5.

2. See Natriello and McDill, "Title I," 31–45.

3. Richard Rothstein, *Class and Schools: Using Social, Economic, and Educational Reform to Close the Black-White Achievement Gap* (Washington, DC: Economic Policy Institute, 2004), 94.

4. Ibid.

5. James Cibulka, "Educational Bankruptcy, Takeovers, and Reconstitution of Failing Schools," in *American Educational Governance on Trial: Change and Challenges* 102nd Yearbook of the National Society for the Study of Education, ed. William Boyd and Debra Miretzky (Chicago: University of Chicago Press, 2003), 249–70; Lynn Olson, "Veterans of State Takeover Battles Tell a Cautionary Tale," *Education Week*, February 12, 1997.

6. Heinrich Mintrop, "The Role of Sanctions for Improving Persistently Low-Performing Schools," in *A Race Against Time: The Crisis in Urban Schooling*, ed. James Cibulka and William Boyd (Westport, CT: Praeger, 2003), 185.

7. Christopher Edley, Jr., personal communication, December 2001; see also James Liebman and Charles Sabel, "The Federal No Child Left Behind Act and the Post-desegregation Civil Rights Agenda," *North Carolina Law Review* 81, no. 4 (May 2003), 1703–49.

8. Margaret Goertz, "Implementing the No Child Left Behind Act: Challenges for the States," *Peabody Journal of Education* 80, no. 2 (2005), 73–89.

9. See Kathryn McDermott and Elizabeth DeBray, "Incremental Revolution: Nationalizing Education Accountability Policy," in *The Rising State: How State Power is Transforming Our Nation's Schools*, ed. Bruce Cooper, Lance Fusarelli, and Bonnie Fusarelli (Albany: State University of New York Press, 2005); Lorraine McDonnell, "NCLB and the Federal Role in Education: Evolution or Revolution?" *Peabody Journal of Education*, 80, no. 2 (2005), 19–38.

10. Jennings, *Why National Standards and Tests?*, 6.

11. Jimmy Kim, "The Initial Response to the Accountability Requirements in the No Child Left Behind Act: A Case Study of Virginia and Georgia." Paper presented at the annual meeting of the American Educational Research Association, Chicago, IL, April 21–25, 2003.

12. David Broder, "Education Reform Controversy Lingers," *Washington Post*, April 6, 2002, http://www.washingtonpost.com (accessed April 8, 2002).

13. Paul Weckstein, "Who Represents Parents and Students?" *Legal Services Reporter*, August 2002, 13.

14. Ibid.

15. Broder, "Education Reform Controversy Lingers."

16. Erik Robelen, "Senate Panel Examines Education Department Efforts to Enforce New ESEA," *Education Week*, May 1, 2002, 24.

17. Diana Schemo, "Law Overhauling School Standards Seen as Skirted," *New York Times*, October 15, 2002, http://www.nytimes.com/.

18. Gregg Toppo, "Vermont Governor Considers Refusing Federal Funds So Schools Can Opt Out of Testing," *Associated Press*, April 19, 2002, http://www.ap.org/.

19. Greg Toppo, "States Strain to Keep Up with 'No Child Left Behind,'" *USA Today*, January 29, 2003, http://www.usatoday.com/.

20. Michael Fletcher, "States Worry New Law Sets Schools Up to Fail," *Washington Post*, January 1, 2003.

21. Linda Jacobson, "Hawaii House Oks Resolution against No Child Left Behind," *Education Week*, April 23, 2003, 21.

22. U.S. General Accounting Office, *Title I: Education Needs to Monitor States' Scoring of Assessments* (GAO-02-393) (Washington, DC: GPO), 2002), 9.

23. See Daniel Koretz, "Discerning the Effects of the NCLB Accountability Provisions on Learning," paper presented at the annual meeting of the American Educational Research Association, Chicago, Illinois, April 22, 2003; Robert Linn, Eva Baker, and Damian Betebenner, "Accountability Systems: Implications of Requirements of the No Child Left Behind Act of 2001," *Educational Researcher* 31, no. 6 (2002), 3–16; Kane and Staiger, "Unintended Consequences," 152–76.

24. Citizens' Commission on Civil Rights, *Closing the Deal: A Preliminary Report on State Compliance with Final Assessment and Accountability Requirements under the Improving America's Schools Act of 1994* (Washington, DC: author, 2001).

25. Erik Robelen, "States Sluggish on Execution of 1994 ESEA," *Education Week*, November 28, 2001.

26. U.S. General Accounting Office, *Title I*, 13.

27. Richard Elmore, "Unwarranted Intrusion," *Education Next*, Spring 2002, http://www.educationnext.org/.

28. U.S. Department of Education, *Letter from Secretary of Education Roderick Paige to State Education Officials* (Washington, DC: GPO, October 22, 2002).

29. Schemo, "Law Overhauling School Standards."

30. Ibid.

31. Bess Keller, "Michigan Lists Schools That Miss Progress Marks," *Education Week*, April 23, 2003, 18.

32. Julie Miller, "Educators, Assessment Experts Fear Accountability 'Train Wreck,'" *Title I Report*, May 2002, 1.

33. Julie Miller and Jeanne Sweeney, "ED Faulted for Belief that 'Reading First' is Limited to a Few Programs," *Title I Report*, May 2002, 10.

34. Ibid.

35. Victor Balta, "End Creative Teaching, Official Says," *Stockton California Record*, October 25, 2002.

36. Diana Schemo, "Few Exercise New Right to Leave Failing Schools," *New York Times*, August 28, 2002, http://www.nytimes.com/.

37. Ibid.

38. Diana Schemo, "Schools Face New Policy on Transfers," *New York Times*, December 10, 2002.

39. Rick Karlin, "TV Ads Stress School Options," *Albany Times-Union*, January 29, 2003.

40. Jen Sansbury, "Augusta Ordered to Follow School Transfer Law," *Atlanta Journal-Constitution*, September 6, 2002.

41. Erik Robelen, "Paige, Bush Upbeat on Making ESEA Work," *Education Week*, September 11, 2002, 23.

42. Elizabeth DeBray, "NCLB Accountability Collides with Court-Ordered Desegregation: The Case of Pinellas County, Florida," *Peabody Journal of Education* 80, no. 2 (2005), 170–188.

43. Jennifer Loven, "Bush Renews Fight for School Vouchers after Supreme Court Decision," *Associated Press*, July 1, 2002, http://www.ap.org/.

44. Ibid.

45. Jeanne Sweeney, "Voucher Case Expected to Have Little Impact on Federal Programs," *Title I Report*, July 2002, 15.

46. Ibid.

47. Alan Richard, "Governor Owens Pledges to Sign Colorado Voucher Bill," *Education Week*, April 9, 2003, 22.

48. Caroline Hendrie, "Paige Calls for Wider Support of School Choice," *Education Week*, February 4, 2004, 25.

49. "Private Agenda," *Bill Moyers' NOW*, television program aired March 26, 2004 on Public Broadcasting Service.

50. Rep. George Miller, quoted in Bruni, "Bush Pushes."

51. Michael Fletcher, "Education Law Reaches Milestone amid Discord," *Washington Post*, January 8, 2003.

52. Noy Thrupkaew, "A Dollar Short: Bush's Budget Defunds Bush's Education Plan," *American Prospect*, June 3, 2002.

53. Dana Milbank, "For Bush, Facts Are Malleable," *Washington Post*, October 21, 2002, A6.

54. Bess Keller, "Wisconsin Review Invites `No Child' Lawsuit. *Education Week*, May 26, 2004, 1.

55. Michael Fletcher, "No School Choice But to Improve," *Washington Post*, April 14, 2003, http://www.washingtonpost.com/.

56. U.S. Congress, Senate, Letter from Senate HELP Committee Democrats to the Secretary of Education Roderick Paige (108th Cong., 2nd sess., January 8, 2004).

57. Sam Dillon, "U.S. Set to Ease Some Provisions of School Law," *New York Times*, March 14, 2004, A21.

58. William Mathis, "Financial Impact of NCLB in the States," *Peabody Journal of Education*, 80, no. 2 (2005), 90–119.

59. Lance Fusarelli, "Gubernatorial Reactions to NCLB: Politics, Pressure, and Education Reform," *Peabody Journal of Education*, 80, no. 2 (2005), 120–136.

60. Eidenberg and Morey, *Act of Congress*, 175.

Chapter 10

1. Rosemary Salomone, *Equal Education under Law: Legal Rights and Federal Policy in the Post-Brown Era* (New York: Palgrave-Macmillan, 1986), 168–92.

2. Frederick Hess and Patrick McGuinn, "Seeking the Mantle of Opportunity: Presidential Politics and the Educational Metaphor, 1964–2000," *Educational Policy* 16, no. 1 (March 2002), 90.

3. Patrick McGuinn and Frederick Hess, "Freedom from Ignorance? The Great Society and the Evolution of the Elementary and Secondary Education Act of 1965," in *The Great Society and the Rights Revolution*, ed. Sidney Milkis and Jerome Mileur (Amherst: University of Massachusetts Press, forthcoming).

4. Hugh Davis Graham, "Short-Circuiting the Bureaucracy in the Great Society Policy Origins in Education," *Presidential Studies Quarterly* 12, no. 3 (Summer 1982), 416–17.

5. Kingdon, *Agendas*, 146–49.

6. McDonnell, "NCLB and the Federal Role."

7. Julia Koppich, "A Tale of Two Approaches—the AFT, the NEA, and NCLB," *Peabody Journal of Education* 80, no. 2 (2005), 137–155.

8. Quoted in Koppich, "A Tale of Two Approaches."

9. Andrew Rich, *Think-Tanks, Public Policy, and the Politics of Expertise* (Cambridge, England: Cambridge University Press, 2004).

10. Ibid., 210.

11. Ibid.

12. James Gimpel, "Grassroots Organizations and Equilibrium Cycles," in *The Interest Group Connection: Electioneering, Lobbying, and Policymaking in Washington*, ed. Paul Herrnson, Ronald G. Shaiko, and Clyde Wilcox (Chatham, NJ: Chatham House Publishers, 1998), 135.

13. Fenno, *Congressmen in Committees*, 29.

14. Kathryn McDermott and Laura Jensen, "Dubious Sovereignty: Federal Conditions of Aid and the No Child Left Behind Act," *Peabody Journal of Education* 80, no. 2 (2005), 39–56.

15. Ibid.

16. Fusarelli, "Gubernatorial Reactions to NCLB" (2005), 120–136.

17. McDonnell, "NCLB and the Federal Role."

18. Professor Goodwin Liu and Dean Christopher Edley, Jr., of Boalt Hall Law School, Berkeley, are co-directors of a new civil rights initiative, entitled "Rethinking Rodriguez: Education as a Fundamental Right." See also Liebman and Sabel, "The Federal NCLB Act and the Post-Desegregation Civil Rights Agenda."

19. Robin Toner, "Southern Democrats' Decline Is Eroding the Political Center," *New York Times*, November 15, 2004, http://nytimes.com/.

20. Bruce Fuller, "Are Test Scores Really Rising?" *Education Week*, October 13, 2004, 40, 52.

21. Children's Defense Fund, *The State of America's Children 2004* (Washington, DC: author).

22. Jeffrey, *Education for Children of the Poor*, 170.

Appendix A

1. See Robert Yin, *Case Study Rearch: Design and Methods*, Vol. 5, 2nd ed. (Thousand Oaks, CA: Sage, 1994).

2. See Ripley and Franklin, *Congress, the Bureaucracy*.

3. See Kingdon, *Agendas, Alternatives, and Public Policies*, 2nd ed.

4. Yin, *Case Study Research*, 81.

5. Yin, *Case Study Research*, 99.

Bibliography

Alvarez, Lizette. "In a Vote on Teacher Hiring, Winning Streak Ends for Senate Democrats." *New York Times*, May 16, 2001, A20.

Alvarez, Lizette. "Senate Education Bill Stalls Despite Its Bipartisan Support." *New York Times*, March 9, 1999. http://www.nytimes.com/.

Alvarez, Lizette. "Senate Rejects Tuition Aid, a Key to Bush Education Plan." *New York Times*, June 13, 2001. http://www.nytimes.com/.

American Association of School Administrators. *Letter to Representative John Boehner*. November 8, 2001. http://www.aasa.org/government_relations/esea/11-08-01_ESEA_Boehner_letter.htm (accessed November 20, 2001).

American Conservative Union. "2000 Ratings of Congress." http://www.conservative.org/ratings2000.htm (accessed March 20, 2001). [The information from which the tables were derived may now be found at http://www.acuratings.org/default.asp?ratingsyear-2000]

Associated Press. "Assessment Board Delays National Student Testing." *Washington Post*, January 23, 1998, A4.

Ayres, B. Drummond, Jr. "Despite Split on Bush, Governors Find Common Ground." *New York Times*, August 6, 2001. http://www.nytimes.com/.

Bailey, Stephen, and Edith Mosher. *ESEA: The Office of Education Administers a Law*. Syracuse, NY: Syracuse University Press, 1968.

Bailey, Stephen, and Howard Samuel. *Congress at Work*. Hamden, CT: Archon Books, 1965.

Baker, Peter. "Clinton Takes Governors to Task over Education." *Washington Post*, July 26, 1997, A9.

Balta, Victor. "End Creative Teaching, Official Says." *Stockton California Record*, October 25, 2002.

Bendiner, Robert. *Obstacle Course on Capitol Hill*. New York: McGraw-Hill, 1964.

Bibby, John, and Roger Davidson. *On Capitol Hill: Studies in the Legislative Process*. 2nd ed. Hinsdale, IL: Dryden Press, 1972.

Binder, Sarah. "Congress, the Executive, and the Production of Public Policy: United We Govern?" In *Congress Reconsidered*, 7th ed., edited by Lawrence Dodd and Bruce Oppenheimer, 293–313. Washington, DC: Congressional Quarterly Press, 2001.

Blair, Julie. "Testing Opponents Speak Out in ESEA Homestretch." *Education Week*, August 8, 2001. http://www.edweek.org (accessed November 1, 2001).

Bond, Jon, and Richard Fleisher, eds. *Polarized Politics: Congress and the President in a Partisan Era*. Washington, DC: Congressional Quarterly Press, 2000.

Borman, Geoffrey, and Jerome D'Agostino. "Title I and Student Achievement: A Meta-Analysis of Federal Evaluation Results." *Educational Evaluation and Policy Analysis* 18, no. 4(1996): 309–26.

Brademas, John. *The Politics of Education: Conflict and Consensus on Capitol Hill.* Norman: University of Oklahoma Press, 1987.

Broder, David. "Education Reform Controversy Lingers." *Washington Post*, April 6, 2002. http:// www.washingtonpost.com (accessed April 8, 2002).

Broder, David. "Long Road to Reform: Negotiators Forge Education Legislation." *Washington Post*, December 17, 2001, A1.

Broder, David, and Michael Fletcher. "State Officials, School Groups Worried about Education Bill." *Washington Post*, October 10, 2001, A2.

Bruni, Frank. "Bush Pushes His Education Plan, and in a Calculated Forum." *New York Times*, August 2, 2001. http:// www.nytimes.com (accessed August 2, 2001).

Carl, Jim. "Parental Choice as National Policy in England and the United States." *Comparative Education Review* 38, no. 3 (1994), 294–322.

Carter, Dan. *From George Wallace to Newt Gingrich: Race in the Conservative Counterrevolution, 1963–1994*. Baton Rouge: Louisiana State University Press, 1996.

Cater, Douglass. *Power in Washington*. New York: Vintage, 1964.

Children's Defense Fund. *The State of America's Children 2004*. Washington, DC: author, July 2004.

Chun, Tammi, and Margaret Goertz. "Title I and State Education Policy: High Standards for All Students?" In *Hard Work for Good Schools: Facts Not Fads in Title I Reform*, edited by Gary Orfield and Elizabeth DeBray, 120–29. Cambridge, MA: Civil Rights Project, Harvard University, 1999.

Cibulka, James. "Educational Bankruptcy, Takeovers, and Reconstitution of Failing Schools." In *American Educational Governance on Trial: Change and Challenges*, 102nd Yearbook of the National Society for the Study of Education, edited by William Boyd and Debra Miretzky, 249–70. Chicago: University of Chicago Press, 2003.

Citizens' Commission on Civil Rights. *Closing the Deal: A Preliminary Report on State Compliance with Final Assessment and Accountability Requirements under the Improving America's Schools Act of 1994*. Washington, DC: author, 2001.

"Clinton Urges $250 Million to Lift Ailing Public Schools." *Associated Press*, February 27, 2000. http://www.ap.org/.

"Clinton's National Testing Plan Defeated." *Education Reporter*, December 1997. http://www.eagleforum.org/educate/1997/dec97/test.html (accessed July 31, 2004).

Cooper, Kenneth. "As School Aid Is Relaxed, So Is Response of Many States." *Washington Post*, March 27, 2000, A6.

Cooper, Kenneth. "Senate GOP Draws Lines on Education." *Washington Post*, March 10, 2000.

Cooper, Michael. "Cheney Finds That Bush Plan for Public Schools Hits Nerves." *New York Times*, September 19, 2000.

Council of Chief State School Officers. "Oppose National Governor's Association Amendment for Governors to Administer ESEA" (Washinton, DC: Author), May 9, 2001.

Cross, Christopher. *Political Education: National Policy Comes of Age*. New York: Teachers College Press, 2004.

Davidson, Roger, and Walter Oleszek. *Congress and Its Members*. 7th ed. Washington, DC: Congressional Quarterly Press, 2000.

DeBray, Elizabeth. "NCLB Accountability Collides with Court-Ordered Desegregation: The Case of Pinellas County, Florida." *Peabody Journal of Education* 80, no. 2, 2005.

"Democrats Unveil Education Plan." *Associated Press*. November 16, 1999. http://www.ap.org/.

"Despite Booming Economy, Poverty Rates Remain High, While States Refuse to Utilize Flexibility to Help Welfare Recipients, Low-Wage Workers in Poverty." *Associated Press*, February 24, 2000. http://www.ap.org/.

Dewar, Helen. "Recasting the Senate as Great Guerrilla Theater." *Washington Post*, May 30, 2000, A8.

Dewar, Helen. "Senate Moves Toward Action on Education." *Washington Post*, May 2, 2001, A4.

Dillon, Sam. "U.S. Set to Ease Some Provisions of School Law." *New York Times*, March 14, 2004, A21.

Dodd, Lawrence, and Bruce Oppenheimer. "Congress and the Emerging Order: Conditional Party Government or Constructive Partisanship." In *Congress Reconsidered*, 6th ed., edited by Lawrence Dodd and Bruce Oppenheimer, 390–414. Washington, DC: Congressional Quarterly Press, 1997.

Doherty, Carroll, and Jeffrey Katz. "Firebrand GOP Class of '94 Warms to Life on the Inside." *Congressional Quarterly*, January 24, 1998; 155–63.

Dorgan, The Hon. Byron. *Congressional Record*. 106th Cong., 2nd sess., May 9, 2000.

Drew, Elizabeth. *Showdown: The Struggle between the Gingrich Congress and the Clinton White House*. New York: Simon & Schuster, 1996.

Education Leaders Council. Press Release, January 10, 2002. http://www.educationleaders.org/elc/pressreleases/020110nclbceremony.html (accessed August 9, 2004).

Eidenberg, Eugene, and Roy Morey. *An Act of Congress: The Legislative Process and the Making of Education Policy*. New York: W. W. Norton, 1969.

Elementary and Secondary Education Act of 1965. Pub. L. No. 89-10, 79 *Stat*. 27, 20 *U.S.C.* secs. 236–41.

Elmore, Richard. "Unwarranted Intrusion." *Education Next*, Spring 2002, http://www.educationnext.org/.

Elmore, Richard, and Milbrey McLaughlin. *Steady Work: Policy, Practice, and the Reform of American Education*. Santa Monica, CA: Rand Corporation, 1988.

Evans, Lawrence. "Committees, Leaders, and Message Politics." In *Congress Reconsidered*, 7th ed., edited by Lawrence Dodd and Bruce Oppenheimer. Washington, DC: Congressional Quarterly Press, 2001.

Evans, Lawrence, and Walter Oleszek. "The Procedural Context of Senate Deliberation." In *Esteemed Colleagues: Civility and Deliberation in the U.S. Senate*, edited by Burdett Loomis. Washington, DC: Brookings Institution, 2000.

"Excerpts from the Republican Party's Response to the President's Address." *New York Times*, January 28, 2000.

"Federal File: The Word on Tests." *Education Week*, May 23, 2001.

"Federal File: Without DeLay?" *Education Week*, August 8, 2001.

Fenno, Richard. *Congressmen in Committees*. Boston: Little, Brown, 1973.

Finn, Chester. "First Do No Harm: The Federal Role in Education Reform." *Congressional Digest* 78 (August-September 1999): 213–21.

Fletcher, Michael. "Congress Still Divided on Education Reform."

Fletcher, Michael. "Education Law Reaches Milestone amid Discord." *Washington Post*, January 8, 2003.

Fletcher, Michael. "More Funds Sought for Ailing Schools: Black State Lawmakers Criticize Bush Plan." *Washington Post*, November 28, 2001, A33.

Fletcher, Michael. "No School Choice But to Improve." *Washington Post*, April 14, 2003. http://www.washingtonpost.com/.

Fletcher, Michael. "States Worry New Law Sets Schools Up to Fail." *Washington Post*, January 1, 2003.

Fletcher, Michael, and Dana Milbank. "Bush Urges Realistic Education Standards." *Washington Post*, August 2, 2001, A2.

"For the Record: Ed-Flex." *Congressional Quarterly Weekly*, November 27, 1999, 2867–68.

"Forum: The Educational Excellence for All Children Act of 1999." *Education Week*, June 9, 1999, 28–54.

Freeman, J. Leiper. *The Political Process*. New York: Random House, 1965.

Frist, The Hon. William. *Congressional Record*. 106th Cong., 2nd sess., May 3, 2000.

Fuhrman, Susan, and Richard Elmore. "Governors and Education Policy in the 1990s." In *The Governance of Curriculum: 1994 Yearbook for the Association for Supervision and Curriculum Development*, edited by Richard Elmore and Susan Fuhrman, 56–74. Alexandria, VA: Association for Supervision and Curriculum Development, 1994.

Fuller, Bruce. "Are Test Scores Really Rising?" *Education Week*, October 13, 2004. http://www.edweek.org/.

Fusarelli, Lance. "Gubernatorial Reaction to NCLB: Politics, Pressure, and Education Reform." *Peabody Journal of Education* 80, no. 2, 2005.

Gimpel, James. "Grassroots Organizations and Equilibrium Cycles." In *The Interest Group Connection: Electioneering, Lobbying, and Policymaking in Washington*, edited by Paul S. Herrnson, Ronald G. Shaiko, and Clyde Wilcox, 100–115. Chatham, NJ: Chatham House Publishers, 1998.

Goertz, Margaret. "Implementing the No Child Left Behind Act: Challenges for the States." *Peabody Journal of Education* 80, no. 2, 2005.

Gorman, Siobhan. "Bipartisan Schoolmates." *Education Next*, Summer 2002.

Graham, Hugh Davis. "Short-Circuiting the Bureaucracy in the Great Society: Policy

Origins in Education." *Presidential Studies Quarterly* 12, no. 3 (1982): 407–20.

Graham, Hugh Davis. *The Uncertain Triumph: Federal Education Policy in the Kennedy and Johnson Years*. Chapel Hill: University of North Carolina Press, 1984.

Gregg, The Hon. Judd. *Congressional Record*. 106th Cong., 2nd sess., May 3, 2000.

Groves, Martha. "Voters Ready to Give Vouchers a Drubbing." *Los Angeles Times*, October 26, 2000, A 3.

Hall, Thad. "Congress and School Vouchers." In *Public School Choice Versus Private School Vouchers*, edited by Richard Kahlenberg, 115–22. New York: Century Foundation Press, 2003.

Harrington, Michael. *The Other America: Poverty in the United States*. New York: Macmillan, 1962.

Haycock, Kati, and David Hornbeck. "Making Schools Work for Children in Poverty." In *National Issues in Education: Elementary and Secondary Education Act*, edited by John Jennings. Bloomington, IN: Phi Delta Kappa International, 1995.

Heclo, Hugh. *A Government of Strangers: Executive Politics in Washington*. Washington, DC: Brookings Institution, 1977.

Heclo, Hugh. "Issue Networks and the Executive Establishment." In *The New American Political System*, edited by Anthony King. 87–123. Washington, DC: American Enterprise Institute, 1978.

Hendrie, Caroline. "Paige Calls for Wider Support of School Choice." *Education Week*, February 4, 2004.

Hess, Frederick, and Patrick McGuinn. "Seeking the Mantle of Opportunity: Presidential Politics and the Educational Metaphor, 1964–2000." *Educational Policy* 16, no. 1 (March 2002): 72–95.

Hoff, David. "Political Shift Emboldens Clinton to Urge Tests." *Education Week*, February 19, 1997. http://www.edweek.org/.

Hollings, The Hon. Ernest. *Congressional Record*. 107th Cong., 1st sess., June 13, 2001. 147 *Cong. Rec.* S 6147.

Hornbeck, Mark, and Charlie Cain. "Backers Keep Up the Fight, Despite Polls." *Detroit News*, November 3, 2000.

"House Passes Title I Overhaul Bill Minus Vouchers and Broad Block Grants." *Congressional Quarterly Weekly*, October 23, 1999, 2521–22.

Improving America's Schools Act of 1994. Pub. L. No. 103-382, 108 *Stat.* 3519, 20 U.S.C. secs. 2701 *et. seq.*

"Intra-GOP Sparring on Education Continues." *White House Bulletin*, May 16, 2001.

Ivins, Molly, and Lou Dubose. *Shrub: The Short But Happy Political Life of George W. Bush*. New York: Random House, 2000.

Jacobson, Gary. "Party Polarization in National Politics: The Electoral Connection." In *Polarized Politics: Congress and the President in a Partisan Era*, edited by Jon Bond and Richard Fleisher, 9–30.Washington, DC: Congressional Quarterly Press, 2000.

Jacobson, Linda. "Hawaii House OKs Resolution against No Child Left Behind." *Education Week*, April 23, 2003.

Jeffords, James. "Back to School." *New York Times*, December 13, 2001. http://www.nytimes.com (accessed December 13, 2001).

Jeffrey, Julie Roy. *Education for Children of the Poor: A Study of the Origins and Implementation of the Elementary and Secondary Education Act of 1965*. Columbus: Ohio State University Press, 1978.

Jennings, John. "Chapter I: A View from Congress." *Educational Evaluation and Policy Analysis* 13, no. 4 (Winter 1991): 335–338.

Jennings, John. "Title I: Its Legislative History and Its Promise." *Phi Delta Kappan*, March 2000, 516–522.

Jennings, John. *Why National Standards and Tests? Politics and the Quest for Better Schools*. Thousand Oaks, CA: Sage, 1998.

Jung, Richard, and Michael Kirst. "Beyond Mutual Adaptation, into the Bully Pulpit: Recent Research on the Federal Role in Education." *Educational Administration Quarterly* 22, no. 3 (1986): 80–109.

Kaestle, Carl. "Mobilizing School Reform from Above: Five Decades of Federal and National Strategies." American Educational Research Association Distinguished Lecture, Chicago, IL, April 21, 2003.

Kaestle, Carl, and Marshall Smith. "The Historical Context of the Federal Role in Education." *Harvard Educational Review* 52, no. 4 (1982): 383–408.

Kane, Thomas, and Douglas Staiger. "Rigid Rules Will Damage Schools." *New York Times*, August 13, 2001. http:// www.nytimes.com (accessed August 16, 2001).

Kane, Thomas, and Douglas Staiger, "Unintended Consequences of Racial Subgroup Rules." In *No Child Left Behind? The Politics and Practice of School Accountability*, edited by Paul Peterson and Martin West, 152–176. Washington, DC: Brookings Institution, 2003.

Kanstoroom, Marci, and Chester Finn, eds. *New Directions: Federal Education Policy in the Twenty-First Century*. Washington, DC: Thomas B. Fordham Foundation, 1999.

Kantor, Harvey. "Sustaining the Liberal Educational State: Title I of the ESEA and the Politics of Federal Education Policy, 1965–1994." Unpublished paper, 2002.

Kaplan, George, and Michael Usdan. "Education's Policy Networks." *Phi Delta Kappan* 73, no. 9 (May 1992: 664–72.

Karlin, Rick. "TV Ads Stress School Options." *Albany Times-Union*, January 29, 2003.

Keller, Bess. "Michigan Lists Schools That Miss Progress Marks." *Education Week*, April 23, 2003.

Keller, Bess. "Wisconsin Review Invites 'No Child' Lawsuit. *Education Week*, May 26, 2004.

Kim, Jimmy. "The Initial Response to the Accountability Requirements in the No Child Left Behind Act: A Case Study of Virginia and Georgia." Paper presented at the annual meeting of the American Educational Research Association, Chicago, IL, April 21–25, 2003.

Kingdon, John. *Agendas, Alternatives, and Public Policies*. 2nd ed. New York: HarperCollins College Publishers, 1995.

Kirchoff, Sue. "House Panel Gives and Takes, Setting Tighter Federal Regulations, Giving States Title I Flexibility." *Congressional Quarterly Weekly*, October 16, 1999, 2463.

Kirchoff, Sue, and Andrew Beadle. "House Bill to Revamp Title I Still Faces Pile of Amendments." *Congressional Quarterly Weekly*, October 9, 1999), 2376–77.

Koopman, Douglas. *Hostile Takeover: The House Republican Party, 1980–1995*. Lanham, MD: Rowman & Littlefield, 1996.

Koppich, Julia. "A Tale of Two Approaches—the AFT, the NEA, and NCLB." *Peabody Journal of Education* 80, no. 2, 2005.

Koretz, Daniel. "Discerning the Effects of the NCLB Accountability Provisions on Learning." Paper presented at the annual meeting of the American Educational Research Association, Chicago, IL, April 22, 2003.

Landrieu, The Hon. Mary. *Congressional Record*. 107th Congress, 1st sess., April 24, 2001. 147 *Cong. Rec.* S 3813.

Lee, Christopher. "Paige Predicts Education Accord." *Dallas Morning News*, November 1, 2001. http://www.dallasnews.com/.

Liebman, James, and Charles Sabel. "The Federal NCLB Act and the Post-desegregation Civil Rights Agenda." *North Carolina Law Review* 81, no. 4 (May 2003): 1703–49.

Lindblom, Charles. "The Science of Muddling Through." *Public Administration Review* 14 (1959): 79–88.

Linn, Robert, Eva Baker, and Damian Betebenner. "Accountability Systems: Implications of Requirements of the No Child Left Behind Act of 2001." *Educational Researcher* 31, no. 6 (2002): 3–16.

Loomis, Burdett. "Civility and Deliberation: A Linked Pair?" In *Esteemed Colleagues: Civility and Deliberation in the U.S. Senate*, edited by Burdett Loomis. Washington, DC: Brookings Institution, 2000.

Loomis, Burdett. *The Contemporary Congress*. New York: St. Martin's Press, 1996.

Loomis, Burdett, ed. *Esteemed Colleagues*. Washington, DC: Brookings Institution, 2000.

Loomis, Burdett, and Wendy Schiller, *The Contemporary Congress*. 4th ed. Belmont, CA: Thomson-Wadsworth, 2004.

Loven, Jennifer. "Bush Renews Fight for School Vouchers after Supreme Court Decision." *Associated Press*, July 1, 2002. http://www.ap.org/.

Lowi, Theodore, and Benjamin Ginsberg. *Embattled Democracy: Politics and Policy in the Clinton Era*. New York: W.W. Norton, 1995.

Manna, Paul. "Leaving No Child Behind." In *Political Education: National Policy Comes of Age*, edited by Christopher Cross. New York: Teachers College Press, 2004.

Mathews, Jay. "Group Pushes for Vouchers." *Washington Post*, December 19, 2000.

Mathis, William. "Financial Impact of NCLB in the States." *Peabody Journal of Education* 80, no. 2, 2005.

Matusow, Allen. *Unraveling America: A History of Liberalism in the 1960s*. New York: Harper & Row, 1984.

Mayhew, David. *Congress: The Electoral Connection*. New Haven, CT: Yale University Press, 1974.

McClure, Phyllis, and Ruby Martin. *Title I of ESEA: Is It Helping Poor Children?* Washington, DC: Washington Research Project and NAACP Legal Defense and Education Fund, 1969.

McDermott, Kathryn, and Elizabeth DeBray. "Incremental Revolution: Nationalizing Education Accountability Policy." In *The Rising State: How State Power is Transforming Our Nation's Schools*, edited by Bruce Cooper, Lance Fusarelli, and Bonnie Fusarelli. Albany: State University of New York Press, 2005.

McDermott, Kathryn, and Laura Jensen. "Dubious Sovereignty: Federal Conditions of Aid and the No Child Left Behind Act." *Peabody Journal of Education* 80, no. 2 (forthcoming).

McDonnell, Lorraine. "NCLB and the Federal Role in Education: Evolution or Revolution?" *Peabody Journal of Education* 80, no. 2 (forthcoming).

McGuinn, Patrick, and Frederick Hess. "Freedom from Ignorance? The Great Society and the Evolution of the Elementary and Secondary Education Act of 1965." In *The Great Society and the Rights Revolution*, edited by Sidney Milkis and Jerome Mileur. Amherst: University of Massachusetts Press (forthcoming).

McLaughlin, Milbrey, and Lorrie Shepard, with Jennifer O'Day. *Improving Education through Standards-Based Reform.* Stanford, CA: National Academy of Education, 1995.

Meckler, Laura. "Gore Offers Education Plan." *Associated Press*, April 28, 2000, http://www.ap.org/.

Metcalf, Stephen. "Reading between the Lines." *New Republic*, January 28, 2002. http://www.thenewrepublic.com/.

Milbank, Dana. "For Bush, Facts Are Malleable." *Washington Post*, October 21, 2002, A6.

Miller, Julie. "Educators, Assessment Experts Fear Accountability 'Train Wreck.'" *Title I Report*, May 2002. http://www.titlei.com/.

Miller, Julie. "Key Lawmakers Close to ESEA Deal . . . But Will It Stick?" *Title I Report*, October 2001. http://www.titlei.com/.

Miller, Julie. "Senate Committee Approves Bipartisan ESEA Bill." *Title I Report*, March 2001. http://www.titlei.com/.

Miller, Julie. "Senate Passes ESEA Bill." *Title I Report*, June 2001. http://www.titlei.com/.

Miller, Julie. "Senate Votes to Fund Targeted Grants." *Title I Report*, November 2001. http://www.titlei.com/.

Miller, Julie, Michael Levin-Epstein, and Lynn Cutler. "Congress Moves toward Bipartisan ESEA Bill." *Title I Report*, May 2001. http://www.titlei.com (accessed June 11, 2001).

Miller, Julie, and Jeanne Sweeney. "ED Faulted for Belief That 'Reading First' is Limited to a Few Programs." *Title I Report*, May 2002.

Mintrop, Heinrich. "The Role of Sanctions for Improving Persistently Low-Performing Schools." In *A Race against Time: The Crisis in Urban Schooling* edited by James Cibulka and William Boyd, 185–201. Westport, CT: Praeger, 2003.

Moe, Terry. "The Politics of Bureaucratic Structure." In *Can the Government Gov-*

ern? edited by John Chubb and Paul Peterson, 267–329. Washington, DC: Brookings Institution, 1989.

Moe, Terry. *Schools, Vouchers, and the American Public.* Washington, DC: Brookings Institution, 2001.

Murphy, Jerome. "The Education Bureaucracies Implement a Novel Policy: The Politics of Title I of ESEA, 1965–72." In *Policy and Politics in America: Six Case Studies*, edited by Alan P. Sindler. Boston: Little, Brown, 1973.

Nathan, Richard. *Social Science in Government: Uses and Misuses.* New York: Basic Books, 1988.

Nather, David. "Education Bill Passes in House with Strong Bipartisan support." *Congressional Quarterly Weekly*, May 26, 2001, 1256.

Nather, David. "Finding Education's Center." *Congressional Quarterly Weekly*, January 13, 2001, 112.

National Commission on Excellence in Education. *A Nation at Risk.* Washington, DC: U.S. Department of Education, 1983.

National Committee for Responsive Philanthropy. *One Billion Dollars for Ideas: Conservative Think Tanks in the 1990s.* Washington, DC: author, 1999.

National Conference of State Legislatures. Letter from Education Committee to Congress. Washington, DC: author, September 26, 2001.

National Governors' Association. Letter from Vice Chairman Parris Glendening and John Engler to Majority Leader Trent Lott and Democratic Leader Thomas Daschle, Washington, DC: author, May 9, 2001.

National Governors' Association. Letter from Co-chairs John Engler and Paul Patton to Reps. Boehner and Miller and Sens. Kennedy and Gregg. Washington, DC: author, August 17, 2001.

Natriello, Gary, and Edward McDill. "Title I: From Funding Mechanism to Educational Program." In *Hard Work for Good Schools: Facts Not Fads in Title I Reform*, edited by Gary Orfield and Elizabeth DeBray, 31–45. Cambridge, MA: The Civil Rights Project, Harvard University, 1999.

Neal, Terry. "Bush Unveils a Reading Skills Plan." *Washington Post*, March 29, 2000, A6.

No Child Left Behind Act of 2001. Pub. L. No. 107-110, 115 *Stat.* 1425 (2002).

Office of Hon. Representative Betty McCollum. "Press Release, 12/13/01." http://www.house.gov/mccollum/pr_121301edubill_nochild behind.html.

Office of Hon. Representative Patsy Mink. *Statement of Congresswoman Patsy Mink of Hawaii on H.R. 2300, The Academic Achievement for All Act, Committee on Education and the Workforce, October 13, 1999.* Washington, DC, 1999.

Office of Hon. Representative Thomas Petri. *On the Air with Thomas Petri.* Transcript of Radio Show #638. Washington, DC, October 27, 1999.

Office of Hon. Representative Thomas Petri. *Support the Petri Amendment to Title I: Let the Money Follow the Child.* Washington, DC, 1999.

Office of Hon. Senator Joseph Lieberman. *The Three R's Bill: A Detailed Summary.* Summary of Proposed Legislation. Washington, DC, 2000.

Office of Hon. Senator Judd Gregg. *The Child-Centered Education Act.* Summary of Proposed Legislation. Washington, DC, 1999.

Olson, Lynn. "Veterans of State Takeover Battles Tell a Cautionary Tale." *Education Week*, February 12, 1997.

Oppenheimer, Bruce. "Abdicating Congressional Power: The Paradox of Republican Control." In *Congress Reconsidered*, 6th ed., edited by Lawrence Dodd and Bruce Oppenheimer. Washington, DC: Congressional Quarterly Press, 1997.

Orfield, Gary. "Strengthening Title I: Designing a Policy Based on Evidence." In *Hard Work for Good Schools: Facts Not Fads in Title I Reform*, edited by Gary Orfield and Elizabeth DeBray, 1–20. Cambridge, MA: Civil Rights Project, Harvard University, 1999.

Owens, The Hon. Major. *Congressional Record*. 107th Cong., 1st sess., December 12, 2001.

Peterson, Paul, Barry Rabe, and Kenneth Wong. *When Federalism Works*. Washington, DC: Brookings Institution, 1986.

"Private Agenda." *Bill Moyers' NOW*. Television program aired March 26, 2004 on Public Broadcasting Service.

Puma, Michael, Nancy Karweit, Cristofer Price, Anne Ricciuti, William Thompson, and Michael Vaden-Klernan. *Prospects: Final Report on Student Outcomes*. Cambridge, MA: Abt Associates, 1997.

Rae, Nicol. *The Decline and Fall of the Liberal Republicans*. New York: Oxford University Press, 1989.

Ravitch, Diane. "Clinton's School Plan Is a Good Start. Let's Go Further." *Wall Street Journal*, January 20, 1999.

Ravitch, Diane. *National Standards in American Education: A Citizen's Guide*. Washington, DC: Brookings Institution, 1995.

Ravitch, Diane. "Student Performance: The National Agenda in Education." In *New Directions: Federal Education Policy in the Twenty-First Century*, edited by Marci Kanstoroom and Chester Finn. Washington, DC: Thomas B. Fordham Foundation, 1999.

Rees, Nina. *The NGA's Phony Education Reform Plan*. Washington, DC: Heritage Foundation, 2000.

"Remarks of the President on the Signing of the No Child Left Behind Act." *Public Papers of the Presidents of the United States*. January 14, 2002.

Rich, Andrew. *Think Tanks, Public Policy, and the Politics of Expertise*. Cambridge, England: Cambridge University Press, 2004.

Rich, Andrew. "War of Ideas: Why Mainstream and Liberal Foundations and the Think Tanks They Support Are Losing in the War of Ideas in American Politics." *Stanford Social Innovation Review*, Spring 2005.

Rich, Andrew, and R. Kent Weaver. "Advocates and Analysts: Think Tanks and the Politicization of Expertise." In *Interest Group Politics*, edited by Allan Cigler and Burdett Loomis. Washington, DC: Congressional Quarterly, 1998.

Richard, Alan. "Governor Owens Pledges to Sign Colorado Voucher Bill." *Education Week*, April 9, 2003.

Ripley, Randall, and Grace Franklin. *Congress, the Bureaucracy, and Public Policy*. 5th ed. Pacific Grove, CA: Brooks/Cole, 1991.

Robelen, Erik. "Bush Has a Loyal Lieutenant in New Education Panel Chairman." *Education Week*, January 21, 2001.

Robelen, Erik. "Democrats in House Offer Their Own Agenda on Education." *Education Week*, June 22, 2005.

Robelen, Erik. "Education Bill Ready to Face Final Hurdles." *Education Week*, June 20, 2001.

Robelen, Erik. "Federal File: Testy about Testing." *Education Week*, May 2, 2001.

Robelen, Erik. "Lawmakers at Odds as Debate Begins in Senate on ESEA Bill." *Education Week*, May 20, 2000.

Robelen, Erik. "Miller Brings Independent Approach to School Concerns." *Education Week*, October 25, 2000.

Robelen, Erik. "Off Target? Political Considerations Cause Title I to Bypass Many Needy Schools." *Education Week*, September 5, 2001.

Robelen, Erik. "Paige, Bush Upbeat on Making ESEA Work." *Education Week*, September 11, 2002.

Robelen, Erik. "Secondary Schools Search for Role in ESEA." *Education Week*, June 9, 1999.

Robelen, Erik. "Senate Panel Examines Education Department Efforts to Enforce New ESEA." *Education Week*, May 1, 2002.

Robelen, Erik. "States Sluggish on Execution of 1994 ESEA." *Education Week*, November 28, 2001.

Rohde, David. "Agenda Change and Partisan Resurgence in the House of Representatives." In *The Atomistic Congress: An Interpretation of Congressional Change*, edited by Allen Hertzke and Ronald Peters. London: M.E. Sharpe, 1992.

Rose, Lowell, and Alec Gallup. "The 32nd Annual Phi Delta Kappa/Gallup Poll of the Public's Attitudes toward the Public Schools." *Phi Delta Kappan* 82, no. 1 (2000): 41–57.

Rotherham, Andrew. *Toward Performance-Based Federal Education Funding: The Reauthorization of Elementary Secondary Education Act*. Washington, DC: Progressive Policy Institute, 1999.

Rothstein, Richard. *Class and Schools: Using Social, Economic, and Educational Reform to Close the Black-White Achievement Gap*. Washington, DC: Economic Policy Institute, 2004.

Rudalevige, Andrew. "Accountability and Avoidance in the Bush Education Plan: The No Child Left Behind Act of 2001." Paper presented at Taking Account of Accountability Conference, Kennedy School of Government, Harvard University, Cambridge, MA, June 10–11, 2002.

Sack, Joetta. "ESEA Negotiators Near Accords, But Snags Remain." *Education Week*, December 5. 2001.

Sack, Joetta. "Heritage Makes Its Mark in Education Debate." *Education Week*, November 10, 1999.

Sack, Joetta. "No Longer a 'Splinter,' ELC Flexes New Political Muscle." *Education Week*, October 10, 2001.

Salomone, Rosemary. *Equal Education under Law: Legal Rights and Federal Policy in the Post-Brown Era*. New York: Palgrave-Macmillan, 1986.

Sanchez, Rene. "House Votes Down Clinton Plan for National Reading, Math Achievement Tests." *Washington Post*, February 19, 1997, A20. http://www.washingtonpost.com/.

Sanger, David. "Bush Pushes Ambitious Education Plan." *New York Times*, January 24, 2001, A1.

Sansbury, Jen. "Augusta Ordered to Follow School Transfer Law." *Atlanta Journal-Constitution*, September 6, 2002.

Schemo, Diana. "Congress May Ease Plans for School Accountability." *New York Times*, August 10, 2001. http://www.nytimes.com (accessed August 10, 2001).

Schemo, Diana. "Few Exercise New Right to Leave Failing Schools." *New York Times*, August 28, 2002. http://www.nytimes.com/.

Schemo, Diana. "Law Overhauling Schools Standards Seen as Skirted." *New York Times*, October 15, 2002. http://www.nytimes.com/.

Schemo, Diana. "School Leaders Contend Laws May Cause Lower Standards." *New York Times*, July 13, 2001. http:// www.nytimes.com (accessed July 18, 2001).

Schemo, Diana. "Schools Face New Policy on Transfers." *New York Times*, December 10, 2002.

Schemo, Diana. "Senators Start Work on Bill to Require State Tests for Students." *New York Times*, March 8, 2001. http://www.nytimes.com (accessed March 8, 2001).

"Scorned School Bill Dies in Senate." *Congressional Quarterly Almanac* 48 (1992): 455–60.

Seelye, Katharine, and Adam Clymer. "Senate Republicans Step Out and Democrats Jump In." *New York Times*, May 25, 2001, A1.

Sinclair, Barbara. "Individualism, Partisanship, and Cooperation in the Senate." In *Esteemed Colleagues: Civility and Deliberation in the U.S. Senate*, edited by Burdett Loomis. Washington, DC: Brookings Institution, 2000.

Sky, Theodore. "Concentration under Title I of the Elementary and Secondary Act." *Journal of Law and Education* 1, no. 2 (1972): 171–211.

Smith, Marshall, Jessica Levin, and Joanne Cianci. "Beyond a Legislative Agenda: Education Policy Approaches of the Clinton Administration." *Educational Policy* 11, no. 2 (1997): 209–26.

Smith, Marshall, and Jennifer O'Day. "Systemic School Reform." *Politics of Education Association Yearbook*, 1990, 233–67.

Smith, Steven, and Eric Lawrence. "Party Control of Committees." In *Congress Reconsidered*, 6th ed., edited by Lawrence Dodd and Bruce Oppenheimer. Washington, DC: Congressional Quarterly Press, 1997.

Snow, Catherine, M. Susan Burns, and Peg Griffin, eds. *Preventing Reading Difficulties in Young Children*. Washington, DC: National Academy Press, 1998.

"State Group: ESEA Bills 'Seriously Flawed.'" *Education Week*, October 10, 2001.

Stout, David. "Bush to Launch Federal Education Plan." *New York Times*, January 23, 2001. http://www.nytimes.com (accessed January 23, 2001).

Sundquist, J. L. *Politics and Policy*. Washington, DC: Brookings Institution, 1968.

Sweeney, Jeanne. "Voucher Case Expected to Have Little Impact on Federal Programs." *Title I Report*, July 2002.

Thrupkaew, Noy. "A Dollar Short: Bush's Budget Defunds Bush's Education Plan." *American Prospect*, June 3, 2002.

Tiedt, Sidney. *The Role of the Federal Government in Education*. New York: Oxford University Press, 1966.

Toner, Robin. "Southern Democrats' Decline Is Eroding the Political Center." *New York Times*, November 15, 2004. http://www.nytimes.com/.

Toppo, Greg. "States Strain to Keep Up with 'No Child Left Behind.'" *USA Today*, January 29, 2003. http://www.usatoday.com/.

Toppo, Greg. "Vermont Governor Considers Refusing Federal Funds So Schools Can Opt Out of Testing." *Associated Press*, April 19, 2002. (accessed April 22, 2002). http://www.ap.org/.

Tyack, David, and Larry Cuban. *Tinkering toward Utopia: A Century of Public School Reform*. Cambridge, MA: Harvard University Press, 1995.

U.S. Congress. House. Committee on Education and the Workforce. *Report No. 106-386* (*Academic Achievement for All Act*). 106th Cong., 1st sess. 1999.

U.S. Congress. House. Committee on Education and the Workforce. *Statement of the Honorable Richard W. Riley, Secretary, U.S. Department of Education*. 106th Cong., 2nd sess., October 2000.

U.S. Congress. House. *P.L. 106-25: The Education Flexibility Partnership Act*. 106th Cong., 1st sess., 1999.

U.S. Congress. House. *Report No. 106-394, Part I*. (*HR2: Student Results Act of 1999*). 106th Cong., 1st sess., 1999.

U.S. Congress. House. *Report of the Committee on Education and the Workforce on HR1 Together with Additional and Dissenting Views, Report 107-63 Part I*. 107th Congress., 1st sess., 2001.

U.S. Congress. Senate. Committee on Health, Education, Labor, and Pensions. *S. Hearing 106-4: Education Reform: Governors' Views*. 106th Cong., 1st sess., 1999.

U.S. Congress. Senate. *Educational Opportunities Act: Report of the Committee on Health, Education, Labor, and Pensions, to Accompany S. 2*. 106th Cong., 2nd sess., 2000.

U.S. Congress. Senate. *S. 2254: The Public Reinvestment, Reinvention, and Responsibility Act*. 106th Cong., 2nd sess., 2000.

U.S. Congress. Senate. *Letter from Senate HELP Committee Democrats to Secretary of Education Roderick Paige*. 108th Cong., 2nd sess., 2004.

U.S. Department of Education. *Challenging the Status Quo: The Education Record, 1993–2000*. Washington, DC: GPO, 2000.

U.S. Department of Education. *Educational Excellence for All Children Act of 1999: An Overview of the Clinton Administration's Proposal to Reauthorize the Elementary and Secondary Education Act of 1965*. Washington, DC: GPO, 1999.

U.S. Department of Education. *Improving America's Schools Act of 1993: Reauthorization of the Elementary and Secondary Education Act*. Washington, DC: GPO, 1993.

U.S. Department of Education. *Letter from Secretary of Education Roderick Paige to Rep. Rob Andrews*. August 13, 2001. http://www.ed.gov/News/Letters/010813a.html (accessed November 22, 2002).

U.S. Department of Education. *Letter from Secretary of Education Roderick Paige to State Education Officials*. Washington, DC: GPO, 2002.

U.S. Department of Education. *Measured Progress: The Report of the Independent Review Panel on the Evaluation of Federal Education Legislation*. Washington, DC: GPO, 1999.

U.S. Department of Education. *Targeting Schools: Study of Title I Allocations within School Districts*. Washington, DC: GPO, 1999.

U.S. Department of Education. Planning and Evaluation Service. *Promising Results, Continuing Challenges: Final Report of the National Assessment of Title I*. Washington, DC: GPO, 1999.

U.S. General Accounting Office. *Title I: Education Needs to Monitor States' Scoring of Assessments* (*GAO-02-393*). Washington, DC: GPO, 2002.

U.S. Government Printing Office. *No Child Left Behind Act of 2001: Conference Report to Accompany H.R. 1*. Washington, DC: author, 2001.

Uslaner, Eric. *The Decline of Comity in Congress*. Ann Arbor: University of Michigan Press, 1993.

Vinovskis, Maris. *History and Educational Policymaking*. New Haven, CT: Yale University Press, 1999.

Von Drehle, David. "Political Split Is Pervasive." *Washington Post*, April 24, 2004. http://www.washingtonpost.com/.

Weaver, R. Kent. *Ending Welfare as We Know It*. Washington, DC: Brookings Institution, 2000.

Weckstein, Paul. "Who Represents Parents and Students?" *Legal Services Reporter*, August 2002, 11–13.

Weiner, Tim, and Abby Goodnough. "Education Deal a Victory in Politics, If Not Yet Schools." *New York Times*, November 12, 1999, A20.

Wellstone, The Hon. Paul. *Congressional Record*, 106th Cong., 2nd sess., May 3, 2000.

Wellstone, The Hon. Paul. *Congressional Record*, 107th Cong., 1st Sess., June 6, 2001. 147 *Cong. Rec.* S 5846.

Wildavsky, Aaron. *The Politics of the Budgetary Process*. Boston: Little, Brown, 1979.

Wilgoren, Jodi. "State School Chiefs Fret over U.S. Plan to Require Testing." *New York Times*, July 17, 2001. http://www.nytimes.com (accessed July 19, 2001).

Wilgoren, Jodi. "Vouchers' Fate May Hinge on Name Alone." *New York Times*, December 20, 2000. http:// www.nytimes.com/.

Wu, The Hon. David. *Congressional Record*. 107th Congress, 1st sess., May 22, 2001. 147 *Cong. Rec.* H 2396.

Yin, Robert. *Case Study Research: Design and Methods*. Vol. 5. 2nd ed. Thousand Oaks, CA: Sage, 1994.

Index

About the Author

Elizabeth H. DeBray is an assistant professor in the College of Education at the University of Georgia. She earned her masters in teaching and curriculum in 1992 and her doctorate in administration, planning, and social policy in 2001, both from Harvard University's Graduate School of Education. Her major interests are the implementation and effects of federal and state elementary and secondary school policies, and the politics of education. She has authored articles on school desegregation, school choice, high schools' organizational response to state accountability policies, and compensatory education. DeBray served as program analyst at the U.S. Department of Education from 1992 to 1996, research assistant with the Consortium for Policy Research in Education (CPRE) from 1997 to 2001, and research associate with the Civil Rights Project at Harvard from 1998 to 2002. She was a fellow in the Advanced Studies Fellowship Program on Federal and National Strategies of School Reform at Brown University from 2002 to 2005. In 2005, she was awarded the National Academy of Education/Spencer Postdoctoral Fellowship, which is supporting her new study of the changing relationship between national education interest groups and Congress.